URBAN ABORIGINAL POLICY MAKING
IN CANADIAN MUNICIPALITIES

FIELDS OF GOVERNANCE:
POLICY MAKING IN CANADIAN MUNICIPALITIES
Series editor: Robert Young

Policy making in the modern world has become a complex matter. Much policy is formed through negotiations between governments at several different levels, because each has particular resources that can be brought to bear on problems. At the same time, non-governmental organizations make demands about policy and can help in policy formation and implementation. In this context, works in this series explore how policy is made within municipalities through processes of intergovernmental relations and the involvement of social forces of all kinds.

The Fields of Governance series arises from a large research project, funded mainly by the Social Sciences and Humanities Research Council of Canada, entitled Multilevel Governance and Public Policy in Canadian Municipalities. This project has involved more than eighty scholars and a large number of student assistants. At its core are studies of several policy fields, each of which was examined in a variety of municipalities. Our objectives are not only to account for the nature of the policies but also to assess their quality and to suggest improvements in policy and in the policy-making process.

The Fields of Governance series is designed for scholars, practitioners, and interested readers from many backgrounds and places.

Urban Aboriginal Policy Making
in Canadian Municipalities

Edited by

EVELYN J. PETERS

McGill-Queen's University Press
Montreal & Kingston • London • Ithaca

DISCARD

HUMBER LIBRARIES LAKESHORE CAMPUS
3199 Lakeshore Blvd West
TORONTO, ON.   M8V 1K8

© McGill-Queen's University Press 2011

ISBN 978-0-7735-3948-8 (cloth)
ISBN 978-0-7735-3949-5 (paper)

Legal deposit fourth quarter 2011
Bibliothèque nationale du Québec

Printed in Canada on acid-free paper that is 100% ancient forest free
(100% post-consumer recycled), processed chlorine free

McGill-Queen's University Press acknowledges the support of the
Canada Council for the Arts for our publishing program. We also
acknowledge the financial support of the Government of Canada
through the Canada Book Fund for our publishing activities.

Library and Archives Canada Cataloguing in Publication Data

Urban Aboriginal policy making in Canadian municipalities / edited
by Evelyn J. Peters.

(Fields of governance : policy-making in Canadian municipalities ; 2)
Includes bibliographical references and index.
ISBN 978-0-7735-3948-8 (bound). – ISBN 978-0-7735-3949-5 (pbk.)

1. Native peoples – Urban residence – Canada. 2. Native peoples –
Canada – Government relations. 3. Urban policy – Canada. 4.Native
peoples – Services for – Canada. I. Peters, Evelyn J. (Evelyn Joy),
1951– II. Series: Fields of governance ; 2.

E78.C2U735 2012   305.897'071   C2011-904852-3V7233.144 20

Typeset by Jay Tee Graphics Ltd. in 10.5/13 Sabon

Contents

Preface

This collection of papers about policies affecting urban Aboriginal people in Canada represents an incursion into an important field, and one that is fascinating for students of public policy. The focus is on two key determinants of policy. First is the complex set of relations between governmental actors from the municipal, provincial, and federal levels. Second is the dense array of organized interests that represent Aboriginal people living in urban areas or that are concerned with their issues and that in many cases actually deliver services to them.

The problems and opportunities that face urban Aboriginal people in Canada are of great importance. Increasingly, Indigenous Canadians are living in municipalities and especially in large cities. In big cities in the West, they make up a very substantial proportion of the population. Governments have become attuned to this reality and have responded with a wide range of new programs and projects. An intriguing issue, one with great consequences for urban residents, is the extent to which Aboriginal people themselves have control over the policies that are designed to help them. This is the central focus of the chapters that follow.

This collection presents original research that stands alone and makes a significant contribution to our knowledge about urban Aboriginal policy in Canada. The authors are all well known experts in the field. Their work is also part of a much larger project, one that explores multilevel governance and public policy in Canadian municipalities. This project has many components, but the bulk of the work has been done on six policy areas, of which urban Aboriginal policy is one. It also covers various provinces and municipalities of different sizes, as in the studies collected here. The objectives of this work are to document what policies exist in a variety of fields, to explain their character by focusing on the processes of intergovernmental relations through which they were shaped, and to concentrate on the "social forces" (organized interests of all kinds) that were involved – or not – in the policy process. More information about the overall project is available at www.ppm-ppm.ca.

Some acknowledgements are in order. First, we thank the Social Sciences and Humanities Research Council of Canada for its support through the Major Collaborative Research Initiatives program. The University of Western Ontario and other universities have contributed generously to the project. We thank McGill-Queen's University Press for its continued interest in our research. Professor Carol Agòcs of the project's Advisory Committee worked closely with this group of researchers, and we appreciate her insights. We are also grateful for the contributions of Mr Alfred Gay. Kelly McCarthy has served as manager for the larger project. She coordinated various meetings of the research team, and she also helped prepare this manuscript. Thanks, Kelly. Finally, we thank David Kanatawakhon-Maracle of Western who kindly read the manuscript from a First Nations perspective and contributed his own expert views.

URBAN ABORIGINAL POLICY MAKING
IN CANADIAN MUNICIPALITIES

Aboriginal Public Policy in Urban Areas: An Introduction

EVELYN J. PETERS

Increasingly Canada's Aboriginal[1] people live in urban areas. In the 1940s, almost all Aboriginal people lived on reserves or in rural areas. While changing census definitions make it difficult to make exact comparisons between urban Aboriginal populations, available data show that the urban Aboriginal population has increased steadily. In 1951, 6.5 per cent of the population with Aboriginal ancestry lived in cities (Peters 2002, 76). The Royal Commission on Aboriginal Peoples estimated that in 1991 44.4 per cent of the individuals who identified as Aboriginal lived in urban areas (Royal Commission 1996, 602). By 2006, the Canadian census showed that over half (53.2 per cent) were urban dwellers. While urbanization rates for Aboriginal people are considerably lower than those for non-Aboriginal people (81 per cent of non-Aboriginal people lived in cities in 2006), the increasing urbanization of Aboriginal people has created unique opportunities and challenges for public policy.

The contributors to this volume have each addressed some of these challenges and opportunities in their approaches to answering the main question of this project: "What combinations of multilevel governance and social forces are most conducive to good public policy in Canadian municipalities?" "Social forces" are here defined as non-governmental institutions and movements affecting urban Aboriginal policy. While project guidelines for assessing the normative aspects of good policy in municipalities were defined in terms of effectiveness, efficiency, equity, and optimality (Young 2007), chapter authors identified additional elements necessary for good policy that were unique to the urban Aboriginal policy field. All of the criteria for defining good public policy in this field are reviewed in the Conclusion.

In tracing the role of the federal government in the dynamics of urban Aboriginal policy making historically, Frances Abele and Katherine Graham argue that consistent engagement with citizens' organizations is required to provide a basis for good policy making. According to Abele and Graham, the growing maturity of urban Aboriginal organizations plays a key role in how the federal government looks at urban Aboriginal issues. Karen Murray traces historical shifts in how Aboriginal peoples and their relationship to city-space have been defined as policy considerations by non-Aboriginal political officials from first contact to the present day. Her analysis stresses the need for a critical examination of the categories that shape the urban Aboriginal policy-making process. Frances Abele, Russell LaPointe, David J. Leech, and Michael McCrossan found that in Ontario cities, where urban Aboriginal populations are often not visible to municipal government officials, Aboriginal organizations have had major roles in educating municipal officials about Aboriginal issues and shaping appropriate municipal responses. Chris Andersen and Jenna Strachan argue that, in the absence of a strong federal co-coordinating role, provinces and municipalities have taken responsibility for Aboriginal programming. The result is that most programs that Aboriginal people access are grounded in need-based approaches, which marginalize Treaty and Aboriginal rights as well as Aboriginal actors. They argue, therefore, that good urban Aboriginal policy should recognize Aboriginal and Treaty rights. Ryan Walker, James Moore, and Maeengan Linklater suggest that urban Aboriginal policy needs to be co-produced with Aboriginal community leaders and experts. Co-production involves meaningful participation in policy generation and implementation, and it is consistent with Aboriginal peoples' inherent right to self-government as recognized by the federal government.

This introduction attempts to provide background information on some basic characteristics of the public policy landscape of urban Aboriginal issues. Interpretations of the urban Aboriginal experience are shaped by a number of assumptions that view urban Aboriginal communities primarily through the lens of poverty, represent Aboriginal cultures as incompatible with urban life, and hold that urban Aboriginal people complicate the implementation of the right to self-government. These assumptions have been resisted in various ways by Aboriginal communities.

It is appropriate here, briefly, to set the municipal context for the studies that follow. As is commonly known, Canada is a highly urbanized country. Many analysts argue that cities have become much more important in the globalized economy, with the largest ones dominating economic activity and forging inter-city links that marginalize peripheral areas (Courchene 2007). Certainly there is more competition between municipalities for investment and immigrants, at both the national and international levels. In Canada, there are significant demographic changes that have occurred as a consequence of economic restructuring. New migrants create growth pressures in the major metropolitan areas, but there is also the strain of depopulation in rural and small-town Canada (Bourne 2003). Aboriginal people are part of the wave of "in-migration," but municipal governments have no explicit responsibility to serve them. On the other hand, municipalities have been given greater latitude in policy making by most provincial governments: their range of authority has been broadened (Garcea and LeSage 2005). Through the 1990s and 2000s there was much pressure to expand the federal presence in cities, and this resulted in the New Deal for Cities and Communities introduced by Paul Martin's government. This program brought several new initiatives, as well as substantially increased cash transfers to municipalities. Under the subsequent government of Stephen Harper, there have been no new urban initiatives, except for the Economic Action Plan, which was aimed at stimulating the economy. However, no significant federal programs affecting municipalities have been terminated: this includes the Urban Aboriginal Strategy, which is discussed in the chapters that follow. For the municipalities, the major concern is finances. Lack of funds partly explains the lack of activity on the Aboriginal file in some municipalities, but there are other factors as well that are identified in the studies that follow.

It is also appropriate here to explain how provinces and municipalities were selected for the study. In the larger research project of which work on urban Aboriginal policy is part, there were six policy fields to be studied. These fields were first allocated to the ten provinces: in each province, two of the six fields were to be studied. This initial allocation was not a perfectly random procedure. The availability of expert researchers was one factor in the allocation of fields to provinces. More importantly, it was essential not only to have provinces where the issues in the field are significant, highly visible, and pertinent to policy makers and the public but also to have provinces where the issues in the field are not highly visible, so that the findings will be representative. To choose only places

where the policy field is a highly significant one would be to intro-
duce selection bias, a problem that is now well understood in the
social sciences (Geddes 1990). Once the initial allocation of fields
to provinces was made, the researchers were to explore the dynamics of policy making within four municipalities of various sizes. The
researchers themselves made the selection of municipalities, with the
restriction that the largest city in the province had to be among the
four. Again, the goal was to achieve representativeness in the findings. Were we to examine only the largest cities or only those municipalities that have active policies about urban Aboriginal people,
then our results would be biased: the description of policies and the
analysis of their formation would not accurately reflect reality. The
result of these choices is that this book does not cover urban Aboriginal policy in some important places. However, interested readers
should note that the larger project includes separate studies of the
largest city in each province. Additionally, four policy fields (the
ones not allocated to the province as a whole) were explored in each
big city. So the studies of Calgary, Montreal, and Halifax do contain
accounts of how urban Aboriginal policy is formed. For various reasons, the Vancouver study did not cover this field, but every other
large city has a study of urban Aboriginal policy.

The first section of this chapter describes the socio-economic
characteristics of urban Aboriginal communities, summarizing the
implications of a perspective that views Aboriginal people primarily
in terms of their marginalization in urban areas. A discussion of
Aboriginal peoples' perspectives on the role of Aboriginal culture
in urban areas follows. The third section describes the implications
of government decisions about responsibility for urban Aboriginal
people. The importance of the Aboriginal right to self-government
and its implementation in urban areas is found in the fourth section.
By way of conclusion, the chapter summarizes the contributions of
the various authors to the issue of defining good public policy in the
urban Aboriginal arena.

URBAN ABORIGINAL COMMUNITIES AND
SOCIO-ECONOMIC CHARACTERISTICS

There is a literature beginning around the 1940s that suggests that
Aboriginal migration to cities would create challenges for migrants,
but that, because of their poverty, their movement into cities would

also challenge government capacity to provide for them (Peters 2007). These concerns are echoed in contemporary research, which shows that Aboriginal people are over-represented among the urban poor in Canadian cities and are more likely than the non-Aboriginal population to live in poor urban neighbourhoods (Heisz and McLeod 2004, 7). Much of the literature on urban Aboriginal communities has seen them primarily in terms of their socio-economic marginalization (Cooke and Bélanger 2006).

Clearly, urban Aboriginal people are disproportionately poor. A comparison of socio-economic indicators for Aboriginal and non-Aboriginal people in Canada's largest cities demonstrates their marginalization in contrast to non-Aboriginal people (Peters 2005, 366–74). Aboriginal unemployment rates are more than double those of the non-Aboriginal population in most cities, and Aboriginal people are under-represented in managerial, supervisory, and professional occupations. Many more Aboriginal than non-Aboriginal individuals in private households have incomes below the poverty line, and many more Aboriginal than non-Aboriginal families are led by lone parents. Aboriginal people are more likely to live in dwelling units that need major repairs (Walker 2008a). Poor housing quality is a major contributor to the high levels of residential mobility among urban Aboriginal families, which affects Aboriginal children's abilities to perform well in school (Skelton 2002). Aboriginal people's difficulty finding quality housing also means that they are more likely to have to depend on kin, friends, or services to find shelter and are more vulnerable to becoming absolutely homeless (Indian and Northern Affairs Canada 2008). Aboriginal people are much less likely than non-Aboriginal people to have a university degree. Aboriginal gangs are increasingly being identified in urban areas, particularly in the Prairie provinces, and their emergence is viewed, in part, as evidence of poverty and marginalization in urban areas (Andersen 2007).

While attention to urban Aboriginal marginalization can highlight social inequalities and create pressure on governments to bring about change, a focus only on this aspect of urban Aboriginal life can have some negative consequences. First, it can turn attention away from the historic context for urban Aboriginal poverty. Increasingly, researchers have emphasized the importance of situating challenges facing urban Aboriginal people within the larger context of colonization, including their dispossession from their own land and cultures, and the intergenerational effects of residential schools (Cedar Project Partnership et al. 2008). Silver et al.'s (2006, 11–15) interviews with twenty-six urban Aboriginal community leaders identified a number of factors affecting Aboriginal people's economic situation in urban areas, including the failure of both residential and non-residential schools to provide them with the skills required for urban employment and the experience of racism, often on a daily basis, with the resulting destruction of self-esteem and positive identity. The urbanization of Aboriginal people in Canada occurred at a time when urban economies increasingly required education and skill levels that relatively few Aboriginal people had received during their educational experience. Some contemporary research suggests that education and employment conditions in many rural Aboriginal communities continue to create disadvantages for migrants to cities (Levitte 2003, 58–70).

Second, an emphasis primarily on marginalization homogenizes urban Aboriginal communities and deflects attention away from the diversity within these communities. Some of the diversity is geographic. Table 1 provides some summary data about Aboriginal people in the cities studied in the following chapters. Data were not available for the two smaller communities in Alberta. Clearly these characteristics do not provide detailed descriptions of Aboriginal communities in particular urban areas, but they do identify some variations between cities. Employment rates (proportions of the populations fifteen and older that are employed) and average incomes are generally lower in Saskatchewan, Manitoba, and New Brunswick than they are in Alberta and Ontario. The proportion of census family members who are lone parents is higher in cities in Saskatchewan and Manitoba than in other cities. Levels of education (as measured by a university degree or certificate) are highest in Saskatoon and in the cities in Ontario and lowest in New Brunswick. These data suggest that a perspective that sees Aboriginal people only as a marginalized population is not equally applicable to all cities.

Finally, a perspective that privileges marginalization also perpetuates negative stereotypes that depict all urban Aboriginal people as destitute. It can deflect attention from the success that many urban Aboriginal residents experience and it can create the perception that Aboriginal people cannot contribute to either Aboriginal or non-Aboriginal communities in urban areas. Siggner and Costa's (2005)

Table 1
Percentage of Aboriginal Identity Population with Selected Characteristics, Selected
Urban Areas, 2006

	Employment Rate	Average Income	Lone Parents	University Degree or Certificate
Edmonton	63.3	28,828	9.2	5.9
Calgary	71.6	33,097	7.3	9.4
Regina	55.7	26,784	11.8	8.4
Saskatoon	54.0	24,467	10.9	11.2
Winnipeg	58.1	25,379	10.5	8.3
Brandon	64.2	20,808	13.2	7.1
Thompson	56.4	28,377	10.0	5.9
Thunder Bay	50.0	27,173	9.2	8.8
Kingston	60.3	28,835	5.8	10.5
Toronto	63.3	35,082	7.5	12.8
Ottawa	66.0	35,508	7.5	15.5
Fredericton	62.8	23,911	5.6	3.5
Moncton	59.9	21,690	6.4	4.4
Saint John	58.0	20,290	8.4	6.5

Source: Statistics Canada Aboriginal Population Profiles, 2006

study of urban Aboriginal people between 1981 and 2001 reported gains in education and employment as well as growth in the proportion of Aboriginal people earning good wages. Wotherspoon (2003, 155) noted that in urban areas, "many public and private sector agencies in both Aboriginal and non-Aboriginal sectors have created initiatives, programs, and hiring policies to attract highly qualified Aboriginal candidates." According to Wotherspoon (2003, 156), this process replicates the way that the non-Aboriginal middle class emerged historically. Focus groups with Aboriginal middle-class Toronto residents highlighted the importance of recognizing the socioeconomic diversity of urban Aboriginal people (Urban Aboriginal Task Force 2006). The Toronto study indicated that middle-class urban Aboriginal people did not access Aboriginal organizations because these organizations are mostly service organizations focusing on a variety of social problems. Instead, they emphasized the need for Aboriginal language and cultural programs that address their aspirations.

Clearly, urban Aboriginal people are disproportionately poor. However, focusing only on marginalization ignores the roots of poverty and homogenizes urban Aboriginal communities. Finally, it constructs urban Aboriginal people primarily in terms of "needs" and fails to recognize capabilities within that population.

ABORIGINAL CULTURES AND URBAN LIFE

There is a long history in western thought that sees urban and Aboriginal cultures as incompatible (Berkhoffer 1979). Goldie's (1989) review of literature about Aboriginal people in Canada, Australia, and New Zealand pointed out that Aboriginal cultures were viewed as authentic only when they were far from urban centres in distance and in time. Early writing about Aboriginal migrants to urban areas in Canada reflected ideas that Aboriginal cultures were an impediment to successful adjustment to urban society. As a result, early services to Aboriginal migrants emphasized integration (Peters 2002). Ideas about the incompatibility of urban and Aboriginal cultures have not dissipated (Royal Commission 1993, 2).

In resistance to perspectives that viewed them primarily as marginalized populations in the urban milieu, Aboriginal people emphasized the importance of Aboriginal cultures in supporting healthy communities. Aboriginal presenters to the Public Hearings of the Royal Commission saw vibrant urban Aboriginal cultures as important elements of Aboriginal people's success in cities. For example, David Chartrand (1993, 565), president of the National Association of Friendship Centres, had this to say:

> Aboriginal culture in the cities is threatened in much the same way as Canadian culture is threatened by American culture, and it therefore requires a similar commitment to its protection. Our culture is at the heart of our people, and without awareness of Aboriginal history, traditions and ceremonies, we are not whole people, and our communities lose their strength ... Cultural education also works against the alienation that the cities hold for our people. Social activities bring us together and strengthen the relationship between people in areas where those relationships are an important safety net for people who feel left out by the mainstream.

Chartrand told the Commission that the most effective way to solve problems that Aboriginal people faced in the city was to catch them before they start through strengthening individuals' identities and awareness of the urban Aboriginal community. Building on testimonies such as these, the Commission recommended that all levels of government initiate programs to support Aboriginal cultures in urban areas (Royal Commission 1996, 537). The Commission suggested that support should be provided for urban Aboriginal institutions, initiatives concerning languages, and access to land and elders.

The continuing importance of cultural identities has implications for the growth of urban populations. The urban Aboriginal population almost doubled between 1991 and 2006, growing from 320,000 in 1991 to 623,920 in 2006. This rapid growth cannot be explained only by demographic factors such as fertility, mortality, and migration (Guimond 2003). Legislation allowing for the reinstatement of First Nations people who had lost their legal status as Registered Indians accounts for part of the increase because many individuals who lost their status were living in urban areas. Much of the population increase came about because individuals who did not identify as Aboriginal in previous Census years now chose to do so. Most of the increase associated with changes in self-identification has occurred in urban areas (Guimond and Robitaille 2008), with the largest proportionate increase among Métis people. Siggner (2003) suggested that the changing attitudes towards Aboriginal peoples in Canada were important in changing patterns of self-identification. Researchers have documented a similar phenomenon in the United States, identifying as contributing factors American ethnic polities that have embraced cultural pride and Indian activism (Nagel 1995).

The continuing significance of Aboriginal cultures and identities in urban areas is accompanied by an expectation that Aboriginal rights are also relevant in urban locations. Presenters to the Royal Commission on Aboriginal Peoples rejected the artificial geographies that associated their rights as Aboriginal people with rural and remote locations (Peters 2006). As a result, urban Aboriginal people do not arrive in cities like other migrants, national or international. Clearly, they face some of the same challenges as other migrants – finding employment, shelter, schooling, and welcoming communities. Unlike other migrants, many Aboriginal people are travelling within their traditional territories. Many expect that their Aboriginal rights will make a difference to the ways that they structure their lives in cities. The clarification of Aboriginal rights in urban areas is an important policy challenge for various levels of government.

The emphasis on Aboriginal cultural identities and rights in urban centres can create enormous complexity in dealing with their situation in urban areas. One element of this has to do with differences between First Nations and Métis people. In many prairie cities, Métis comprise half or more of the urban Aboriginal population, and these Métis communities wish to receive programs and services that support their distinct cultures. Many First Nations people identify with their particular cultures of origin and, as a result, urban First Nations populations are quite culturally complex (Clatworthy 2000; Royal Commission 1996, 591–97). A participant in a recent study of urban Aboriginal identities in Saskatoon gave an example of the challenges faced by Aboriginal groups whose culture was in a minority in the Aboriginal population. He expressed the difficulty of being Saulteaux in a city where Cree culture was dominant: "Like if you wanna talk about being Saulteaux, what our culture is all about, the language and the value systems and also the traditions or if there's a council dance or a sweat on my reserve and I have no way to get there then I'm, you know, I'm hooped. I can't do it because it's all the way over there. So, I mean, if I wanna go to a sweat then I have to, say, call [Cree elders] which, if it's as good as it gets then okay, I'll sweat, but I'm sweating with Cree culture not Saulteaux culture and there goes the beginning of Pan Indianism" (Peters et al. 2008).

The significance of Aboriginal culture and rights in the urban milieu creates a complex context for processes of public policy making. Aboriginal communities expect governments to work with them in different ways than they work with other minority groups in the city (Walker 2006). This context also contributes to a complex policy environment that involves many different Aboriginal groups and cultures.

JURISDICTIONAL ISSUES

Because of the lack of clarity about which level of government has jurisdiction over Aboriginal people in urban areas, both federal and provincial governments have avoided taking responsibility. The conflict between federal and provincial governments about jurisdiction over urban Aboriginal people has contributed to the association of Aboriginal culture and rights with non-urban areas. Under the *Constitution Act, 1867*, section 9(24), jurisdiction over "Indians and Lands reserved for Indians" is assigned exclusively to the federal government. By the early decades of the 1900s, almost all First

Nations people were settled on reserves, and almost all reserves were located at a distance from urban centres. Through a variety of mechanisms, these largely segregated patterns of settlement persisted into the mid-1940s. This assignment of jurisdiction meant that the federal government provided services to First Nations people living on reserves through the Indian Affairs Branch.

Conflict over jurisdiction emerged as increasing population pressure and a chronic lack of economic possibilities on the small and often resource-poor reserves resulted in a gradually rising number of First Nations people migrating from reserves to cities after the Second World War. In 1957, interpreting the decision to migrate to cities as a decision to integrate into mainstream Canadian society, the federal government assigned responsibility for "urban Indians" to the Citizenship Branch of Canada, an agency with experience in aiding international immigrants (Peters 2002, 82). The Citizenship Branch's responsibility was exercised through the establishment of Friendship Centres, with the first one opening in Winnipeg in 1959. The Indian Affairs Branch retained its historic role with respect to reserve residents. The Indian Affairs Branch-sponsored research into constitutional obligations concluded that there were no barriers against the involvement of provincial governments and other federal government departments in providing and funding services for First Nations migrants, and by the early 1950s the Indian Affairs Branch had adopted the position that it was responsible only for Indians living on reserves (Barron 1997, 119; Peters 2002).[2] The federal government continues to maintain this position (Morse 1989).

There is little in the way of publicly available documentation about how the position of the Indian Affairs Branch was translated into actual funding arrangements, but it is clear that this position was hotly contested by provincial governments. Barron's (1997, 119–21) description of negotiations between the Branch and Saskatchewan in the early 1950s indicated that federal officials agreed to deliver welfare services only for Registered Indians who had lived off the reserve for less than twelve months. Arrangements for other social services were a "patchwork of confusing and conflicting jurisdictions", where federal officials denied responsibility but made exceptions in practice.[3] The federal government's 1969 White Paper was a logical extension of the federal government's devolution policy. It proposed dismantling reserves and the *Indian Act* and shifting program and financial responsibility for First Nations people to the provinces. The withdrawal of the White Paper in the face of strong First Nations resistance resulted in a change of strategy for the federal government to a "pragmatic approach" that involved "exploiting every opportunity" to devolve program and fiscal responsibility for First Nations to the provinces and to other federal departments (Bostrom 1984, 524). Federal compensation for provincial expenditures varied by province pursuant to specific federal-provincial agreements, and these expenditures also varied for different social services (Breton and Grant 1984). Research for the Royal Commission on Aboriginal Peoples found that the federal government's cessation of reimbursement to provinces for social assistance to Registered Indians during the first year they lived off-reserve created considerable hardships for some provincial governments (Royal Commission 1996, 542–5).

The federal government has never recognized a constitutional responsibility for Métis people. In the early 1950s, the Saskatchewan government's attempt to negotiate federal support for the delivery of social services to Métis people was met with the response that Indian Affairs had no mandate for Métis people (Barron 1997, 120). Despite the inclusion of the Métis as Aboriginal peoples in section 35 of the *Constitution Act, 1982*, the federal government resists arguments that Métis people are included in the scope of section 91(24) (Morse and Giokas 1995, 140). As a result of judicial interpretation, federal jurisdiction does apply to the Inuit.[4] Issues of jurisdiction for Inuit living in urban areas have not received much attention, possibly due to the low numbers of Inuit people living in cities in the south relative to First Nations and Métis, and because contemporary land claims have addressed funding arrangements for many Inuit people.

A few federally funded services are available to Registered Indians and Inuit generally, no matter where they live. The most notable of these are non-insured health benefits and postsecondary educational assistance. However, a participant in the Royal Commission on Aboriginal People's (1993, 17) round table on urban issues summarized the implications of decades of debates over jurisdiction: "[W]e give people the runaround now when they come into the city. Well, you're Treaty and you've not been here one year so you go to this place. But, oh no, you've been here one year so you go to this place. But, oh no, you've been here a year already so you go to this place. Well, you're Métis, you have to go somewhere else.

It's too confusing for people." Federal devolution of program and fiscal responsibility has had a number of implications for urban Aboriginal people. First Nations people living on reserves and Inuit living in their communities receive programs and services for which urban Aboriginal people are not eligible, for example, social housing or band-administered social assistance. Urban Métis and non-Registered Indians do not have access to non-insured health benefits and support for post-secondary education, while these benefits are available to urban Registered Indians and Inuit. Urban Aboriginal people may have difficulty accessing provincial programs available to the general population either because provincial governments have taken a stance that these programs should be provided by the federal government or because individual service providers do not have complete information about the services that are available.

However, debates about jurisdiction over and responsibility for urban Aboriginal people do not mean that federal, provincial, and municipal governments provide no funding for programs and services that focus on the particular needs of Aboriginal people in cities. Hanselmann's (2001) study found that, despite the federal government's stated position with respect to its responsibility for urban Aboriginal people, it was involved in programming for urban Aboriginal people in a large number of program fields. In some cases the federal government's involvement was through programs specifically designed for Aboriginal people in urban areas (for example, the Aboriginal Friendship Centre Program and the Urban Multipurpose Aboriginal Youth Centres). In other cases, federal government involvement was primarily through funding (for example, the Winnipeg Urban Circle Training Centre, funded by the governments of Canada and Manitoba). Finally, the federal government was involved in Aboriginal-specific programs that were located in urban areas but were not urban-specific (for example, the Department of Justice's Legal Studies for Aboriginal People Program found in urban universities). Despite having shifted funding responsibilities for many services to provincial governments, the federal government remains involved in a substantial number of programs for urban Aboriginal people, mostly through departments other than the Department of Indian and Northern Affairs. In turn, in spite of their rhetorical position that Aboriginal people are the responsibility of the federal government, provincial governments also provided programming for urban Aboriginal people in a wide variety of fields

(Hanselmann 2001). Finally, despite a limited resource base and limited formal responsibility, many municipal governments with large numbers of urban Aboriginal people have played important roles in creating and supporting initiatives for urban Aboriginal peoples.

The report of the Royal Commission on Aboriginal Peoples (1996, 545) indicated that "[t]here is a critical need for the federal and provincial governments to clarify their respective legal and fiscal responsibilities" for urban Aboriginal people. The Commission made a number of recommendations for clarifying funding arrangements, including areas that should be funded by provincial governments. However, there is no evidence that issues of federal and provincial jurisdiction and responsibility for urban Aboriginal people are currently being addressed. Instead, the currently preferred way of dealing with urban Aboriginal issues appears to be through agreements or funding arrangements between various levels of government, often involving different ministries and departments. The advantage of these approaches include the ability to create initiatives that avoid the "silos" of government organization responsibilities as well as the ability to respond to local needs. No single level of government is required to take sole responsibility for the complex issues challenging urban Aboriginal communities, and no government is seen as establishing a precedent in assuming responsibility.

While current approaches to policy making for urban Aboriginal people have been successful in some programming and service initiatives, the current approach to jurisdiction and responsibility has some major shortcomings. A relationship with the federal government is an important symbol of what it means to be an Aboriginal person in Canada. The federal government's insistence that it is not responsible for urban Aboriginal peoples reinforces an association of authentic Aboriginal identities with reserves and non-urban places and reinforces historic ideas about urbanization and assimilation. Current arrangements also lead to complexity and lack of shared information: Hanselmann (2002) reported that many of the civil servants who gathered information about programs and services for urban Aboriginal people for his research were not aware of what other initiatives were in place. Finally, the current system creates programs and services that are not equally accessible to Aboriginal people with different legal status, and it means that access to programs and services is uneven across different urban locales.

SELF-GOVERNMENT

Increasingly, Aboriginal people in urban areas emphasize their right to play a substantial role in setting public policy and defining and delivering programs and services to urban populations. By emphasizing their Aboriginal rights in the city, urban Aboriginal people distance themselves from policies of multiculturalism. Meaningful participation in creating and administering programs and services acknowledges Aboriginal rights to self-government, recognized by the Government of Canada as an inherent right of all Aboriginal people (Government of Canada 1997). However, there are practical and political challenges facing the implementation of the right to self-government in urban areas.

Not all urban Aboriginal people are represented by existing Aboriginal political bodies and, as a result, they are denied a strong political voice in this arena. This lack of representation derives both from geographic variations in organizational structures and because of differential access to these organizations for different categories of Aboriginal people. The Congress of Aboriginal Peoples (CAP), formerly the National Council of Canada, has defined itself as the voice of off-reserve Aboriginal people in Canada since 1971. While CAP has been an important political voice for urban Aboriginal peoples, it currently has very limited support in the Prairies and Ontario. The Assembly of First Nations' (AFN) stated interest in urban issues is relatively recent, sparked in part by assumption of responsibility for off-reserve member services by some First Nations governments and tribal councils. The 1999 Supreme Court of Canada's Corbiere decision, which gave First Nations band members living off-reserve the right to vote in band elections and referendums, also influenced the AFN's interest in urban issues.[5] In 1999, the AFN established a task force on urban issues. In response, the 1999 AFN General Assembly resolved to create an Urban Issues Secretariat. That decision has not yet occurred and the AFN has little involvement in urban First Nations issues. In the recent election of the Grand Chief of the AFN, there was virtually no attention paid to urban First Nations issues. The Métis National Council, which is working to affirm Métis rights more generally, also does not have a strong presence in urban areas. Provincial First Nations and Métis organizations similarly do not have a strong focus on the urban Aboriginal situation.

At the level of particular cities, however, some political organizations have emerged with a particular focus on urban Aboriginal issues. Arrangements are extremely variable, geographically. One approach is an urban-focused organization that represents all Aboriginal people (First Nations, Métis, and Inuit) in the city, for example, the Aboriginal Council of Winnipeg (ACW). Founded in 1990 with the union of the Urban Indian Association and the Winnipeg Council of Treaty and Status Indians, it serves as a political and advocacy voice that represents the interests of the Aboriginal community of Winnipeg regardless of its legal status. While there have been attempts to establish similar organizations in other cities, none appears to have been as stable as the ACW. For example, the BC United Native Nations (UNN) has a longer history than the Aboriginal Council of Winnipeg, but it has closed down several times during its history. In some cities, individual First Nations have set up urban offices to represent and provide services to their members. In a few cities, there are separate organizations that represent and provide services for urban First Nations and Métis people. For example, in Saskatoon, political representation for First Nations is provided by the Saskatoon Tribal Council, which also delivers a wide range of services, some to First Nations and some to all Aboriginal people living in Saskatoon. The Central Urban Métis Federation Inc. (CUMFI) is a Métis local that provides a political voice as well as programs and services to Métis people in Saskatoon. Finally, the location of some reserves within city boundaries of a few urban areas means that members of those First Nations have political representation within the city.

In most cities, though, urban Aboriginal people do not have political representation. Even where there are urban-focused organizations, such as the ones in Saskatoon, they do not necessarily provide a voice (as opposed to services) for all urban Aboriginal people, as they leave out First Nations people who are not registered or who do not belong to First Nations that are represented on the tribal council. Moreover, as Walker (2003; 2008b) has described, urban Aboriginal people often do not participate in non-Aboriginal community organizations and consultations. This, in addition to their uneven access to political representative bodies, means that they often do not have a direct voice in public policy making.

Most urban Aboriginal people experience some level of self-government through the emergence of a variety of urban Aboriginal organizations that deliver programs and services in a wide range of policy sectors. Hibbard and Lane (2004, 97) note that Indigenous movements for sovereignty rights around the world have emphasized three interlocking matters: "how to have some measure of political autonomy; how to maintain particular sets of social relations and more or less distinct cultural orders; and how to maintain or regain control over resources, especially land." While resource issues are not central in most urban Aboriginal communities, the Royal Commission suggested that the development of urban Aboriginal organizations creates meaningful levels of control over some of the issues that affect urban Aboriginal residents' everyday lives (Royal Commission 1996, 584). Aboriginal-controlled social services generally have greater scope in delivering programs that incorporate Aboriginal principles, beliefs, and traditions; they create important employment opportunities for urban Aboriginal residents; and they result in significant economic benefits for Aboriginal communities (Hylton 1999, 85–6). Aboriginal participation can also contribute to more effective policies and services for urban Aboriginal people. The Royal Commission on Aboriginal Peoples' round table on urban issues (1993, 14) reported that "participants said non-Aboriginal agencies have different goals and priorities from Aboriginal social service agencies. Aboriginal agencies, such as friendship centres, view an individual person's problems as 'symptoms of deeper problems' that are rooted in 'racism, powerlessness and cultural breakdown.' The non-Aboriginal agencies, they said, tended to look at conditions as isolated problems and to view the individual as deficient. As a result, the workshop participants said, Aboriginal agencies are trusted more than non-Aboriginal agencies by Aboriginal urban people." Roberts et al. (2001, 196) explained how the creation of Métis-focused organizations supports cultural distinctiveness: "For the Metis, such organizational arrangements require the establishment of a set of parallel organizations in the major institutional sectors including education, employment, social services, religion, family, and recreation. Such institutional completeness provides the organizational structures by which the Metis community can control and shape the conduct of its membership as guided by its distinctive cultural ideas and ideals."

The ability of urban Aboriginal communities to create programs and institutions is affected by population size and the proportion of urban populations Aboriginal people comprise. Table 2 provides

Table 2
Aboriginal Identity Population Size and Proportion of Urban Population

	Total Population	Aboriginal Identity Population	% Aboriginal
Edmonton	1,024,825	52,105	5.1
Calgary	1,070,295	26,575	2.5
Regina	192,440	17,105	8.9
Saskatoon	230,850	21,535	9.3
Winnipeg	686,040	68,385	10.0
Brandon	40,705	3,995	9.8
Thompson	13,405	4,915	36.7
Thunder Bay	121,050	10,055	8.3
Kingston	148,475	3,290	2.2
Toronto	5,072,075	26,575	0.5
Ottawa	1,117,120	20,590	1.8
Fredericton	49,980	725	1.5
Moncton	124,055	1,175	0.9
Saint John	120,875	1,250	1.0

Source: Statistics Canada, Population Profiles, 2006

statistics for most of the municipalities studied in this volume. Winnipeg had the largest Aboriginal population (nearly 70,000) in 2006, followed by Edmonton. There were a number of cities with populations around the 20,000 range (Regina, Saskatoon, Toronto, and Ottawa). Cities in New Brunswick had small Aboriginal populations of around 1,000. The proportion of a city's population that is Aboriginal may also affect levels of attention in public policy. Cities like Toronto, Ottawa, and Montreal may have larger or similar numbers of Aboriginal people compared to Prairie cities, but Aboriginal people comprised a larger proportion of the latter's urban population. In Winnipeg, the Aboriginal population made up one-tenth of the total population of that city. In Saskatoon, Regina, and Thunder Bay, more than eight per cent of the total Census Metropolitan Area (CMA) population was Aboriginal. As in other small and more northern cities (for example, Prince Albert), Aboriginal people are a large component (almost thirty seven per cent) of Thompson's population. In contrast, in most eastern cities, Aboriginal people comprise around two per cent or less of the total urban population. Cities like Toronto and Montreal have many other minority groups living in them, and as a result, Aboriginal issues receive relatively less attention. This may help to explain the results of Abele and Graham's (1989) comparison of policies for Aboriginal people in

Alberta and Ontario, which showed that Alberta had a wider range of practical initiatives focused on urban Aboriginal initiatives than did Ontario.

The number of Aboriginal organizations providing services to the urban Aboriginal population has increased rapidly since the establishment of the first urban Aboriginal organizations. Howard-Bobiwash's (2003) history of professional Aboriginal women in Toronto documented their important role in creating the first urban Aboriginal organizations in that city, including the Toronto Friendship Centre. Newhouse (2003, 244) notes that many urban organizations evolved from programs originally established and individuals originally trained in Friendship Centres: "Growing out of the friendship centre movement, a huge network of institutions has emerged within the urban Aboriginal communities. Over the last four decades (1960–2000), urban Aboriginal landscapes have been transformed through the emergence of Aboriginal organizations designed to meet the many needs of growing urban populations."

A case study of urban Aboriginal organizations in Winnipeg illustrates some of the characteristics of urban Aboriginal organizations, particularly in cities with large Aboriginal populations (Peters 2005). In 2002 there were twenty-eight Aboriginal organizations in Winnipeg, with the number of clients served monthly representing about one-fifth of the population that identified themselves as Aboriginal in that city. By 2002 the majority of organizations were a decade old or more. The oldest organizations were the Indian Métis Friendship Centre, established in 1959, two housing corporations, and four other organizations established in the 1970s and still in existence today. The range of services was extensive, with services for a variety of age groups and addressing a variety of policy sectors, including housing, culture and religion, language, employment, and family violence. Many organizations were created out of the Friendship Centre. Others emerged from a core of Aboriginal activists involved in many initiatives over several decades (Loxley and Wien 2003). Newhouse (2000) characterized urban Aboriginal organizations as reformulating western institutions and practices to support Aboriginal cultures and identities so that Aboriginal people could survive as distinct people in contemporary societies.

However, unstable and fragmented funding arrangements make it difficult for organizations to plan and deliver services (Graham and Peters 2002). Staff are trained, collaborative relationships are established, clients become aware of the program, and then the end of the project means either that staff are let go or organizations scramble to reconfigure programs to meet new granting criteria in order to retain staff and support clients. A large amount of time that should be directed towards service delivery is diverted to applying for funding and writing reports (Royal Commission 1996, 554–7). In this context, the Royal Commission recommended five-year funding arrangements in order to maintain some stability and efficiency. There is also a need for coordination and planning: at present, Aboriginal organizations often end up competing with each other. This makes it difficult to ensure that there is adequate coverage of different policy areas and creates duplication and confusing information (Royal Commission 1996, 556). Often there are also tensions between service delivery and political organizations because both are in need of funding dollars and, as a result, they compete for programs. In Hanselmann's interviews (2002, 7), service delivery personnel emphasized the importance of separating politics from service delivery: "Interview subjects from service delivery organizations spoke very strongly of the importance of keeping roles separated. The message that came through is that governments have to be clear about the intentions of funding decisions: if a policy decision is made to build capacity among political organizations, then do so through core funding, not by encouraging, however unintentionally, political organizations to chase programming dollars. When political organizations apply to deliver programs, governments should try to find an existing service organization instead." At the same time, political organizations may feel the need to deliver services in order to meet the needs of their constituents, act as a voice for urban Aboriginal people, and access government funding.

In general though, urban Aboriginal people generally do not access self-government over urban issues through existing Aboriginal political organizations. Their main channel for exerting some control over aspects of their lives in cities is a variety of urban Aboriginal services organizations that have emerged in the last half century. Current funding strategies for these organizations have created a confusing array of programs and services with duplication in some areas and lack of attention in others. Sustainability is a major challenge for many organizations. Differences in the structure of organizations (political and service delivery) in different cities and frequent competition between organizations for funding dollars means that governments find it difficult to identify who represents the urban Aboriginal community. Public policy making for urban Aboriginal people takes place in this complex, fragmented, and often conflict-ridden environment.

SUMMARY OF FOLLOWING CHAPTERS

Each of the following chapters makes an original contribution to our understanding of the challenges facing the crafting of public policy for Aboriginal communities in urban areas.

Frances Abele and Katherine Graham describe the evolution of federal government policies and programs concerning urban Aboriginal people. They focus on the dynamics of policy engagement between governments and non-governmental institutions in different economic, political, and social circumstances in cities. According to Abele and Graham, attention to urban Aboriginal issues waxed and waned depending on the degree to which cities were on the federal agenda and on the extent to which other issues (for example, constitutional negotiations or Aboriginal grassroots conflicts) took centre stage. They argue that the period since 1993 represents one in which there is federal recognition of the importance of cities, urban Aboriginal organizations are mature and increasingly influential, and there is sustained federal interest in urban Aboriginal issues. As a result, they are cautiously optimistic that the preconditions for good urban Aboriginal policy making currently exist.

Karen Murray's main question addresses how urban areas were defined (as problems or solutions) in relation to New Brunswick's Aboriginal peoples. Beginning at the time of contact, she identifies four stages in the evolution of policy making. Initially, the proximity of reserves to cities was viewed positively as a mechanism facilitating assimilation. By the late nineteenth century, there were concerns about the negative effects of reserves on cities, and cities on reserves, with the result that measures were introduced to segregate Aboriginal people from urban life. Viewed as a drain on the public purse towards the end of the Second World War, reserve residents were the target of policies that promoted migration to urban areas and integration into White labour markets, with an emphasis on eradicating reserves. After the 1970s, a variety of developments in federal and provincial policy making for Aboriginal peoples shifted the emphasis to Registered Indians living on reserves, a transformation that sidelined the policy importance of Aboriginal people living in cities. Reserve and city political economies were viewed as being mutually dependent. Murray's analysis highlights the significance of local specificities in creating unique outcomes and emphasizes the historic malleability of the categories used to frame urban Aboriginal policy making.

Frances Abele, Russell LaPointe, David J. Leech, and Michael McCrossan studied urban Aboriginal policy making in four cities in Ontario: Thunder Bay, Kingston, Toronto, and Ottawa. They argue that there were several reasons why municipalities found it challenging to make good Aboriginal policies. These were that municipalities generally did not recognize special attributes of citizens in the ways that federal and provincial governments did and, as a result, Aboriginal issues were not on their horizons; federal and provincial governments were seen as having jurisdiction over Aboriginal issues; and Aboriginal populations were small and diverse relative to other population groups in cities. Abele et al. found that all four cities had taken different approaches to urban Aboriginal policy, reflecting different historical legacies and Aboriginal demographics. Of particular importance in generating positive municipal responses to Aboriginal issues were strong, pro-active Aboriginal organizations, which took responsibility for educating politicians and bureaucrats about urban Aboriginal issues and appropriate responses to them.

Chris Andersen and Jenna Strachan emphasize the need for leadership from the federal government in order to coordinate policy making and programming for urban Aboriginal communities. They point out that the lack of a federal coordinating role resulted in a "patchwork of short-term, overlapping, and inefficient urban Aboriginal programs and policies." Unlike the situation in Ontario and New Brunswick, Alberta cities demonstrated an enormous amount of programming that urban Aboriginal people access in the absence of clearly articulated policies connected to particular programs and services. The resulting jurisdictional maze had a number of implications. First, programs and services varied enormously by city, which created geographic unevenness in access. Second, there was a lack of coordination between various government departments, with resulting gaps and overlap in programming. Finally, the approach to programming through funding numerous short-term projects marginalized Aboriginal actors by encouraging competition between organizations, which created a necessity for Aboriginal service providers to constantly meet various program criteria with the result that they were unable to set their own agendas.

Ryan Walker, James Moore, and Maeengan Linklater focus on urban Aboriginal policy making in Swan River, Thompson, Brandon, and Winnipeg, Manitoba, examining seven policy areas. Arguing that co-production is an essential element of good policy making in the urban Aboriginal policy arena, they explore the extent to which the appropriate combinations of leadership and expertise were present in the processes of creating these policies through agenda setting, problem definition, production, and decisions about alternatives and implementation. Walker et al. found that, in general, urban Aboriginal policy was being produced by governments and implemented with Aboriginal communities, and the authors suggest that Aboriginal participants needed to be co-producers at all stages of the policy-making process. Walker et al.'s case studies show that the current involvement of Aboriginal stakeholders is complex and variable. They suggest that governments had often assumed that urban community leadership was found in political organizations. Based on the experience of urban Aboriginal policy making in Manitoba, these authors suggest that co-production should involve Aboriginal community leaders and community-based policy and program-based expertise, as well as political organizations. They indicate that a community nomination process could provide an appropriate mechanism for selecting participants in the co-production of urban Aboriginal policy.

By way of conclusion, Robert Young identifies some of the general themes evident in the chapters of this volume. He addresses the involvement of different levels of government, inter-governmental relations, the role of social forces (the organized interests of all kinds that are involved (or not) in the policy process), and the elements that make good public policy. Two themes stand out. One is the complexity and geographic variability of urban Aboriginal policy making. This is generated in part because most initiatives are provincial, and provincial engagement is extremely variable. Some of the complexity is also due to the extreme variability of Aboriginal organizations in different cities; these organizations can influence government responses. As a result, the services and opportunities available to urban Aboriginal residents are very uneven, geographically. The second theme is Young's argument that the degree to which urban Aboriginal policy delegates decision making to Aboriginal people is an important criterion for evaluating urban Aboriginal policies: "Aboriginal people have special rights to determine the policies that affect them, especially those that target them. They have a claim for resources to support these policies and programs ... In general, participation in policy making is not a criterion of a good policy: poor policies may have involved a lot of participation and at times citizen participation can make policies worse by any reasonable measure. But policies about Aboriginal people are different. *By definition*, policies that do not rest on their full participation are sub-optimal." By this definition, existing urban Aboriginal policy falls short. However, Young is optimistic that there are grounds for improvement as the field grows and matures.

There is virtually no research available that explores the subjects that are the focus of these chapters on the nature of and challenges involved in crafting policies and programs for urban Aboriginal communities. These chapters demonstrate the extensive variations between provinces and cities in the recognition of urban Aboriginal people as a distinct group requiring particular approaches and they provide some hints concerning the question of why initiatives regarding urban Aboriginal peoples seem to work in some cities but are less smoothly implemented in others. They also touch on some of the unique issues related to policy making in the urban Aboriginal field – issues of historic definitions of "Aboriginal" in relation to cities, the important role of urban Aboriginal organizations, the need to address Aboriginal and Treaty rights, including the right to self-government, and the lack of leadership that produces a complex jurisdictional and programming maze in urban areas. Together these chapters make a unique contribution to our understanding of policy making for Aboriginal people in cities.

NOTES

1 Following the *Constitution Act* (1982 as amended), we use the term "Aboriginal peoples" to refer to the Indian, Métis, and Inuit peoples of Canada. Most contemporary writers use "First Nations" instead of "Indian." When discussing official government policies, we adopt the terms used in colonial and Canadian government policies and statistics (for example, Registered Indian, Native). Registered Indians are individuals who are registered under the *Indian Act*. When referring to a specific

First Nations community, we use particular names such as Mi'kmaq, Cree, and Ojibway. We also recognize that the term Métis has different and contested meanings; sometimes it refers to descendants of First Nations and European people, and sometime it refers to descendants of the Métis Nation that emerged in the Prairie provinces. Although the particular meaning of Métis is not always specified, we acknowledge these differences here.

2 Despite this position, the Indian Affairs Branch introduced its Placement Program in 1956, aimed at facilitating urban integration of carefully selected migrant families. The program was debated within the Branch. As a result of conflict emerging from the support of local Indian Affairs personnel for the administration of this program by a group of Blackfoot in Calgary in the 1960s, the program was cancelled (Ryan 1972; Peters 2002).

3 Bostrom (1984, 523) presented a slightly different perspective, maintaining that the federal government had developed "no evident strategy" to shift costs for urban First Nations to provinces until 1964, when it "made its first concerted effort to transfer some of its program and fiscal responsibilities for Indians to the provinces." Negotiations with provinces focused on provincial delivery of services with financial compensation from the federal government for Registered Indians living off reserves. Bostrom indicates that this initiative had dissolved by 1968 and was replaced with the federal government's 1969 White Paper.

4 Re Term "Indians", [1939] 1 S.C.R. 104 at 121; and [1939] 2 D.L.R. 417 at 433.

5 Corbiere v. Canada (Minister of Indian and Northern Affairs) [1999] 2 S.C.R. 203.

REFERENCES

Abele, Frances and Katherine A.H. Graham. 1989. "High Politics is Not Enough: Policies and Programs for Aboriginal Peoples in Alberta and Ontario." In Aboriginal Peoples and Government Responsibility: Exploring Federal and Provincial Roles, ed. David Hawkes, 141–72. Ottawa: Carleton University Press.

Andersen, Chris. 2007. "Aboriginal Gangs as a New Form of Aboriginality." Paper presented at the annual meeting of the Canadian Indigenous Native Studies Association, Congress of the Humanities and Social Sciences, 26 May – 2 June, at the University of Saskatchewan.

Barron, F. Laurie. 1997. Walking in Indian Moccasins. The Native Policies of Tommy Douglas and the CCF. Vancouver: UBC Press.

Berkhoffer, Robert F. 1979. *The White Man's Indian: Images of the American Indian from Columbus to the Present*. New York: Vintage.

Bostrom, Harry. 1984. "Recent Evolution of Canada's Indian Policy." In *The Dynamics of Government Programs for Urban Indians in the Prairie Provinces*, eds. Raymond Breton and Gail Grant, 519–44. Montreal: The Institute for Research on Public Policy.

Bourne, Larry S. 2003. "Elastic Cities; Inelastic Governments: Urban Growth and Urban Governance in Canada." *Canadian Issues*, February: 14–18.

Breton, Raymond and Gail Grant, eds. 1984. *The Dynamics of Government Programs for Urban Indians in the Prairie Provinces*. Montreal: The Institute for Research on Public Policy.

Canada. 1997. *Gathering Strength: Canada's Aboriginal Action Plan*. Ottawa: Minister of Public Works and Government Services.

Canada. 1969. *Statement of the Government of Canada on Indian Policy* (The White Paper, 1969). Available: http://www.ainc-inac.gc.ca/ai/arp/ls/pubs/cp1969/cp1969-eng.asp. Accessed 23 November 2008.

Cedar Project Partnership, Pearce, Margo E., Wayne M. Christian, Katherina Patterson, Akm Moniruzzaman, Kevin J.P. Craib, Martin T. Schechter, and Patricia M. Spittal. 2008. "The Cedar Project: Historical Trauma, Sexual Abuse and HIV Risk among Young Aboriginal People who Use Injection and Non-injection Drugs in two Canadian Cities." *Social Science and Medicine* 66 (11): 2185–94.

Chartrand, David. 1993. *The Electronic Series: Public Hearings*, Public Hearings, Royal Commission on Aboriginal Peoples, Toronto, CD-ROM. Ottawa: Minister of Supply and Services.

Clatworthy, Stewart. 2000. *First Nation Affiliation Among Registered Indians Residing in Select Urban Areas*. Ottawa: Minister of Public Works and Government Services Canada.

Cooke, Martin and Danièle Bélanger. 2006. "Migration Theories and First Nations Mobility: Towards a Systems Perspective." *Canadian Review of Sociology and Anthropology* 43 (2): 141–65.

Courchene, Thomas J. 2007. *Global Futures for Canada's Global Cities*. IRPP Policy Matters 8 (2).

Garcea, Joseph and Edward C. LeSage Jr., eds. 2005. *Municipal Reform in Canada: Reconfiguration, Re-Empowerment, and Rebalancing*. Don Mills: Oxford University Press.

Geddes, Barbara. 1990. "How the Cases You Choose Affect the Answers You Get: Selection Bias in Comparative Politics." *Political Analysis* 2 (1): 131–50.

Goldie, Terry. 1989. *Fear and Temptation: The Image of the Indigene in Canadian, Australian, and New Zealand Literatures.* Kingston and Montreal: McGill-Queen's University Press.

Graham, Katherine A.H. and Evelyn J. Peters. 2002. *Aboriginal Communities and Urban Sustainability.* Ottawa: Canadian Policy Research Network.

Guimond, Eric and Norbert Robitaille. 2008. "Aboriginal Populations in Canadian Cities: Why Are They Growing So Fast?" Paper presented at the conference on Aboriginal Population in Transition – Demographic, Sociological and Epidemiological Dimensions, 17–18 October, at the University of Alberta.

Guimond, Eric. 2003. "Fuzzy Definitions and Population Explosion: Changing Identities of Aboriginal Groups in Canada." In *Not Strangers in These Parts: Aboriginal People in Cities*, eds. David Newhouse and Evelyn J. Peters, 35–50. Ottawa: Policy Research Initiative.

Hanselmann, Calvin. 2002. *Uncommon Sense: Promising Practices in Urban Aboriginal Policy-Making and Programming.* Calgary: Canada West Foundation.

– 2001. *Urban Aboriginals: Opportunities and Challenges.* Calgary: Canada West Foundation.

Heisz, Andrew and Logan McLeod. 2004. *Low Income in Census Metropolitan Areas, 1980–2000.* Catalogue no. 75-001-XIE. Ottawa: Statistics Canada.

Hibbard, Michael and Marcus B. Lane. 2004. "By the Seat of Your Pants: Indigenous Action and State Response." *Planning Theory and Practice* 5 (1): 97–104.

Howard-Bobiwash, Heather. 2003. "Women's Class Strategies as Activism in Native Community Building in Toronto, 1950–75." *American Indian Quarterly* 27 (3–4): 566–82.

Hylton, John H. 1999. "The Case for Self-Government: A Social Policy Perspective." In *Aboriginal Self-Government in Canada*, ed. John Hylton, 78–91. Saskatoon: Purich Publishing.

Indian and Northern Affairs Canada. 2008. *Aboriginal Housing.* Available: http://www.ainc-inac.gc.ca/ai/mr/is/abhsg-eng.asp. Accessed 3 December 2008.

Levitte, Yael. M. 2003. *Social Capital and Aboriginal Economic Development: Opportunities and Challenges.* PhD diss., Geography Department, University of Toronto.

Loxley, John and Fred Wien. 2003. "Urban Aboriginal Development." In *Not Strangers in These Parts: Aboriginal People in Cities*, eds. David

Newhouse and Evelyn J. Peters, 217–42. Ottawa: Policy Research Initiative.

Morse, Bradford. 1989. "Government Obligations, Aboriginal Peoples and Section 91 (24): Aboriginal Peoples." In *Government Responsibility and Aboriginal Peoples: Exploring Federal and Provincial Roles*, ed. David C. Hawkes, 59–92. Ottawa: Carlton University Press.

Morse, Bradford W. and John Giokas. 1995. "Do the Métis Fall Within Section 91(24) of the *Constitution Act 1867?*" In *Aboriginal Self-Government: Legal and Constitutional Issues*. Ottawa: Royal Commission on Aboriginal Peoples.

Nagel, Joan. 1995. "American Indian Ethnic Renewal: Politics and the Resurgence of Identity." *American Sociological Review* 60 (6): 947–65.

Newhouse, David. 2003. "The Invisible Infrastructure: Urban Aboriginal Institutions and Organizations." In *Not Strangers in These Parts: Urban Aboriginal Peoples*, eds. David Newhouse and Evelyn J. Peters, 243–53. Ottawa: Policy Research Initiative.

– 2000. "From the Tribal to the Modern: The Development of Modern Aboriginal Societies." In *Expressions in Canadian Native Studies*, eds. Ron F. Laliberté, Priscilla Settee, James B. Waldram, Rob Innes, Brenda Macdougall, Lesley McBain, and F. Laurie Barron, 395 409. Saskatoon: University of Saskatchewan Extension Press.

Newhouse, David and Evelyn J. Peters. 2003. *Not Strangers in These Parts: Urban Aboriginal Peoples*. Ottawa: Policy Research Initiative.

Peters, Evelyn J., Roger Maaka, and Ron Laliberte. 2008. *Urban First Nations and Métis Identities in Saskatoon*. Unpublished Data. Saskatoon: University of Saskatchewan.

Peters, Evelyn J. 2007. "First Nations and Métis people and Diversity in Canadian Cities." In *Belonging? Diversity, Recognition and Shared Citizenship in Canada*, eds. Keith Banting, Tom J. Courchene, and F. Leslie Seidle, 207–46. Ottawa: Institute for Research on Public Policy.

– 2006. "[W]e Do not Lose Our Treaty Rights Outside the ... Reserve: Challenging the Scales of Social Service Provision for First Nations Women in Canadian Cities." *Geojournal*. 65 (4): 315–27.

– 2005. "Indigeneity and Marginalization: Planning for and with Urban Aboriginal Communities in Canada." *Progress in Planning* 63 (4): 325–404.

– 2002. "Our City Indians": Negotiating the Meaning of First Nations Urbanization in Canada, 1945–75. *Historical Geography* 30: 75–92.

Reeves, William and Jim Frideres. 1981. "Government Policy and Indian Urbanization: The Alberta Case." *Canadian Public Policy* 7 (4): 584–95.

Roberts, Lance, Susanne von Below, and Mathias Bos. 2001. "The Métis in a Multicultural Society: Some Reflections on the Macro Picture." In *Métis Legacy: A Historiography and Annotated Bibliography*, eds. Lawrence J. Barkwell, Leah Dorion, and Darren R. Prefontaine, 193–98. Winnipeg: Pemmican Press.

Royal Commission on Aboriginal Peoples. 1996. *Perspectives and Realities*. Vol. 4 of the *Report of the Royal Commission on Aboriginal Peoples*. Ottawa: Minister of Supply and Services Canada.

Royal Commission on Aboriginal Peoples. 1993. *Aboriginal People in Urban Centres: Report of the National Round Table on Aboriginal Urban Issues*. Ottawa: Minister of Supply and Services.

Ryan, Joan. 1972. *Wall of Words*. Edmonton: Hurtig Publishers.

Siggner, Andrew. 2003. "The Challenge of Measuring the Demographic and Socio-Economic Condition of the Urban Aboriginal Population." In *Not Strangers in These Parts: Urban Aboriginal Peoples*, eds. David Newhouse and Evelyn J. Peters, 119–39. Ottawa: Policy Research Initiative.

Siggner, Andrew and Rosalinda Costa. 2005. *Aboriginal Conditions in Census Metropolitan Areas, 1981–2001*. Catalogue no. 89-613-MIE, No. 008. Ottawa: Statistics Canada.

Silver, Jim, Parvin Ghorayshi, Joan Hay, and Darlene Klyne. 2006. *In a Voice of Their Own: Urban Aboriginal Community Development*. Winnipeg: Canadian Centre for Policy Alternatives.

Skelton, Ian. 2002. "Residential Mobility of Aboriginal Single Mothers in Winnipeg: An Exploratory Study of Chronic Moving." *Journal of Housing and the Built Environment* 17 (2): 127–44.

Statistics Canada. 2008. *Aboriginal Peoples in Canada in 2006: Inuit, Métis and First Nations, 2006 Census*. Available: http://www12.statcan.ca/english/census06/analysis/aboriginal/urban.cfm. Accessed 3 December 2008.

Urban Aboriginal Task Force. 2006. *Progress Report Phase I*. Available: http://www1.servicecanada.gc.ca/eng/on/epb/uas/reports/uatfphase1.shtml#1. Accessed 3 December 2008.

Walker, Ryan. 2008a. "Social Housing and the Role of Aboriginal Organizations in Canadian Cities." *IRPP Choices* 14 (4): 1–18.

– 2008b. "Improving the Interface Between Urban Municipalities and Aboriginal Communities." *Canadian Journal of Urban Research* 17 (1 Supplement): 20–36.

– 2006. "Searching for Aboriginal/Indigenous Self-determination: Urban Citizenship in the Winnipeg Low-cost Housing Sector, Canada." *Environment and Planning* A.38 (12): 2345–63.

– 2003. "Engaging the Urban Aboriginal Population in Low-Cost Hous-
  ing Initiatives: Lessons from Winnipeg." *Canadian Journal of Urban
  Research* 12 (1): 99–118.
Wotherspoon, Terry. 2003. "Prospects for a New Middle Class Among
  Urban Aboriginal Peoples." In *Not Strangers in These Parts: Aboriginal
  People in Cities*, eds. David Newhouse and Evelyn J. Peters, 147–66.
  Ottawa: Policy Research Initiative.
Young, Robert. 2007. *Good Public Policy in Municipalities*. Handout.
  Montreal: Research meeting, 30 April – 1 May in Ottawa.

2

Federal Urban Aboriginal Policy: The Challenge of Viewing the Stars in the Urban Night Sky

FRANCES ABELE AND KATHERINE A.H. GRAHAM

In 1996, the Canadian Royal Commission on Aboriginal Peoples (RCAP) observed that "[t]he issues confronting urban Aboriginal people – governance, access to culturally appropriate services, cultural identity, and intercultural relationships – have been woefully neglected by Canadian governments and Aboriginal authorities in the past" (RCAP 1996b, 5). The Commission's finding raises two important questions for those interested in public policy and municipalities:

- What were the causes of past deficiencies?
- What are the necessary social, economic, and political conditions necessary for good urban Aboriginal policy?

This chapter considers these questions as they relate to the evolving federal government policies and programs concerning urban Aboriginal people. It complements the studies of Aboriginal policy in the cities of four provinces – Alberta, Manitoba, Ontario, and New Brunswick. These studies focus on how policy is made in Canadian municipalities and attempt to assess what constitutes good public policy in local contexts. They consider the interplay of all three levels of government, the economic, political, and social state of the cities, and the extent to which urban Aboriginal issues were recognized and acted upon. They also consider non-governmental institutions and movements, namely, the social forces that contribute to the shape and impact of urban Aboriginal policy.

Understanding federal urban Aboriginal policy requires consideration of all of these matters. In this chapter, we ask: what would be the best alignment of social forces, conditions in municipalities, and federal priorities and institutions that would result in good urban Aboriginal policy? Our analysis is based on the premise that good policy follows from the consistent engagement of federal and municipal governments with social forces, that is, citizen organizations and movements that seek to bring about change. Good public policy is fluid; it constantly adapts to changing social circumstances, responds to the needs of the people for whom it is relevant, and balances their concerns with the welfare of the general population. In this chapter, we do not attempt a comprehensive assessment of the various phases of federal urban policy, but focus instead on the factors that make for good Aboriginal urban policy.

While all levels of government are important, no other level of government has the financial resources and the reach of the federal government. One way or another, federal sponsorship or direct participation affects virtually all aspects of urban life in Canada, and in this regard, Aboriginal policy is no exception. We provide an answer to our two main questions by briefly reviewing the history of federal urban Aboriginal policy and then assessing at some length the current (post-1993) policy situation in light of this history. We examine the extent to which there is a necessary alignment among social forces, conditions in cities, and federal approaches for urban Aboriginal policy to be effective. Metaphorically, we investigate whether or not the stars can actually be seen to align in a busy and often hazy urban night sky.

THE EVOLVING FEDERAL PROBLÉMATIQUE

Federal governments have long been ambivalent about their urban Aboriginal responsibilities. For decades, policy limited attention to the needs of First Nations people living on reserves. Only gradually have federal policies and programming recognized that First Nations people live in cities as well as on reserves and that, along with Inuit, Métis, and the other "Section 35" groups,[1] they require urban-based programming.

Clearly, one factor driving the recent change in federal policy has been the relatively rapid urbanization of Aboriginal peoples. Today, more than half of the Aboriginal people of Canada live in cities. These people, regardless of how they may have come to live in urban areas, remain Aboriginal and their constitutional rights are unchanged. Furthermore, they are connected with Aboriginal peoples living in home territories (i.e., reserves, settlements, and regions) through family, culture, law, and politics (Peters, this volume). While policy must focus on the distinct needs and contributions of urban Aboriginal people, it must also recognize their connections with the broader and equally diverse polity of Aboriginal peoples in Canada as a whole.

Federal initiatives relevant to urban Aboriginal people date back to 1957 and generally have been marked by degrees of ambivalence about the boundaries of federal responsibility, both geographical and jurisdictional. A full review of the history of federal Aboriginal policy and programming is outside the scope of this chapter, which focuses principally on policy changes that occurred during the last fifteen years. We have found that the evolution of federal programs in the urban Aboriginal policy field is best understood as consisting of four distinct time periods. We have labeled these periods according to the general characteristics of the political and policy-making processes that shaped them.

The first period, 1955 to 1977, may be seen as the period in which significant activity in urban Aboriginal affairs began. We have dubbed it the period of "activist engagement." It includes the earliest stirrings of federal activity in urban Aboriginal affairs, as well as the run-up to and the immediate aftermath of the release of the 1969 *White Paper on Aboriginal Policy,* which many identify with the rising of a grassroots and nationally organized Aboriginal political movement.[2] This was also a period of heightened federal government interest in cities, manifested, for example, by the establishment of the first-ever Ministry of State for Urban Affairs,[3] and the federal convening of a series of intergovernmental conferences with provinces and municipal governments, represented by the Federation of Canadian Municipalities. Federal initiatives with respect to Aboriginal peoples and (independently) with respect to cities reflected the fiscal buoyancy and general readiness to take executive action of the time as well as the relatively undeveloped state of mutual expectations in this period. The federal role with respect to programming for Aboriginal peoples *in* cities was minimal and indeed the object of considerable conflict (Ryan 1978; Peters 2001).

The "activist engagement" period was full of overt conflict and some confusion, and, ultimately, considerable success for Aboriginal activism. Political representative organizations[4] focused increasingly on the recognition of Aboriginal rights, a new term that gained considerable traction during this period, partly as a result of a series of rights-based court cases. By contrast, (although not in complete contradiction) broader social forces and other Aboriginal organizations (for example, women's organizations) sought social justice and poverty reduction. Aboriginal people and their organizations formed alliances with others who were working for social justice, poverty reduction, and environmental protection. In the cities, a new municipal government activism was shaped considerably by the demands of these broader social forces, which also shaped the activism of the federal government. This is the context for the first major foray by the federal government into specifically defined "urban Aboriginal policy," which was cast as a matter of good social policy rather than as a recognition of Aboriginal rights. Funding for Indian Friendship Centres dates from this period, as do debates over what programs were required for the growing urban Aboriginal population, how these should be conceived, and what the balance of federal and provincial involvement should be. As Evelyn Peters (2001, 77) notes, "Competing frameworks for understanding Indian urbanization made the exercise of program development and administration unstable and unpredictable."

The second period, from 1978 to 1986, is overwhelmingly the period of "high politics" in matters both intergovernmental and constitutional. The constitutional patriation debates and the constitutional aftermath dominated public affairs and consumed the energies of leaders, governments, and organizations. Throughout this period, most active members of the political elites inside and outside government focused on the constitution and the law, while matters of daily life and community well-being tended to receive less attention. The specific needs and unique circumstances of Aboriginal people living in cities were universally recognized, but they did not fit readily into the national debates about rights, land, and political institutions. Like their political counterparts, social groups and organizations – especially those committed to advocacy – were caught up in the high politics of the period. Any discussions about social justice and social inclusion were subsumed under the rubric of "constitutional negotiations." The high politics associated with patriation and its aftermath underlined concerns of governance at the expense of all others and created a line of public discourse in which the specific, local, and heterogeneous concerns of urban

Aboriginal life were difficult to situate. This situation was to persist for a number of years.

In parallel fashion, this period saw the concerns of Canadian cities take a back seat to the high-stakes issues of national unity and economic restructuring that were being discussed by federal, provincial, and territorial elites. Though their concerns were indeed implicated in these discussions to the extent that they would reap the benefits and bear the brunt of political and economic restructuring, their voices were otherwise eclipsed.

The third period, from 1987 to 1992, is a period of "deteriorating relations" between Aboriginals and the state. This period also featured a great deal of civil disobedience. In the aftermath of the failure of the last First Minister's Conference on Aboriginal Rights either to advance the Aboriginal agenda or establish alternative frameworks for policy discussion, a period of Aboriginal protest ensued (Peach 2004). Grassroots conflicts over land rights spilled into municipalities small and large. The most prominent example is probably the conflict over "the Pines" at Kanesatake/Oka near Montreal.[5] In response to the armed standoff at Oka (and perhaps gathering protests across the country) in 1991, the federal Cabinet established the long-promised Royal Commission on Aboriginal Peoples (RCAP) as a body responsible for fostering collective reflection, research, and debate, and founded the Indian Specific Claims Commission (ISCC) as an arms-length body responsible for reviewing (but not adjudicating) allegations of specific infringements of Treaty rights (Indian Specific Claims Commission 2008).

The five years of deteriorating relations after 1987 saw Aboriginal peoples and governments coping with the aftermath of patriation, including the consequences of the Meech Lake and Charlottetown accords. It was also a period in which the fundamental issues of Aboriginal rights spilled into the everyday life of one of Canada's largest cities (Montreal) and into the consciousness of all Canadians and their governments. While the specific needs and unique circumstances of Aboriginal people living in cities were subordinated to other concerns during the previous period, these same concerns now moved to the centre of the national stage and, not coincidentally, to the agendas of provinces and cities.

The final period, from 1993 to the present, we have dubbed a period of "consolidation and construction." For various reasons, the stars seem to have aligned and made possible a positive change in urban Aboriginal policy. The 1996 publication of the Royal Commission's report, and the public and political reaction to it, led to a number of measures that were particularly helpful to urban Aboriginals. In the same period, there was perhaps a growing shift in the way city life was perceived, especially with respect to the increasing role of ethnic diversity within the urban landscape. With the reductions in public expenditures during the 1990s, the dimensions of urban poverty became more visible. Public discussion of the whole system of social provision and the challenges of homelessness led to debates about the role of different levels of government and civil society organizations in dealing with both diversity and poverty. From the federal perspective, a myriad of policy issues began, to varying extents, to be viewed through an urban lens. This period is our central focus. In analyzing it, we will compare it to the three earlier periods in terms of the interplay among social forces, the state of our cities and towns, and federal government initiatives, all of which have shaped urban Aboriginal policy in Canada.

STARS IN ALIGNMENT: 1993–2006

Two events in the early 1990s set the stage for major changes in urban Aboriginal politics. The first was the defeat of the Charlottetown Accord in 1992. The defeat of the Accord was the final act in the long drama that was twentieth-century constitutional politics in Canada. A document drafted by a wide selection of elite representatives (including Aboriginal representatives) after a very public participatory process, the Accord envisioned a new constitution for Canada in which Aboriginal governments formed a third order in the federation. When the Accord was put to a Canada-wide referendum, it was defeated. With the end of the Charlottetown process, the high politics of constitutional negotiation subsided; the political space and funding for the institutions and processes of high politics in Aboriginal affairs disappeared.[6]

The second inaugural event of this period was the election of the new Liberal government of Jean Chrétien in 1993. Chrétien and his minister of finance, Paul Martin, became convinced that it was necessary to make reduction of the federal deficit a priority and ended years of increased federal expenditures. A Program Review carried out during the fiscal year 1994–95 affected all Canadians because it changed the pattern of federal spending in all areas of social provision.

City governments began to feel the effects of federal fiscal restraint and, in some cases, perhaps most dramatically in Ontario, of provincial cutbacks as well (Marquardt 2007). The federal and provincial governments' withdrawal of funding from programs like social housing and social assistance had an impact on the health of many Canadian cities. One manifestation of this impact was the rise of homelessness as a visible fact of urban life in the mid-1990s. The funding shortfall began to place increasing financial pressure on city governments as well as voluntary organizations; it occurred at the same time as the economic infrastructure of many Canadian cities felt the effects of recent free trade agreements (Canada-United States and the North American Free Trade Agreement) and increasing internationalization (Gertler and Wolfe 2002). Extremes of wealth and poverty became more visible all across the country, albeit unevenly.

In Aboriginal affairs, the effects of the fiscal changes of the early 1990s were mixed. Aboriginal people, as all other Canadians, found their life prospects reorganized not only by the restructuring economy but also by the restructuring state: a new model of federal funding of Aboriginal social programs emerged (Abele 2004). The new model involved support for the establishment of numerous small Aboriginal-controlled service organizations, most of which were situated in cities. Some examples of these organizations include the Vancouver Native Health Society walk-in clinic, Poundmakers Lodge (Edmonton), the Joe Duquette High School (Edmonton), the Saskatchewan Urban Native Teacher Education Program (Regina and Saskatoon), the Estey School Aboriginal Employment Program (Saskatoon), and Anishinaabe Oway-Ishi – an Aboriginal youth employment preparation and placement program in Winnipeg (Newhouse 2003, 248–9). This was also a period in which some long-standing organizations reached institutional maturity, with established lines of operation, a network of contacts, and experienced staff (Peters 2005).

At the same time, in a number of areas of service provision, policy deliberations were opened to Aboriginal participation through the use of advisory and, in some cases, decision-making appointed councils. New initiatives in Aboriginal service provision emphasized mutual respect and partnership – a more collaborative approach between government and Aboriginal organizations in the development of programs (Abele 2004). Although the new policy councils and committees were introduced for programs that affected Aboriginal people in the cities and in the countryside, they engaged mainly the urban-dwelling organizational representatives and staffers with the side effect that the relationship these urban individuals maintained with federal institutions was altered. In earlier periods, political leaders and their support staff maintained regular contact with federal institutions, while people in social service and health professions were employees of governments or non-governmental organizations. The changes of the early 1990s drew some of these staffers into advisory roles, even while they created a large number of new organizations (Abele and Papillon 2008). The effect was to broaden the exposure of federal officials to urban Aboriginal activists working as advocates and service providers.

As these changes were occurring, the ethnic character of major Canadian cities began to change as a result of an amended immigration policy and current world events. For example, the Asian population of Vancouver began to grow rapidly as the new immigration policy that gave priority to immigrants with significant capital resources intersected with the immanent transfer of Hong Kong from British to Chinese jurisdiction. Immigration, however, was by no means confined to the rich. In fact, the number of newcomers to Canadian cities who did not bring substantial financial resources with them was so large, that there was an increasingly strong link during this period between being a recent immigrant and being poor (Graham and Phillips 2007). The challenges of diversity and prosperity in Canadian cities now propelled a broad-based constellation of local social forces into action. Social forces and city governments have been working "at the coal-face" to address these challenges and they have been dealing with constrained or reduced federal and provincial funding. The new challenges facing Canada's cities has induced co-operation and competition among the organizations representing various social and ethnic groups.

It is in this context that Aboriginal people and their representative organizations began to formulate a new agenda for the 1990s in which urban affairs received much more emphasis than in the past. The move towards the "Aboriginalization" of service-delivery organizations created many more institutional actors, each of which had an interest in certain policy areas (Loxley and Wien 2003). Between 1993 and 2000, the number of Aboriginal organizations (for-profit and NGOs) more than tripled (Newhouse 2003). Along with this expansion came significant differences of opinion about how these organizations should be organized; some people favoured "status-blind" approaches while others favoured a segmented approach in which organizations and services are keyed to constitutional status.[7] Meanwhile, the proportion of Aboriginal people living in Canadian cities continued to grow. In the five years between 1996 and 2001, the proportion of the total population in Canada who identified as Aboriginal who lived in urban areas grew from 47 to 49.1 per cent (Statistics Canada 2003).

The increasing prominence of urban issues has been reflected in the politics of Aboriginal organizations at the national level. The Assembly of First Nations (AFN), which asserts that it represents First Nations citizens regardless of age, gender, or place of residence, struggled with the reality that its internal centre of power was the assembly of reserve-based chiefs even as the people it sought to represent were living off-reserve in Canadian cities. The Congress of Aboriginal Peoples (CAP) grew out of the Native Council of Canada, an organization representing "non-status Indians." In the 1990s, CAP began to identify itself firmly as the representative of all urban Aboriginal people, whatever their status. CAP also sought to represent urban Métis people, an increasingly heterogeneous group no longer the exclusive preserve of the Métis National Council. Pauktuutit, the Inuit Women's Association, turned its attention to the needs of Inuit women living in the cities. All of these national organizations were constrained in their advocacy role during the 1990s by reduced federal funding and were consequently forced to survive on overheads generated by federal contracts.

Despite general fiscal restraint, there were some new program initiatives during this period that were relevant to Aboriginal people living in cities, such as the Aboriginal Head Start Initiative (Health Canada 1995) and the Aboriginal Justice Strategy (1995). To these general application programs was added a single program focused on the cities, the Urban Aboriginal Employment Initiative (1996–99).

In more pure policy terms, there was an important change with the 1995 recognition of the inherent right of self-government for Aboriginal peoples of Canada (including the Indian, Inuit, and Métis people) mentioned in Section 35 of the *Constitution Act* of 1982. Released jointly by the Minister of Indian Affairs and Northern Development and the Federal Interlocutor for Métis and Non-Status Indians, the "inherent right policy" explicitly recognized the right of self-government of Métis and Indian groups "Off a Land Base" (Canada 1995). In fact, no negotiations began with Métis and

Indian groups residing off a land base south of the sixtieth parallel, and no policy respecting urban Aboriginal people was developed. Métis Nation proposals for self-government subsequently laid out in the RCAP report did include an urban land dimension, but, despite its mandate, RCAP did not judge their workability (Cairns 2000). The Métis Nation Framework Agreement was signed with the federal government in 2005, and it aimed to address this urban issue as well as other longstanding issues, particularly for members of the Métis Nation of Ontario, the Manitoba Métis Federation, the Métis Nation of Saskatchewan, the Métis Nation of Alberta, and the Métis Provincial Council of British Columbia. However, there is no mention of an urban-specific framework despite the fact that 65 per cent of the Métis population live in urban areas (RCAP 1996c, 604).

In 1996, the Royal Commission on Aboriginal Peoples released its final report. In retrospect, the analytical attention devoted to urban concerns is remarkably scant: just one chapter in its five-volume opus was devoted exclusively to urban Aboriginal issues, with occasional references to urban concerns in the rest of the report. The section on urban economic issues occupies four pages out of 248 devoted to economic development. Nevertheless, the report speaks eloquently about the challenges faced by Aboriginal people in Canadian cities as well as their resiliency and some of their successes. It recognizes the centrality of identity to Aboriginals living in cities and the scourge of the racism frequently experienced by urban Aboriginals, which sometimes came at the hands of the police and other municipal authorities. The special challenges faced by Aboriginal women and youth in cities are also addressed in the report: the Commissioners note that, for some women who gained Indian status through Bill C-31, cities remain a relatively welcoming environment in comparison with reserves. The Commission recommends an enhanced role for the federal government in financing social programs for Aboriginal people living off a land base and it offers a powerful argument for parallel provincial responsibility in this area. The report proposes some ways in which urban governments can reform their institutional arrangements and services to become more understanding and responsive to the needs and interests of the Aboriginal population. Finally, the report offers a range of models for achieving Aboriginal self-government in urban centres, not prescriptively, but by way of illustrating workable alternatives.

One year later, in 1997, the federal Cabinet issued its formal response to the RCAP report. *Gathering Strength: Canada's Aboriginal Action Plan* is thirty-six pages long and has two paragraphs that deal with urban issues. *Gathering Strength* focuses on the need to "strengthen partnerships with provincial governments and Aboriginal groups to develop practical approaches for improving the delivery of programs and services to urban Aboriginal people" (Canada, IAND 1998, 12). The document then gives the example of a new "single window" approach to service delivery in Winnipeg, involving the federal, provincial, and city governments collocating in the Winnipeg Aboriginal Centre. The publication of *A Guide to Federal Initiatives for Urban Aboriginal Peoples* was cited as an example of recent good practice.

From a practical perspective, the impact of RCAP on the urban Aboriginal front was to give urban Aboriginal people a public voice, through its hearing process. It also contributed modestly to increased awareness among municipal governments in Canada of the situation and aspirations of urban Aboriginal people. One part of the hearing process was the Urban Aboriginal Working Group, a group of Aboriginal leaders with an urban focus and city managers from Fredericton, Toronto, and Winnipeg. This group met regularly through the research and policy phase of RCAP and reached consensus on new ways ahead. This was not only a vehicle for education among the participants but also a new opportunity to catalyze broader municipal action on urban Aboriginal issues through the Federation of Canadian Municipalities.

In 1996, the Centre for Municipal-Aboriginal Relations (CMAR) was established as a joint initiative between the Federation of Canadian Municipalities (FCM) and the Indian Taxation Advisory Board (ITAB). Its mandate was to "promote effective municipal-Aboriginal relations based on the principles of mutual recognition, respect, sharing, and mutual responsibility" by undertaking targeted research and acting as a clearing house to develop a database of agreements and effective practices (Aboriginal Council of Winnipeg et al. 1998). The focus was on rationalizing urban-reserve issues in situations where a reserve was located in or near an urban area, not on relations between municipal governments and their Aboriginal residents. The initiative was funded in part by INAC, though it was housed in ITAB's Ottawa offices, had no full-time staff, and operated on a project-to-project basis. An important CMAR project was the 2001 formation of the Municipal Aboriginal Adjacent Community Cooperation Project, a committee whose partners included the FCM, ITAB, and INAC, and whose mandate was to identify best practices in municipal and First Nations' partnership-building (Larbi 1998). Their final report analyzed five municipal case studies, provided recommendations from each of these communities, and demonstrated that mutually beneficial economic development initiatives are possible with the commitment of both parties (Tamera Services Limited 2002). In light of intervening changes in the federal political landscape, it seems likely that had RCAP begun its work perhaps a decade later, in 2000 rather than 1990, urban matters would have had more prominence.

If RCAP devoted comparatively little ink to urban issues, so too did the formal federal policy response. An important contributing factor to this dearth is the Commission's primary focus on the reinterpretation of Canadian history built upon a more solid understanding of the role of Indigenous peoples and on large matters of constitutional status and political change. Above all, RCAP settled upon a "nation-to-nation" perspective[8] that sits somewhat uneasily with urban Aboriginal realities. In many urban centres, particularly large ones such as Vancouver and Toronto, the Aboriginal population represents many nations, rendering urban Aboriginal governance complex. *Gathering Strength*, as the formal federal policy response, had to deal with this central thrust of the RCAP report. The federal response rested on a partnership paradigm between the federal government and Aboriginal peoples, without directly stating the federal view on the Commission's concept of nationhood. Interestingly, this partnership paradigm would inform future federal initiatives related to urban Aboriginal policy. For example, the federal government's National Homelessness Initiative, established in 1999, contained a segmented fund for Aboriginal homelessness and provided for designated Aboriginal organizations to adjudicate projects to be undertaken using these funds.

The partnership paradigm is perhaps most fundamental to what is now arguably the cornerstone of federal urban Aboriginal policy, namely, the 1998 Urban Aboriginal Strategy (UAS). There is, however, another key dimension that distinguishes the UAS. It is founded on the premise that place-based policy making best meets the circumstances of urban Aboriginal people and cities. The judicious extension of federal support in response to local activity also exemplifies the "steering not rowing" paradigm of 1990s public management, in which the role of the state was redefined in the devolution of responsibilities to private or non-profit organizations. The UAS began as a four-year, $50 million initiative that was introduced following the release of *Gathering Strength: Canada's Aboriginal Action Plan.* Funding was renewed in 2003, and from 2003 to 2006 over 300 pilot projects were funded. As of 2007, the federal government has committed another $68.5 million over the next five years. Led by the Federal Interlocutor for Métis and Non-Status Indians in collaboration with eight other federal departments, the UAS aims to address socio-economic needs of at-risk Aboriginal people in urban centres. It is a community-based approach that supports projects and priorities identified by community members, and, in so doing, works to build organizational capacity within urban Aboriginal organizations. The goal of this strategy is to develop partnerships that better align federal, other government, and non-governmental programs to respond to these priorities; to coordinate federal resources across departments; and to test policy and programming ideas in order to provide strategic direction.

The Office of the Federal Interlocutor (OFI) leads the UAS nationally in the coordination and management of an interdepartmental committee structure that oversees its implementation. Steering committees have been formed in each participating city. As of 1 April 2007, the OFI assumed full responsibility for the implementation of the program and took over from Western Economic Diversification Canada (WD) in British Columbia and Manitoba, and Service Canada in Saskatchewan and Ontario.

The same principles of partnership and place-based policy making also form the core of another federal urban initiative that carries implications for urban Aboriginal people. The 2000 Vancouver Agreement between the federal government, the government of British Columbia, and the City of Vancouver is intended to ameliorate the appalling social pathology and impoverishment in Vancouver's Downtown Eastside. Aboriginal people, along with Chinese and Latinos, are the predominant residents of this area. The Vancouver Agreement was a conscious experiment. In the latter days of the Chrétien era and during the Martin prime ministership, there was even some appetite to replicate the agreement in other cities. In Vancouver, the experiment was a success: Aboriginal people were direct beneficiaries of a federal urban initiative that saw them as part of a very complex whole.

While these broad changes were occurring in federal-Aboriginal relations, Canadian cities also formulated a response to the impacts of 1990s fiscal restraint. Faced with continuing financial challenges, economic competitiveness, crumbling public infrastructure, the challenges of immigrant settlement, and managing diversity and homelessness, Canadian cities became increasingly active in lobbying for a new federal urban agenda as the 1990s wore on. Local social forces, from chambers of commerce to social and environmental groups, were also supportive of this goal. The federal government responded with a Task Force on Urban Issues, led by MP and former Toronto city councillor, Judy Sgro. Its objective was to find ways in which the federal government could become more active on urban issues without running afoul of jurisdictional boundaries and without committing significant financial resources. The 2002 Task Force Report proposed three priority programs in urban areas: affordable housing, transit/transportation, and sustainable infrastructure.

Perhaps sensitized by the RCAP report but more likely realizing firsthand urban Aboriginal realities and the experience to date with the UAS, the Sgro Task Force had several recommendations specifically related to urban Aboriginal peoples. The government was called on to coordinate strategic intergovernmental policy delivery; to address issues related to poverty, employment, and housing, especially as they relate to urban Aboriginal youth; to increase the pilot projects that had been started under the Urban Aboriginal Strategy; to encourage the co-operation of urban reserves with the surrounding urban areas; to include the needs of Métis and non-status urban Aboriginal peoples; and to strengthen educational supports at the post-secondary level (Sgro 2002, 30–1).

While the channels of communication between Aboriginal peoples and the federal government were being adjusted during this period, some municipal-Aboriginal frequencies remained fuzzy. A survey undertaken in 1998 by the Centre for Municipal-Aboriginal Relations (since defunct) showed that, while many municipal players were aware that "Aboriginal agencies provided services, many of them were not sure about the number of agencies involved or the types of services provided" (Larbi 1998, 18). At a minimum, however, it can be argued that there is now greater awareness among and interaction between municipal governments, the federal government,

Aboriginal organizations, and other local social forces whose interests intersect with those of Aboriginal people in urban centres that have participated in implementation of the UAS. Participating cities include Vancouver, Prince George, Lethbridge, Calgary, Edmonton, Prince Albert, Regina, Saskatoon, Winnipeg, Thompson, Toronto, and Thunder Bay. As Andersen and Strachan's chapter elsewhere in this volume argues, the federal government can play an important leadership role simply in coordinating the multiple actors in every Canadian city.

The federal government's urban Aboriginal agenda since the Sgro report has, to a considerable degree, rested on the UAS foundation. The period 2002 to the present has seen dramatically shifting political winds in Canada and the fact that the UAS has been sustained may be thought of as remarkable. The Martin government's "Communities Agenda," during its brief life from 2004 to 2005, was more holistic than targeted. It was replaced by a Conservative agenda that, if it is focused on anything "urban," is more about infrastructure and environment. In the case of the UAS, the Conservatives have chosen to place somewhat more emphasis on economic development. Nonetheless, the Urban Aboriginal Strategy has been renewed – something that suggests that the stars may be in alignment for some progress on service delivery capacity, if not, as Walker et al. argue, for movement towards the development of an Aboriginal presence in the politics of Canadian cities.

CONCLUSIONS: GOOD GOVERNANCE?

For most of the twentieth century, federal urban Aboriginal policy was overwhelmed by or subsumed under the meta-policy questions related to Aboriginal rights and self-determination. There has never been a comprehensive urban Aboriginal policy framework in Canada. Aboriginal issues have appeared on the federal policy agenda only when the government of the day or a minister has been seized by some aspect of the "urban Aboriginal fact" due to that government's or minister's preoccupation with cities, poverty, and economic development or with crime or other aspects of social pathology.

The constitutional breakthrough in 1982 entrenched "existing Aboriginal and treaty rights" without reference to place of residence and made no distinctions among "Indians, Inuit and Métis." In spite of this constitutional change, successive Ministers of Indian and

Northern Affairs remained unwilling to pick up the urban file and followed the long-standing federal policy of financing social welfare projects only on reserves. It is notable that the Urban Aboriginal Strategy was originally developed by the minister who served as the Federal Interlocutor for Métis and Non-Status Indians and not by the Minister of Indian Affairs and Northern Development – although both sets of responsibilities have been assigned to the same individual since the election of the Harper government in 2006. This constitutional change, the signing of modern treaties and post-1995 self-government agreements, and the urbanization of the Aboriginal population, have all rendered the federal "on-reserve only" policy untenable because of its limitations.

In light of the seemingly episodic policy interest and action, and the historic dispersion of responsibilities for urban Aboriginal issues within the federal government documented here and discussed in Peters' Introduction to this volume, one would normally ask whether there was consistency in the general direction of federal policies affecting urban Aboriginal people or whether they acted at cross purposes. This is a difficult question to answer because developments were so dispersed and episodic.

Certainly, there are signs that a sustainable federal approach to urban Aboriginal policy and social policy in particular is beginning to emerge. The Urban Aboriginal Strategy, which we have already discussed at length, is one such sign; it is significant that this program has been continued by the Harper Conservative government after it was created under the Martin Liberals. The strengths of the UAS approach include its ability to adapt to local circumstances, its community-based approach, its allowance for federal information sharing and coordination, and its receiving strong provincial support. On the other hand, there are some difficulties with this approach. There is significant tension between the UAS' supposed strategic focus and the reality of project funding pressures, weak communication with the Aboriginal community at large, a lack of clear terms of reference for the steering committees, a lack of ongoing strategic direction, a lack of direction from senior managers in participating federal departments, and a lack of a commonly understood longer-term vision for the UAS (Canada, OFI 2005).

As an evaluation assessing the first five years of the program noted, "Collaboration among federal departments and agencies is generally constructive but limited by: a shortage of funds at the local federal level; well-entrenched policy and program instruments; a lack of impetus from senior management in partner departments/agencies; a focus of project expenditures as opposed to the longer-term strategic focus; [and] a lack of clarity as to how the partner departments/agencies are intended to contribute" (Canada, OFI 2005).

This chapter began by asking a complex question: what would be the best alignment of social forces, conditions in municipalities, and federal priorities and institutions that would result in good urban Aboriginal policy? As defined by this project, good public policy has four characteristics: effectiveness, efficiency, equitability, and optimality. Our historical review suggests that only recently – perhaps only in the last few years – have the stars been aligned to favour positive action on all four of these axes. Many broad challenges and city-specific difficulties remain but the conditions for constructive federal policy and programming are more favourable than in previous periods.

Urban Aboriginal people are more organized than ever before. Many urban Aboriginal organizations have well-developed working relationships with municipal, provincial, and federal governments. They have developed area-specific policy expertise and connections into each general policy area. They benefit, of course, from the growing presence of well-educated Aboriginal professionals who are attracted to the employment opportunities available in cities. At the same time, more and more Canadian city governments are recognizing the need for engagement with Aboriginal residents and neighbouring Aboriginal communities. While there remain many areas of conflict – some cities have yet to establish effective channels of communication – there has been much progress in Aboriginal-government relations overall, a fact that will soon become apparent to all. Most strikingly, in recent years it has been clear that effective federal social policy will require that good working relations be maintained with the Aboriginal policy delivery sector and with Canadian cities.

NOTES

1 Section 35 of the *Constitution Act* recognizes "existing aboriginal and treaty rights of Indians, Inuit and Metis."
2 Indigenous peoples' mobilization on a Canada-wide basis actually pre-dates the White Paper, though resistance to the White Paper provided the

catalyst for a more united and focused movement of First Nations and other peoples and for a proactive federal response (Abele 2000; Weaver 1975; Ponting and Gibbins 1980).

3 The Ministry of State for Urban Affairs closed in 1979.

4 These included the National Indian Brotherhood (now the Assembly of First Nations), the Native Council of Canada (later the Congress of Aboriginal Peoples), Inuit Tapirisat of Canada (now Inuit Tapiriit Kanatami), and the Métis National Council.

5 Other conflicts in this period included the Peigan protests over the Oldman River Dam in 1990 and the Bear Island/Temagami conflict in 1991.

6 Although not all funding disappeared, the extra amounts provided for constitutional deliberations to the Assembly of First Nations and other peak organizations were expended and did not continue. Inuit had formed a separate institution for constitutional negotiation, the Inuit Committee on National Issues, which was wound up after the failure of the Charlottetown Accord referendum.

7 The term "status-blind" refers to measures that are available to all Aboriginal people whether or not they have status under the *Indian Act*. Those who have status are registered in federal records for differentiated services under the *Indian Act* and associated federal policies. People who have status are typically descendants of individuals who signed treaties or who were afforded "status" by administrative action. Today, they make up a large minority of the total Aboriginal population.

8 This concept of Aboriginal-Canada relations is rooted in the treaty relationship, which is comprised of a negotiated contract between two sovereign entities or nations.

REFERENCES

Abele, Frances and Martin Papillon. 2008. "Tracing the Contours of Neoliberal Citizenship: Aboriginal Peoples and Welfare State Restructuring." Paper presented at the annual general meeting of the Canadian Political Science Association, 25 May, at the University of British Columbia.

Abele, Frances. 2004. *Urgent Need: Serious Opportunity: Towards a New Social Model for Canada's Aboriginal Peoples*. Ottawa: CPRN.

– 2000. "Small Nations and Democracy's Prospects: Indigenous Peoples in Canada, Australia, New Zealand, Norway, and Greenland." *Inroads* 10: 137–49.

Aboriginal Council of Winnipeg, Institute on Governance, and Centre for Municipal-Aboriginal Relations. 1998. *Aboriginal Governance in*

Urban Setting: Completing the Circle Conference Summary and Conclusions. Available: http://www.iog.ca/publications/urbanreport_ps.pdf.

Cairns, Alan C. 2000. *Citizens Plus: Aboriginal Peoples and the Canadian State*. Vancouver: UBC Press.

Canada, Minister of Indian Affairs and Northern Development. 1995. *The Government of Canada's Approach to Implementation of the Inherent Right and the Negotiation of Aboriginal Self-Government*. Available: http://www.ainc-inac.gc.ca/al/ldc/ccl/pubs/sg/sg-eng.asp#PartI.

Department of Indian Affairs and Northern Development (DIAND). 1998. *Gathering Strength: Canada's Aboriginal Action Plan*. Ottawa: Minister of Public Works and Government Services Canada.

Canada, Office of the Federal Interlocutor (OFI). 2005. *Urban Aboriginal Strategy Formative Evaluation – Final Report*. Available: http://www.ainc-inac.gc.ca/ai/ofi/pubs/evr/evr-eng.asp.

Canada, Statistics Canada. 2003. *Aboriginal Peoples of Canada: A Demographic Profile* (2001 Census: Analysis Series). Ottawa: Ministry of Industry.

Gertler, Meric S. and David Wolfe, eds. 2002. *Innovation and Social Learning: Institutional Adaptation in an Era of Technological Change*. New York: Palgrave Macmillan.

Graham, Katherine A. and Susan Phillips. 2007. "Another Fine Balance: Managing Diversity in Canadian Cities." In *The Art of the State III: Belonging? Diversity, Recognition, and Shared Citizenship in Canada*, eds. Keith Banting, Tom Courchene, and Leslie Seidle, 155–94. Montreal: IRPP.

Indian Specific Claims Commission. 2008. Available: http://www.tbs-sct.gc.ca/rpp/2008–2009/inst/ICC/icc01-eng.asp.

Larbi, Patrick. 1998. *A Portrait of Municipal-Aboriginal Relations in Canada*. Prepared for CMAR [Ottawa Centre for Municipal-Aboriginal Relations].

Loxley, John and Fred Wien. 2003. *Urban Aboriginal People: History of Discriminatory Laws*. Ottawa: Depository Services Program, Law and Government Division.

Marquardt, Richard. 2007. *The Progressive Potential of Municipal Social Policy: A Case Study of the Struggle over Welfare Reform in Ottawa during the Common Sense Revolution*. PhD diss., School of Public Policy and Administration, Carleton University.

Newhouse, David. 2003. "The Invisible Infrastructure: Urban Aboriginal Institutions and Organizations." In *Not Strangers in These Parts: Urban*

Aboriginal Peoples, eds. David Newhouse and Evelyn J. Peters, 243–53. Ottawa: Policy Research Initiative.

Peach, Ian. 2004. *The Death of Deference: National Policy Making in the Aftermath of Meech Lake and Charlottetown Accords*. Saskatchewan Institute of Public Policy.

Peters, Evelyn J. 2005. "Progress in Planning: Indigeneity and Marginalization." *Planning for and with Urban Aboriginal Communities in Canada* 63 (4): 325–404.

– 2001. "Developing Federal Policy for First Nations People in Urban Areas: 1945–1975." *The Canadian Journal of Native Studies* 21 (1): 57–96.

Ponting, J. Rick and Roger Gibbins. 1980. *Out of Irrelevance: A Sociopolitical Introduction to Indian Affairs in Canada*. Toronto: Butterworth and Company.

Royal Commission on Aboriginal Peoples. 1996c. *Perspectives and Realities*. Vol. 4 of the Report of the Royal Commission on Aboriginal Peoples. Canada: Minister of Supplies and Services.

Ryan, Joan. 1978. *Wall of Words: The Betrayal of the Urban Indian*. Toronto: PMA Books.

Sgro, Judy. 2002. *Canada's Urban Strategy: A Blueprint for Action (Sgro Report)*. Ottawa: Prime Minister's Caucus Task Force on Urban Issues.

Tamera Services Limited. 2002. *Report Governing Relations Between Local Government and First Nation Government*. Available: www.cd.gov.bc.ca/lgd/gov_structure/library/first_nations_report.pdf.

Weaver, Sally. 1975. *Making Canadian Indian Policy*. Toronto: University of Toronto Press.

3

The Silence of Urban Aboriginal Policy in New Brunswick

KAREN BRIDGET MURRAY[1]

INTRODUCTION

New Brunswick might seem an unlikely research site for a study of what constitutes "good" urban Aboriginal policy. Urban Aboriginal policy is typically understood as a field comprising governmental responses to issues arising from the growing number of Aboriginal peoples[2] in cities, often as a result of migration from "reserves," Crown lands set aside for the exclusive use of Status Indians (Canada 2008a; Graham 1999; Graham and Peters 2002; Hanselmann 2001; Peters 2000 and 2002). The federal government's flagship urban Aboriginal program, launched in 1997 and known as the Urban Aboriginal Strategy (Canada 2008b), reinforces this understanding. The strategy, aimed at improving the social and economic conditions of urban communities, is based upon eligibility criteria that, in effect, exclude New Brunswick. For instance, cities with populations larger than 15,000 are eligible, but only where Aboriginal peoples constitute at least 5 per cent of the population. Additionally, a substantial "need" among Aboriginal peoples must be evident. Finally, there must not only be a willingness on the part of the provincial and municipal governments to partner with the federal government but also a demonstrated desire among a "significant" number of Aboriginal peoples "to work together" (Canada 2008c). These expectations de facto disqualify New Brunswick's three largest cities because the municipal governments of Fredericton, Moncton, and Saint John have very limited jurisdictional or fiscal competency for joint undertakings and Census-defined urban Aboriginal populations fall short of the 5 per cent minimum, constituting, in 2006, 2.8 per cent (2,375) in Fredericton (population 85,688), 0.9 per cent (1,175) in Moncton (population 126,424), and 1 per cent (1,250) in Saint John (population 122,384) (Statistics Canada 2006a). As shall be explained later in this chapter, British and (later) Canadian colonial laws,[3] policies, and practices fostered legal, political, and spatial divisions among Aboriginal peoples that render the expectation of Aboriginal peoples uniformly desiring or having the means to "work together" problematic (Canada 2008c). Moreover, the constitutional and economic context of the early twenty-first century has dissuaded the provincial government from expanding its reach into the off-reserve urban Aboriginal policy setting.

Michel Foucault's understanding of discursive silences is instructive for evaluating a part of the country where an express urban Aboriginal policy field is almost completely absent. Foucault defined discourse not as synonymous with language, but rather as a form of "power/knowledge" inherent in practices, spaces, effects, and *silences*. As Foucault (1978) wrote in volume one of the *History of Sexuality*, silence is not the end of discourse but rather the beginning of:

> a new regime of discourses. Not any less [will be] said about [a particular matter]; on the contrary. But things [would be said] in a different way; it [would be] different people [saying] them, from different points of view, and in order to obtain different results. Silence itself – the things one declines to say, or is forbidden to name, the discretion that is required between different speakers – is less the absolute limit of discourse, the other side from which it is separated by a strict boundary, than an element that functions alongside the things said, with them and in relation to them within over-all strategies. (27)

Policy silences, in short, "are an integral part of the strategies that underlie and permeate discourses" (Foucault 1978, 27).

The silence that defines urban Aboriginal policy in New Brunswick follows a long history whereby governments have been preoccupied with shaping the relationship between urban spaces and reserves. The aim of this chapter is to understand this preoccupation in historical perspective. An historical vantage point allows a way to grasp how the lack of urban Aboriginal policy in the contemporary setting emerged and the political and governmental implications arising from this absence. In this manner of analysis, urban and reserve spaces are not hermetically sealed entities defined by demographic, geographical, functional, legal, or administrative boundaries. They are mutually constituted domains of ever-changing relationships, representations, contestations, and identifications (Parker 2004, 149; Peters 2002) shaped in part by official actions and inactions (Pal 1992, 2) and their effects.

Several interrelated questions are posed: How have British and (later) Canadian colonial authorities defined urban space and Aboriginal peoples as interlocking governmental concerns? What were the predominant presuppositions, objectives, and mechanisms brought to bear to address the "problems" relating to the urban-reserve relationship? What conditions gave rise to discursive regime variations? Finally, what were the broader ramifications of each regime? The focus is on British and (later) Canadian official viewpoints and governmental mechanisms pertaining to urban space and reserves, as well as the predominant political, economic, legal, and racial processes to which they gave rise. Such a focus is inherently limited because it leaves out a detailed assessment of the refusal of indigenous peoples to accept colonial and settler policies and conditions. Nevertheless, tracing the surfaces and surfacing of urban Aboriginal policy silence brings out some of the discursive complexities and multiplicities shaping policies relating to Aboriginal peoples in New Brunswick.

The source materials informing this analysis include findings from interviews conducted with twenty-three people between June and September 2008. Interviewees included past and present political leaders and activists (4), front-line service providers (4), academics (2) and municipal (5), provincial (5), and federal authorities (4).[4] Participant selection began with a conspicuous sampling method, whereby individuals known to have knowledge of the history of indigenous peoples and policies relating to urban space in New Brunswick were deliberately chosen. The interview list expanded through a snowball sampling technique, whereby each person interviewed provided the names of people whom she or he felt fit the key informant criteria. Interviewees were ensured confidentiality to the fullest extent possible by law, that their privacy would be protected, that their names would not be released to anyone, and that information obtained in interviews would be compiled and reported in such a manner so as to avoid identifying any specific respondents.

In New Brunswick, where the number of possible participants was small, many of the interviewees would have attended meetings and other events together and would be keenly aware of each other's views. For example, even a reference to a "federal official" or "activist" could potentially reveal a person's identity based on the content to which it refers. For this reason, a numeric coding system is used (i.e., Interview 1, Interview 2, etc.).

Interviewees were asked open-ended questions about their knowledge of the relevance of urban space to Aboriginal policy. Through such questions, they drew attention to the crucial significance of the urban-reserve imbrications that define Aboriginal policy in the province. Interview data served as signposts to specific governmental activities, which were examined in greater depth by drawing upon additional primary and secondary evidence. The collective historical memory of interviewees was vital to the present analysis. Participants, in effect, offered an oral history that made it possible for me to move beyond the simplistic demographic imperative argument that permeates many evaluations of urban Aboriginal policy towards an understanding of the complex, contingent, and problematic political dynamics underlying this largely hidden field of policy in New Brunswick. The people interviewed for the project not only highlighted predominant systems of governance but also directed me to and often generously shared obscure written materials that were not self-evidently relevant to the research questions (for example, program and service pamphlets, etc.). Many participants also read and commented on an initial draft of this report. The data were ordered diachronically as a way to bring into visibility emblematic moments, episodes where predominant policy definitions linking questions of urban space and reserves gave way to new sensibilities. Consideration was given to how these transformations took shape and how they affected the ordering of spatial relations of power with respect to reserves and cities.

In the analysis to follow, I show how the silence of urban Aboriginal policy in New Brunswick constitutes the fourth in a succession of discursive spatial regimes.[5] The first dates back to the pre-Confederation setting, when the town-reserve relationship became a matter of official concern and close *proximity* was considered preferable. The second was already in effect by the late nineteenth century, when industrialization gave rise to *segregation* mentalities and techniques aimed at distancing the city from reserve. The end of the Second World War saw the emergence of attempts at reserve system *eradication* and Aboriginal peoples' integration into urban labour markets. The fourth was a new spatial regime evident as early as the late twentieth century. This *trans-spatial* regime modeled the relationship between cities and reserves as constitutionally and economically interdependent. This chapter concludes by assessing these findings as they pertain to "good" urban Aboriginal policy in New Brunswick.

PROXIMATION

For thousands of years, the Mi'kmaq, Passamaquoddy, and Wolastoqiyik[6] have lived in territories of what became known as Quebec, Prince Edward Island, Nova Scotia, and New Brunswick as well as areas in Maine, Vermont, and New Hampshire (Bartlett 1986, 13–14; Leavitt 1995, 1996, 2000; McGee 1983; Wiseman 2005).[7] In contemporary New Brunswick, Mi'kmaq traditional lands are located in the eastern part of the province, the Wolastoqiyik's along the St John River and its tributaries, as well as above Lake Temiscouata along the south shore of the St Lawrence River, and the Passamaquoddy's territories are close to the St Croix River and its streams and coastal areas bordering Passamaquoddy Bay. The Mi'kmaq and Passamaquoddy are maritime-oriented and the Wolastoqiyik river-oriented people. They have semi-nomadic traditions and rely upon hunting, fishing, and trapping for survival. The Europeans who first encountered these three Algonquian-speaking groups referred to them all as "Indians" (Virginia Miller 2004; Prins 1996; Speck and Hadlock 1946; Upton 1974, 5–6; Wallis and Wallis, 1957; Wicken 2002, 8).

In New Brunswick, the reserve system would become an integral part of British and (later) Canadian officials' attempts to define and address the relationship between cities and reserves (Bartlett 1986, 13–20). Initially reserving lands for "Indians" was part of British war strategy to regulate the Mi'kmaq, Passamaquoddy, and Wolastoqiyik, who were seen as posing a military threat to the British until the end of the War of 1812 (Oliver and Sturgeon 1983, 10–13; Upton 1973, 51, 55; Upton 1974, 4). Reserves also offered a means to dampen land conflicts between the burgeoning Loyalist population and the indigenous peoples after the American Revolution (Krueger 1975; Upton 1979, 98). Promoting New Brunswick's agricultural sector, considered vital to the colony's economic future, was also a key colonial technique for discouraging Aboriginal peoples from pursuing their semi-nomadic traditions (McNutt 1984; Upton 1974, 26). Farming, the British maintained, would "civilize" Indians (Parenteau 1998; Parenteau and Kenny 2002, 51; Upton 1974, 7; Upton 1979, 106).

The British established reserves without any regard for eighteenth-century agreements they had made with the Mi'kmaq, Passama-quoddy, or the Wolastoqiyik (Canada 2006a; Nurse 2004; Saunders 1970; Wicken 1994 and 1995). Authorities saw land access for Aboriginal peoples as a privilege not a right, a position supported by early treaty jurisprudence (Bartlett 1986, 41; Nicholas 1986, 217).[8] In this setting, the Mi'kmaq, Passamaquoddy, and the Wolastoqiyik had little choice but to accept government land grants that entitled them, not to own property outright, but "to occupy and possess" reserves "during pleasure," the latter expression referring essentially to the pleasure of the Crown (1838 Schedule of Indian Reserves quoted in Bartlett 1986, 42). Loyalist squatters routinely encroached upon reserve lands. Officials did very little to stop them (Bartlett 1986, 30–3; Parenteau and Kenny 2002, 51). The Mi'kmaq, Pas-samaquoddy, and Wolastoqiyik requested assistance in transitioning to agriculture. Authorities did very little to help them (Parenteau and Kenny 2002, 55). In the mid-nineteenth century, when British officials found that few reserves had become viable agricultural ventures, they blamed Aboriginal people for leaving the land in an "uncultivated state." In 1838, the New Brunswick Legislative Assembly urged a greater "disposition of land" to settlers, who were considered more likely to make the desired "permanent improve-ments" (Bartlett 1986, 30).

In the mid-nineteenth century, many Mi'kmaq, Passamaquoddy, and Wolastoqiyik were faced with limited land access, limited assist-ance with farming, and limited defenses against threats to their traditional ways of life. They were pushed to the point of starva-tion and left with no other choice than to seek help from the Brit-ish Colonial Office, which, in response, sent a directive to New Brunswick in 1838 asking for recommendations for addressing the "Indian problem" (McNabb 1983, 280–1; Redmond 1998; Upton 1974, 7–14; Upton 1979, 101). As part of its colonial policies more generally, the British pondered "extermination, slavery, insulation, and amalgamation" as solutions to such matters, but only the latter two were deemed practical; local officials, including authorities in New Brunswick, were directed to determine how to proceed. By then, many assumed that Aboriginal peoples in New Brunswick were on the verge of extinction. For instance, in his *Journal of a Mission to the Indians in the British Provinces*, John West (1827), a Church of England missionary, wrote that with respect to the "Indians of New Brunswick ... it is a question ... of extinction of the remnant of a people, who were once sovereigns of the soil, at no very distant period" (252–3). This assumption was evident in the emergence of markets for Wolastoqiyik goods and services that were geared towards assisting European goals or aimed at selling "Indianness" as a passing artifact of history. Parenteau offers a compelling image of these sensibilities when he describes the example of "elite anglers [who] wanted ... not simply someone to help them catch fish, but an authentic 'primitive' man to guide them into an imaged world of primeval wonder – someone to legitimize their adventure as a true wilderness experience" (Parenteau 1998, 2). Markets such as these construed Aboriginal peoples as "pre-modern" (Tully 1995, 62–70) incongruities in the march of progress. The way of life *and* the bodies of Aboriginal people were accorded market value for their assumed rarity and finitude.

Moses Perley, a lawyer and "sportsman," was recruited in the 1830s for the task of reporting on the situation of the New Brunswick Indians (Harring 1998, 182) and he had specific remarks about the location of the French Village reserve and its proximity to Fredericton. French Village (later renamed Kingsclear) was established in 1792 roughly twenty-six kilometres southwest of Fredericton (see Map 1), a small town and a strategic military site. Both town and reserve were in the heart of fertile Wolastoqiyik territory (Oliver and Sturgeon 1983, 10; Squires 1980; Upton 1974, 98).

After visiting every reserve in the province, Perley concluded that Indians were generally "gradually frittering away from the absence of superintendence, and the want of authority of one person or persons to watch over and protect the rights of the unlettered people who, from their situation and utter ignorance of business, are peculiarly open to the schemes of designing persons" (Perley 1841, 3). At French Village, however, Perley saw an anomalous situation. There he found a reserve with sufficient arable land to render farming

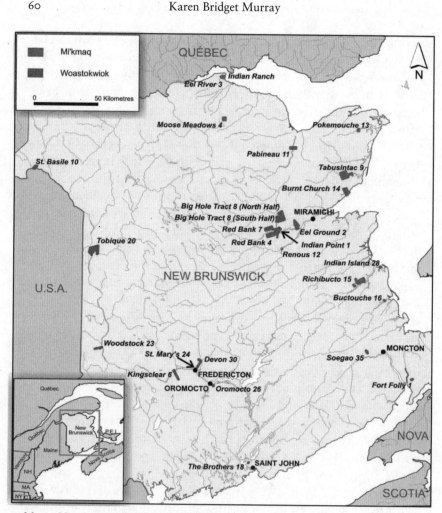

Map 1: New Brunswick Indian Reserves 2008

Source: *Atlas of Canada* 1,000,000 National Frameworks Data
Map by: Elise Pietroniro, University of Saskatchewan; Map Projection: NAD 1983 (CSRS98)
New Brunswick Stenographic

feasible; it lay in close proximity to a nearby town, a fact that allowed for the supervising of Indians (Parenteau and Kenny 2002, 53). He explained:

> the Indians at the Village near Fredericton have of late years become rather industrious; the women work early and late at the manufacture of baskets, while the men provide the materials,

and also till the soil with their own hands. They do not follow the chase as ardently, or for so great a part of the season, as they used to do, and they lead much more settled lives than formerly. Hence, it may be inferred that this would be the most eligible place, for the establishment of a School, and for making the attempt to civilize them. The Village is in a respectable neighbourhood, near the Seat of Government, and could always be kept under effectual supervision, and the immediate eye of the Executive. (Perley 1841, 3)

The Wolastoqiyik at French Village, while near the town, were not to be of the town. Like other legally and politically disadvantaged groups, such as women and non-property holders, Aboriginal peoples were denied the right to vote, run for office, own property, or sit on juries – not that Aboriginal peoples necessarily wanted such things (Krueger 1975; Lawrence 2004, 36). Assimilation was a distinctly racialized process (Upton 1979, 106) that, in effect ensured that the Wolastoqiyik's existence did not interfere with White propertied-class objectives. In this regard too, the British deemed a degree of insulation necessary. As Perley explained, "Indians [would] be benefited by the practical experience and example of the white Settlers," but kept "far removed from town as to prevent their intercourse with the idle and depraved [Whites] as much as possible" (Perley 1843, 87).

SEGREGATION

In the years immediately following Confederation, the constitutional and geographical conditions altered with respect to Fredericton and reserves, and this change fostered a new spatial discourse premised upon segregation. The constitutional setting was transformed with the passing of the *British North America Act* (1867) (hereinafter the BNA *Act*), which established the Dominion of Canada as a federal system that gave the national (hereinafter federal) government legal jurisdiction for and fiduciary duty to "Indians" (Paul 2006, 219–80). With the presumption that Aboriginal peoples would "naturally" die off perhaps waning, a new reserve, Devon/St Mary's (hereinafter St Mary's),⁹ was created in 1867 on the opposite side of the St John River from Fredericton (see Map 1). Not long after, in 1876, the federal government integrated many pre-Confederation laws written for Upper and Lower Canada into a new federal *Indian Act* (1876), thus establishing the legal category "Status Indian." The Status Indian classification was legally intertwined with Indian entitlements to lands set aside for their "collective use and benefit," namely, the Indian reserves (Canada 2008a).

This new constitutional and geographical context gave rise to three distinct governmental orders in the Fredericton area. First, there was the on-reserve governmental setting at St Mary's that fell under the federal government's fiduciary duty to Status Indians under the *Indian Act*. The on-reserve distinction was further entrenched in 1884 with the passing of the *Indian Advancement Act*, which established the terms for municipal-style "band" governments for Status Indians on reserves that had reached a sufficient degree of "civilization" (Shewell 2004, 147). Bands and their respective reserves, including St Mary's, nevertheless remained subject to federal authority.[10] Second, there was the off-reserve setting that was defined by both provincial and federal jurisdiction and trained on the settler populations.

Third, there was a governmental field defined by a lack of express political attention. The *Indian Act* shaped this terrain by providing mechanisms whereby Indian status could be lost voluntarily or involuntarily, a process euphemistically called "enfranchisement." Importantly, for women, involuntary means included marrying a person who was not a Status Indian. As the *Indian Act* (1876) stipulated, "any Indian woman marrying any other than an Indian or non-treaty Indian shall cease to be an Indian in any respect within the meaning of this Act." Research by Gary Gould and Alan Semple attests to some of the effects of this provision on Fredericton's governmental milieu.[11] In *Our Land: The Maritimes: The Basis of the Indian Claim in the Maritime Provinces of Canada* (1980), they describe how, in 1881, a White man named George N. married an Aboriginal woman named Cecilia S. from the St Mary's Indian Reserve. Under the *Indian Act*, Cecilia lost her status upon marriage. Soon after, both the Reserve Chief and the federal government's Indian Agent pressured Cecilia to move off the reserve. After that:

> the couple relocated just outside the Reserve, where they built a small log house. They lived their whole life in this location and raised a large family, perhaps as many as twenty-five children, all of whom followed their parents' footsteps and lived near their

mother's home reserve. They were accepted and mixed with the Indian community, spoke the Malecite language and were indistinguishable from those living on the reserve. From this close association with the reserve Indians nearly all of these children took Indian spouses. Consequently, the next generation of the family had large percentages of Indian blood and lived in an Indian manner. These intermarriages developed complex lines of interrelationship with the St John River reserves of Kingsclear [previously known as French Village], St Mary's, and Oromocto. (Gould and Semple 1980, 95)

People such as George and Cecilia were *in* but not *of* the city, while simultaneously *of* but not *in* the reserve. They found themselves in a constitutional abject zone, excluded from band government and ignored by federal and provincial governments, the latter two of which refused any obligations to Non-Status Indians.

In the late nineteenth century, the goal of "civilizing" Indians endured, although, in 1889, a railway bridge providing direct land egress between town and reserve set the stage for a reassessment of the suitability of St Mary's location. Farming remained a key assimilation technique, but, until the bridge was built, officials had shown little concern about the lack of agriculture at St Mary's, where the Wolastoqiyik's subsistence hinged heavily upon "logging, rafting, guiding, trapping, and the making of baskets, moccasins, and canoes" (Cloney 1993, 118). Even until 1891, annual reports for the Department of Indian Affairs spoke favourably about evidence of assimilation among the Fredericton-area Wolastoqiyik, commenting on "marked improvements" (Dominion of Canada 1891, 35) in "dress" and "ideas" (Dominion of Canada 1889, 38), as well as in "habits and customs" (Dominion of Canada 1891, 35).

The train bridge symbolically and materially embodied the emergent urban industrial economic order, but it also raised the possibility of a new racial order and rendered the reserve too close to the city for comfort in the eyes of British settlers. From one angle, Fredericton was seen as a place of vice that would hinder efforts to civilize Indians. From another angle, the presence of Indians in or nearby the city was regarded as a threat to the city, an emblem of a lack of progress or, worse yet, civilization's decline. These dual and often expressly racist concerns were apparent from the late nineteenth century and into the early twentieth century. In 1889, the federal government's Indian Agent in New Brunswick, James Farrell, wrote in his *Annual Report of the Department of Indian Affairs* that: "[t]he most objectionable feature in connection with [St Mary's] reserve is its situation and close proximity to Fredericton. Since the prosecution of several parties for selling liquor to the Indians it is difficult for them personally to purchase it, but there are indirect means by which it can be procured, and whilst two-thirds of the Indians never use intoxicants there is one-third that will indulge, much to the annoyance of those who avoid its use; and these, when questioned, will not reveal the names of the offending parties or in any way assist the agent in bringing them to justice" (Dominion of Canada 1889, 38). In 1912, the superintendent of the Indian day schools for New Brunswick, J.J. Ryan, reported that: "[o]wing ... to the proximity of this reserve to the city of Fredericton – the highway bridge only separating the two places, it is extremely difficult to maintain a fair attendance at school. The moving picture shows exercise a weird fascination over the Indian, and I have frequently turned the children back whom I found on the bridge, making their way alone to these shows. When I spoke to the parents about it they acknowledged they knew of the children going, and this during school hours, but made light of the matter"(Dominion of Canada 1912, 315). In 1918, Fredericton's Mayor, R.B. Hanson, grumbled about the reserve being "in the heart of the town" and not adequately "removed from certain evil interests surrounding it." The reserve, he asserted, was "more or less untidy and uncleanly" and "in fact an eyesore" (quoted in Walls 2008, 8). Such comments no doubt had moral connotations, as cleanliness was a mark of morality in early twentieth-century Canada (Duplessis 1995, 31; Valverde 1991). Other people complained about Wolastoqiyik "parading the streets of Fredericton" (quoted in Walls 2008, 8). Robert John Cloney (1993), in a master's thesis that focused on how political officials regarded the Wolastoqiyik as a governmental concern, quoted a local observer who claimed the problems were "largely due to the situation of the Reserve. Imagine 120 odd of a population of Indians camped on two acres of land, situated between the rowdy element of Gibson and St Mary's villages ... [T]he rowdy elements of Fredericton that has only to cross the bridge leading from Fredericton to the Reserve" (119). Later on, federal officials began to talk about the reserve's "poor sanitation" (quoted in Walls 2008, 8), but had no regard for their own role in shaping the substandard living conditions of the Wolastoqiyik. Even into the 1960s, for instance, only two houses at St Mary's had flush toilets because no level of government wanted to pay for plumbing hook-ups (Maritime Regional Office, 1958; Interview 17).

At the beginning of the twentieth century, officials launched the first of numerous attempts to move the St Mary's reserve to French Village, which was still valued by officials for its sufficient distance from the city and conduciveness for agricultural undertakings. In 1930, St Mary's was repositioned a short distance from its original site, but the reserve remained adjacent to the city (Nicholas 2005; Walls 2008, 8–13). Right through to the end of the Second World War, however, successive efforts at physically segregating the reserve from the city were consistently thwarted. Euro-Canadian officials faulted the St Mary's Wolastoqiyik, ironically, on their reluctance to "give up their nomadic ways" (Shewell 2004, 108–9). Historian Martha Walls (2008, 8–13) came to a different conclusion, seeing this intransigence as a successful form of resistance. Protecting their land and livelihood, which depended upon (among other things) selling goods and services in the city (La Forest 1980; Parenteau 1998; Parenteau and Kenny 2002), the St Mary's Wolastoqiyik asserted their treaty rights to fend off relocation schemes.

Segregation strategies were pervasive throughout the Fredericton milieu. In 1903, a separate Indian entrance and seating area was secured at the newly built Catholic Church in Devon, a project partially funded by the federal government and championed by a Marysville industrialist who collaborated on the project with a Member of Parliament, Alexander Gibson (Nicholas 2005). At the dawn of the Depression, the opening of the Shubenacadie Residential School launched a sustained period of removal, often by force, of many Aboriginal children from their families, including children from the Fredericton area. The expulsion of Wolastoqiyik to "Shubie," as it was called by students, was part of a broad-based effort to erase Aboriginal peoples' ways of living, being, thinking, and speaking, which placed indigenous children in the hands of abusers running the school (Knockwood and Thomas 1992), abuse that was evident even in the very early years after its opening in 1930 (Murray 2011). Around this time, Euro-Canadian contractors hired by the federal government for housing construction at St Mary's refused to give Indians jobs. In a letter to the Indian Agent, band members asked "if the Government don't give us work we don't know where we can get work, times are hard and we depend on that work." The

Indian Agent did nothing to help. St Mary's residents tried to build their own houses but were told that "no Indian" was "permitted to erect buildings of his own on the new reserve." Status Indians hired for federal projects were paid in-kind rather than in cash, the latter form being a "privilege" accorded to Whites only. Through to the Second World War, it was common for Indians to be denied store credits, a common courtesy extended to Whites. On-reserve education offered by British settlers to Indians was geared towards agricultural and religious instruction, whereas off-reserve education prepared non-Aboriginal students for economic and educational advancement.[12] It would be 1947 before a St Mary's reserve student obtained an education beyond grade eight. This state of affairs is easy to understand given that, in addition to a woman marrying a non-Aboriginal person, a higher level of formal education was another means by which Indian Status could be involuntarily lost. Federal officials needed only to unilaterally decide that White Euro-settler norms had been sufficiently adopted through education for an Indian's status to be revoked (Cloney 1993, 122, 126, 142, 152, and 155). The cessation of legal status, the end of federal entitlements, and the curtailment of public relief went hand-in-hand. Indian status was absolutely essential for piecing together a modicum of subsistence.

ERADICATION

After the Second World War, the federal government began promoting urban labour markets as key arenas through which to "integrate" Aboriginal peoples (Walker 2006). This idea was linked to proposals for the eradication of the reserve system, which emerged as early as 1944, when Dorise Nielsen, a member of the socialist-oriented Cooperative Commonwealth Federation Party and Member of Parliament from Saskatchewan, argued before the House of Commons Committee on Postwar Reconstruction and Re-establishment for the need to "[b]reak down ... the prejudice, and see that Indian people have the same right of employment as anybody else ... that gradually the younger generation of the Indian people are absorbed into the life of Canada, that they live in cities like the rest of us. I think that speaking of that younger generation of Indian people, we should bring them up to take their part in the general life of this country and forget about the reserves" (Shewell 2004, 149–50). In 1947, the *Report of the Commission on Indian Affairs* echoed Nielsen's viewpoint and stressed urban migration as a way to promote citizenship through employment. The report noted that "Indians" working in urban areas had "no objection, as a rule, to paying taxes so earned" (Canada 1947, 5). That same year, local officials were once again trying to relocate St Mary's to Kingsclear (Walls 2008, 22), but at least one member of the Commission saw the contradiction, noting that the "weakness" of the removal scheme was "the idea of taking these Indians back into the hinterland so to speak" (Walls 2008, 30).

Until 1951, individual Indian Agents kept lists that identified who was and who was not an Indian, and this fact led to significant variation across the country concerning the basis upon which official status was determined. That year, however, the federal government altered the *Indian Act*. This change was not the first revision to the act, but it was the first time that a centralized national registry was created (Interviews 13 and 15). After the completion of the new national registration process, the federal government's fiduciary duty to "Indians" would only be to people centrally registered. A new classification of "Registered Indian" emerged. On the one hand, direct descendants of, for instance, the Mi'kmaq, Passamaquoddy, or Wolastoqiyik, even if they had been previously identified as Status Indians, could be denied status as "Registered Indians." One's name need only be left off the list to lose legal status as an Indian. Many people lost status this way, sometimes as a result of simply being unaware of the registration process or its significance (Interview 15). On the other hand, people without direct blood links to the Mi'kmaq, Passamaquoddy, or the Wolastoqiyik, such as non-Aboriginal women who had married Status Indians, could become Registered Indians if their names were placed on the official register (Interviews 13 and 15). Because material benefits could accrue from one's registered status, including, inter alia, the potential for treaty rights, annuity payments, and band revenues (Lawrence 2004, 54; NBAPC n.d.a), legal divisions already apparent among Aboriginal peoples in the Fredericton environs were further entrenched. Eventually as the next section will show, these changes to the *Indian Act* had major ramifications for urban-reserve governing mentalities.

In 1960, Status Indians obtained voting rights and soon after federal attention turned to the reserve system. In 1966, the Department of Citizenship and Immigration released a report entitled *A Survey of the Contemporary Indians of Canada Economic, Political, Educational Needs and Policies*, commonly known as the "Hawthorne Report." The report reignited the national debate about the potential for urban labour markets to absorb reserve populations. It famously coined the term "citizens plus" to capture two key ideas: recognition of traditional treaties and granting of Canadian citizenship rights and responsibilities to Aboriginal peoples. With respect to urban life, the report stated it was essential that "the more specially gifted or qualified Indians [be taken] out of reserves and [brought] into major metropolitan centres to work in a variety of skilled jobs" (Hawthorne 1966, 143). Aboriginal peoples were to be in and of the city, where government officials hoped racial divisions would erode.

Significantly, the Hawthorne Report treated New Brunswick cities as anomalies. Unlike major urban economic hubs, the province's cities were regarded as offering none of the usual benefits of urban living. New Brunswick (along with some other parts of the country) presented a "special problem" that had "no easy solution." As the report explained:

> New Brunswick – generally has the highest rates of unemployment and the lowest per capita income in Canada. Here the basic problems are depletion of resources (especially timber), obsolescence (especially coal), and distance and high transportation costs from major potential markets. Barring massive federal investments and expenditures on an unprecedented scale, coupled with large subsidies and other inducements to entice outside capital to invest in the region, one can see little prospect for substantial improvement in the economic position of the Maritime population, White or Indian. (Hawthorne 1966, 160)

It seems "unavoidable," the report concluded, "that Indians will need the opportunity to participate with Whites in the general migration of surplus rural population to other regions having more remunerative job opportunities. Otherwise the Indians will remain, as they have for decades, a depressed group having no meaningful economic role to play" (Hawthorne 1966, 159). In effect, Hawthorne envisioned making Aboriginal peoples into "citizens plus" in highly differentiated ways according to urban spatial considerations. While the federal government did not accept the Hawthorne Report, some of the mentalities regarding urban space in Atlantic Canada were already circulating in national policy discourses and practices. For instance, in 1965, the federal government purchased property near Halifax known as Wallace Hill to "provide a site for the relocation of Indians close to a centre of employment" (Canada 2007a; Interview 10; Proctor 2001). The plan was never implemented, but the intention was to facilitate urban migration of Aboriginal peoples – not only from New Brunswick but also from across Atlantic Canada – to Halifax by providing housing for Status Indians who wanted to move off reserves (Interview 10).[13]

The discursive ferment that defined the late 1960s was also shaped by the creation of Aboriginal peoples' advocacy groups funded by the federal government, which hoped such entities would contribute to discussions about revisions to Indian policy (Chute 2002, 76; Moore 1983). One such group was the Union of New Brunswick Indians (UNBI), launched in 1967. The UNBI had its headquarters in Fredericton and would later become affiliated with the National Indian Brotherhood (later the Assembly of First Nations), a Registered Indian organization. The UNBI balked when the federal government largely ignored the views of Aboriginal peoples in the now infamous *Statement of the Government of Canada on Indian Policy* (hereinafter "the White Paper") in 1969. In the White Paper, the federal government proposed the eradication of reserves and the migration of Aboriginal peoples to cities. As the White Paper put it:

> [w]ith the technological change of the twentieth century, society became increasingly industrial and complex, and the separateness of the Indian people became more evident. Most Canadians moved to the growing cities, but the Indians remained largely a rural people, lacking both education and opportunity. The land was being developed rapidly, but many reserves were located in places where little development was possible. Reserves were usually excluded from development and many began to stand out as islands of poverty. The policy of separation had become a burden. (Canada 1969)

The White Paper was ultimately rejected, having been met with mounting resistance by Aboriginal peoples (Sappier 1969, 25; Weaver 1981).

Until 1971, it was unclear whether the UNBI represented Registered and Non-Registered Indians. That year, at a meeting at St
Mary's, the matter was settled: the UNBI represented only Registered Indians who descended from the Mi'kmaq and Wolastoqiyik (*Agenutemagen* 1971; Nicholas 1970). The UNBI regarded the
Indian Act as problematic and was specifically concerned with how
it divided Registered and Non-Registered Indians; nevertheless, as
UNBI's first president, St Mary's Chief Harold Sappier asked: "If we
did consent to the abolishment of the *Indian Act* ... what would happen to our negotiating position?" (Sappier 1969). The message was
clear: Registered Indians were in a stronger political position without Non-Registered Indians. An assertion of political agency and a
challenge to federal authority, this decision was, nonetheless, shaped
by and adapting to the mainstream constitutional setting and its colonial premises that had been, and continued to be, imposed upon
Aboriginal peoples.

In 1972, the New Brunswick Association for Métis and Non-Status
Indians (NBAMNI) was launched (Interview 2), also in Fredericton,
to speak for "biologically or culturally" Aboriginal people, generally Non-Registered Indians. NBAMNI would later become affiliated
with the Native Council of Canada, now the Congress of Aboriginal Peoples[14] (Interviews 10, 13, and 17; NBAPC n.d.b, 13; Silman
1987). NBAMNI was in a disadvantaged advocacy position relative
to the UNBI, which had band-based membership that received federal funding under the *Indian Act* (*Agenutemagen* 1985, 1; La Forest and Nicholas 1999). NBAMNI not only lacked the political clout
afforded to the UNBI through the *Indian Act* but also confronted
the provincial and federal governments' denial of any *constitutional*
obligations towards the Non-Registered Indian members that comprised the preponderance of its membership base.

Around this time, the provincial and federal governments offered
NBAMNI funds for mostly small-scale programs centred in Fredericton in areas of housing, labour market-training, youth programming, and, to a small extent, economic development. A new Native
Friendship Center (sic) was also set up (Fredericton Native Friendship Centre n.d.; La Forest and Nicholas 1999, 7; Milne 1994;
NBAPC n.d.a, 13, 17–20). Right into the twenty-first century, many
of these endeavours would come and go and a few new undertakings were launched. Some were more stable than others, but the field
of "urban Aboriginal policy" would always be limited in scope and

primarily Fredericton-focused (Canada 2006b; CBC News 2007; Fredericton Native Friendship Centre n.d.; MacCormac 1999; Milne 1994). Significantly, NBAMNI's urban constituents were typically life-long residents of the capital city or from nearby reserves, specifically Kingsclear, Oromocto, and St Mary's (Interviews 4 and 17). From the start, and unlike many other parts of the country that saw increasing numbers of Aboriginal people moving into the city, New Brunswick was different. There was no "demographic imperative."

TRANS-SPATIALIZATION

In the late twentieth century, a new constitutional order positioned the provincial government as a key player in the formulation of a new urban-reserve model. Until that time, provincial officials had steadfastly denied any constitutional obligation for Aboriginal peoples, registered or not. The year 1973 was cataclysmic because it witnessed the Supreme Court of Canada decision known as *Calder v. British Columbia*, which struck a lethal blow to the assumption that Aboriginal treaty rights had been extinguished (Coates 2000, 76) and set the stage for the entrenchment of Aboriginal and treaty rights in the *Constitution Act* (1982). From that point on, a new sphere of jurisprudence took form that extended various resource entitlements to Aboriginal peoples and imposed upon the provincial and federal governments a duty to consult and accommodate where such rights existed or might exist (Chute 2002, 75; Interview 8; J. R. Miller 2004; Thomas 2003). Across a different plane, the Supreme Court of Canada, in the 1999 case of *Corbiere v. Canada* (Minister of Indian and Northern Affairs), extended voting rights in band elections to off-reserve Registered Indians. Prior to *Corbiere*, band governments assumed that their constituencies ended at the reserve boundary. After *Corbiere*, some band governments saw off-reserve Registered Indians as political constituents (Interview 2; Isaac 1994). As a practical matter, the plight of off-reserve Registered Indians, including treatment by provincial authorities, was potentially a concern for band governments.

In this new legal context, the provincial government began to embark upon a modern-day treaty-making process and to generally rethink its relationship with Aboriginal peoples (Canada 2010). In spite of this new orientation, provincial officials continued to view the situation of Aboriginal peoples who were not legally "Indian" as

a minor, non-pressing matter. Aboriginal peoples who lacked Registered Status were, as far as the province was concerned, politically
and legally the same as all other non-Aboriginal New Brunswickers
– a status beyond the scope of Aboriginal and treaty rights.[15] The
non-reserve setting, therefore, endured into the twenty-first century
as a zone outside of the federal government's fiduciary duty and
beyond the scope of what the provincial government saw as within
its constitutional remit.

The provincial government's new focus on Aboriginal policy was
also shaped by economic concerns and principally an acute urban
labour shortage. In 1996, a Province of New Brunswick discussion
paper on demographic issues raised concerns about declining birth
rates. "New Brunswick's fertility rate," it stated, "is at a very low level
of 1.5. The replacement level is 2.1. In short, we are not replacing
ourselves, a trend that is to have significant implications" (New
Brunswick 1996). By the new millennium, it was widely acknowledged that birth rates among indigenous peoples were going against
wider trends. This younger and growing population offered a solution to labour shortages for key urban economic projects, including,
in Saint John, the refurbishment of the Point Lepreau nuclear plant,
and the building of Irving Oil's new liquefied natural gas facility and
its second oil refinery (Canada 2007b).

Registered Indian workers, and by extension Registered Indian
women giving birth to future workers, became important because
provincial officials could argue that labour cost training fell under
the federal government's fiduciary duty under the *Indian Act*. This
view was stated as early as 1997, when the provincial government's
Select Committee on Demographics reported that higher fertility
rates among Aboriginal peoples compared to non-Aboriginal
peoples could "contribute to the labour force at a time when the
growth of the labour force [was] expected to slow." The report elab-
orated that: "[e]ffective provincial approaches to Aboriginal issues
require a partnership approach with Aboriginal people themselves,
and with the federal government. In many cases, the federal government has the primary jurisdiction, and the programs and resources to address the issues. However, there are many areas where the
provincial government can assist in accomplishing Aboriginal goals.
Although the population is small, statistics show that Aboriginal
people will form a larger percentage of New Brunswick's population
and workforce in the future" (New Brunswick 1997). In 2007, it

was reported in the *Telegraph-Journal* that the minister of Aboriginal Affairs, Bernard Thériault, said that there was "some grey area in native jurisdiction" upon which "certain provinces [were] capitalizing" (Casey 2007), including, it was evident, New Brunswick. That same year, the provincial government and reserve chiefs (Mi'kmaq and Maliseet – New Brunswick 2007) signed a bilateral agreement that committed the parties to, among other things, collaborate on the development of the province's first casino slated for the City of Moncton. Marking the provincial government's first foray into modern-day treaty making, this agreement had the indelible stamp of urbanism (Canada 2007b).

A *trans-spatial model* of the urban-reserve relationship was brought into visibility as the federal government began praising "urban reserves" as "quiet success stories" (Canada 2008d). In New Brunswick, this model did not hinge on reserves and cities being adjacent to or geographically overlapping each other, as is the case in dominant understandings of "urban reserves." Rather, the new spatial regime was defined by interlocking constitutional and economic relationships between city and reserve. In this trans-spatial model, urban space emanated from and in conjunction with reserves. Aboriginal peoples would be in and of city *and* reserve. Crucially, the future of cities was deemed to hinge on an inherent Aboriginal identity tied to the reserve system.

Over the latter years of the twentieth and into the twenty-first century, St Mary's reserve saw pronounced effects of this new trans-spatial discursive regime (Interview 12). St Mary's band government entered into resource agreements with municipal, provincial, and federal authorities in areas such as commercial fishing (Canada 2007c; McGraw 2003; Wildsmith 1995), wood harvesting (Blakney 2003), land purchases (Canada 2002; *Telegraph Journal* 2002), and taxation (Canadian Press 2004a and 2004b). The band developed a new shopping mall and office centre that drew non-Aboriginal peoples to the reserve, a complete reversal of the nineteenth-century patterns of exchange whereby the Wolastoqiyik crossed the river to sell their goods and wares (Nicholas 2005). The band council pursued an autonomous policy agenda for "social policy, health delivery, educational strategies, economic initiatives, environmental management, resource allocation, land use, transportation, public works, housing and so on." It resisted provincial imposition of child welfare standards (St Mary's First Nation Wolastoqiyik n.d.), defined a new role for on-reserve policing (Interviews 3, 5, and 9), determined its own smoking laws in the face of provincial government resistance (St Mary's First Nation Wolastoqiyik n.d.), and secured substantive input over curriculum and pedagogy for Aboriginal students in provincial schools (Canada and New Brunswick 2007; Interview 14). For over a century, Canadian political officials had seen St Mary's reserve as worthless and troublesome. They now viewed it as vital to the city itself (Interview 12). Then Prime Minister Paul Martin captured this attitude in a speech delivered at St Mary's in 2005 when he declared St Mary's was a "kind of model that ... ought to be ... raise[d] in every province and territory in the country" (Chiarelli 2005). The trans-spatial urban model had, politically, arrived.

CONCLUSION

This chapter demonstrates that a focus on "urban Aboriginal policy" in the narrow sense, that is to say, defined in terms of responses to urban migration, marks a space of discursive silence in New Brunswick that has been shaped by a long history of governmental attempts to address shifting "problems" pertaining to the relationship between cities and reserves.

Proximation, segregation, eradication, and trans-spatialization comprised four distinct discursive regimes, each of which was premised upon a particular set of presuppositions about Aboriginal peoples. At different moments and in different ways, these regimes rested upon presuppositions about the political, economic, and racial benefits to be gained by promoting particular types of spatial relations between city and reserve. Mutations in spatial discourses were not ever, nor are they today, innocent. By marking out these spatial frames, we can begin to ponder, for instance, how race, gender, and class relations have been shaped and reshaped in terms of the urban Aboriginal policy nexus; we can reflect upon the proliferation of silences as certain Aboriginal policies have been included, excluded, and reshaped in political discussions; and we can take seriously the ramifications of past and current colonial practices, laws, and policies. This chapter has only scratched the surface of such matters, but it suggests that however one might define "good" policy – the less obvious facets of urban Aboriginal policy, the silent dimensions, must be taken into account. In New Brunswick, the piercing silence of urban Aboriginal policy is impossible to ignore and a crucial entry point for assessing colonial modes of rule past and present.

NOTES

1 The task at hand could not have been seen through to completion without the contributions of the people who gave so kindly of their knowledge and time to be interviewed for this study. Countless archivists and librarians assisted in the research project of which this one paper is a part. I would like to single out Gloria MacKenzie, formerly of Library and Archives Canada, as well as Linda Baier of University of New Brunswick Archives and Special Collection, Diana Moore of the Public Archives of New Brunswick, and Benoît Thériault of the Museum of Civilization. I am indebted to Bill Parenteau, who shared crucial thoughts at the earliest stage of the research. The encouragement from the Urban Aboriginal Policy subgroup members who contributed to this volume is gratefully acknowledged. I extend special thanks to Frances Abele, who helped me navigate through research obstacles along the way. Evelyn Peters not only adroitly directed the chapter through to publication in conjunction with co-editor Robert Young but also provided countless insights that improved the argument herein. I owe both Evelyn and Robert an enormous debt of appreciation. York University graduate students in seminars on urban governance and women and politics significantly elevated the analysis, and graduate students Vera Nikolovski and Anthony Rodgers each provided exemplary research assistance. All errors are of course my own. Research for this chapter was funded in part by Robert Young's MCRI, a grant from the Social Sciences and Humanities Research Council of Canada, Number: 832–2002–011, and by funding from York University.

2 The author acknowledges the problematic use of the term "Aboriginal." See Alfred and Corntassel (2005, 598).

3 For a timeline of legal discrimination against indigenous peoples, see Moss and O'Toole-Gardner (1991).

4 One person was counted in two categories.

5 On shifting governing mentalities in Aboriginal policy see, for example, Abele, Graham, and Maslove (1999), and Tobias (1991).

6 Many writers use the term "Maliseet," but this has fallen into disuse because it has a pejorative meaning in the Mi'kmaq vernacular (Interviews 13 and 15; Oliver and Sturgeon 1983, 2).

7 Neither the provincial nor the federal government recognizes the historical claims of Passamaquoddy in New Brunswick, but this view is contested (Interview 15; Prins 1986, 265; Interviews 10 and 15; Speck and Hadlock 1946, 362). In 2008, a Passamaquoddy Legal Defence Fund was being established to defend Passamaquoddy rights in New Brunswick (see Francis 2008).

8 In 1921, the Judicial Committee of the Privy Council in London, then Canada's highest court, ruled that Aboriginal title "must be presumed to have continued unless the contrary is established" (Canada n.d.b). In 1923, however, the federal government "made it a criminal offence for a First Nation to hire a lawyer to pursue land claims settlements" (Canada n.d.c). This was changed in 1951 under a revised *Indian Act* (Canada n.d.b).

9 In 1895, the Oromocto reserve was established roughly twenty-two kilometres southeast of Fredericton. For the timeline of the creation of New Brunswick reserves, see Bartlett (1983 and 1986); Calbrick (1997); Canada (n.d.a); Fort Folly First Nation (n.d.); and Woodstock First Nation (n.d.).

10 For a discussion of band council jurisdiction under the *Indian Act*, see Peters (2007).

11 The gendered dimensions of discursive spatial regimes in New Brunswick require detailed attention beyond the context of this chapter. For a study of the interconnections between race, gender, and space in the Winnipeg context, see Klodawsky (1999). On the passing of Bill C-31 in 1985, which provided for Indian Status reinstatement resulting from the patriarchal bases of the *Indian Act*, see, for instance, Green (2007), Lawrence (2004), Peters (1998), and Silman (1987).

12 On education at Indian Day Schools in New Brunswick, see Hamilton (1986).

13 The importance of context in how race and space are twinned as governmental techniques is brought into sharp relief in this proposed federal project, which was diametrically opposite to the 1960s wholesale razing of Africville, a community of roughly 400 primarily Black residents on the edge of Halifax.

14 At the time of the formation of NBAMNI, the notion of "Métis" was considered an apt descriptor for the Non-Status Indian Aboriginal peoples and their descendants, including those who had married outside of the Mi'Kmaq, Passamaquoddy, and Wolastoqiyik. The constitutional meaning of "Métis" has since become a key site of contestation (see CBC News New Brunswick 2003; La Nation Autochtone du Québec 2006; *R. v. Lavigne*, 2007, CNLR 268, NBQB, [2005] 3 CNLR 176; *R. v. Powley*, 2003, 2 SCR 207, 2001). In the early 1990s, the NBAMNI changed its name to The New Brunswick Aboriginal Peoples Council (NBAPC n.d.c).

15 While the constitutionality of Aboriginal identity is a complex terrain, the exponential increase in people self-identifying as Métis in the Canadian Census is impossible to ignore. As a statistically defined population, the Métis grew by 350 per cent between 1996 and 2006, that is, from 975 to

4,290 people (Anderson 2008, 359). For an insightful assessment of the political dynamics underpinning this statistical revolution, see Anderson (2008).

INTERVIEWS

Interview 1 (2 people), Fredericton, 16 June 2008

Interview 2 (2 people) Fredericton, 16 June 2008

Interview 3, Fredericton, 17 June 2008

Interview 4, Fredericton, 17 June 2008

Interview 5, Fredericton, 17 June 2008

Interview 6, Fredericton, 17 June 2008

Interview 7, Fredericton, 18 June 2008

Interview 8, Fredericton, 18 June 2008

Interview 9 (3 people), Fredericton, 18 June 2008

Interview 10, Fredericton, 19 June and Toronto and Fredericton 11 August 2008 (phone)

Interview 11, Fredericton, 19 June 2008

Interview 12, Fredericton, 19 June 2008

Interview 13, Fredericton, 19 June 2008

Interview 14 (2 people), Fredericton, 20 June 2008

Interview 15, Devon, 20 June 2008

Interview 16, Toronto, 23 June 2008

Interview 17, Toronto and Fredericton, 9 September 2008 (phone)

Interview 18, Moncton, 15 June 2008

REFERENCES

Abele, Frances, Katherine Graham, and Allan Maslove. 1999. "Negotiating Canada: Changes in Aboriginal Policy over the Last Thirty Years." In *How Canada Spends, 1999–2000*, ed. Leslie Pal, 251–92. Toronto: Oxford University Press.

Agenutemagen. 1971. Execs Meet with St Mary's Band. December.

Agenutemagen. 1985. Provinces Shouldn't Handle Indian Affairs. April/May.

Alfred, Taiaiake and Jeff Corntassel. 2005. "Being Indigenous: Resurgences against Contemporary Colonialism." *Government and Opposition*, 40 (4): 597–614.

Anderson, Chris. 2008. "From Nation to Population: the Racialization of 'Métis' in the Canadian Census." *Nations and Nationalism*, 14 (2): 47–68.

Bartlett, Richard H. 1986. *Indian Reserves in the Atlantic Provinces of Canada*. Studies in Aboriginal Rights No. 9, Saskatchewan: University of Saskatchewan Native Law Centre.

– 1983. "Indian and Native Law: Survey of Canadian Law." *Ottawa Law Review* 15 (2): 431–502.

Blakney, Sherrie. 2003. "Aboriginal Forestry in New Brunswick: Conflicting Paradigms." *Environments* 31 (1): 61–78.

British North America Act, 1867.

CBC News. 2007. Children's Program Aims to Preserve Maliseet. Available: http://www.cbc.ca/canada/new-brunswick/story/2007/03/22/nb-maliseet.html. Accessed 25 August 2008.

CBC News New Brunswick. 2003. "No Métis Rights Here: Green." Available: http://nben.ca/environews/media/mediaarchives/03/sept/metis2.htm. Accessed 18 August 2008.

Calbrick, Mary L. 1997. "Locke's Doctrine of Dispossession and the Dispossession of the Passamoquoddy." Master's thesis, University of New Brunswick. Available: http://www.collectionscanada.gc.ca/obj/s4/f2/dsk2/ftp01/MQ29975.pdf. Accessed 21 September 2008.

Canada. 2010. "Fact Sheet – Progress Report on Aboriginal and Treaty Rights Negotiations in the Maritimes and the Gaspé." Available: http://www.ainc-inac.gc.ca/al/hts/tng/ecn/fs-eng.asp. Accessed 29 January 2011.

– 2008a. Terminology. Indian and Northern Affairs Canada. Available: http://www.ainc-inac.gc.ca/ap/tln-eng.asp. Accessed 7 March 2009.

– 2008b. Urban Aboriginal Strategy: Backgrounder. Indian and Northern Affairs Canada. Available http://www.ainc-inac.gc.ca/interloc/uas/index-eng.asp. Accessed 18 August 2008.

– 2008c. Office of the Federal Interlocutor for Métis and Non-Status Indians, e-mail reply to author concerning a question about location of research materials, 6 November.

– 2008d. "Urban Reserves: A Quiet Success Story." Indian and Northern Affairs

Canada. Available: http://www.ainc-inac.gc.ca/ai/mr/is/urs-eng.asp. Accessed 7 March 2009.

– 2007a. First Nation Members and Indians (as defined in section 2(1) of the *Indian Act*). Flyer distributed by the Atlantic Regional Office of Indian and Northern Affairs Canada re: Attention First Nations. Author's personal files.

– 2007b. Aboriginal Human Resource Council. *Workforce Connex: New Brunswick Forum, Building Strong Aboriginal and Private Sector*

Partnerships. Available: http://www.workforceconnex.com/planning/ documents/NB_WFC_Report.pdf. Accessed 25 August 2009.

– 2007c. Fisheries and Oceans Canada. Marshall Response Initiative – St Mary's: One Year Fisheries Agreement 2000–2001. Available: http:// www.dfo-po.gc.ca/communic/Marshall/Fish_Agreement/new_fa/ SaintMarys_e.htm. Accessed 25 August 2008.

– 2006a. *Peace and Friendship Treaties in the Maritimes and Gaspé*. Indian and Northern Affairs Canada. Available: http://www.ainc-inac. gc.ca/ps/clm/atr/wkn_e.html. Accessed 25 August 2008.

– 2006b. Completed Projects: Aboriginal Head Start Projects: Under One Sky Development Phase, Fredericton and Saint John. Canadian Public Health Agency. Available: http://www.phac-aspc.gc.ca/canada/regions/ atlantic/project/a_1_comp.html#under_one_sky. Accessed 25 August 2008.

– 2002. "Expanded Land Base for Saint Mary's First Nation." Indian and Northern Affairs Canada. Online. Available: http://www.ainc-inac.gc.ca/ nr/prs/s-d2002/2–02205_e.html. Accessed 25 August 2008.

– 1969. *Statement of the Government of Canada on Indian Policy (The White Paper, 1969)*. Available: http://www.ainc-inac.gc.ca/ai/arp/ls/pubs/ cp1969/cp1969-eng.asp. Accessed 23 November 2008.

– 1947. *Report of the Commission on Indian Affairs*. Indian Affairs Branch.

– n.d.a. "First Nation Profiles." Indian and Northern Affairs Canada. Available: http://sdiprod2.inac.gc.ca/FNProfiles/. Accessed 25 August 2008.

– n.d.b. "Fact Sheet: Aboriginal Rights in BC." Indian and Northern Affairs Canada. Available: http://www.ainc-inac.gc.ca/ai/mr/is/abr-eng. asp. Accessed 22 April 2011.

– n.d.c. "Fact Sheet: Treaty Negotiations." Indian and Northern Affairs Canada. Available: http://www.ainc-inac.gc.ca/ai/mr/is/trn-eng.asp. Accessed 23 January 2009.

Canada and New Brunswick. 2007. "Memorandum of Understanding Concerning Education and First Nation Students and Communities in the Province of New Brunswick." Indian and Northern Affairs Canada. Available: http://www.ainc-inac.gc.ca/nr/prs/j-a2008/2-3025-eng.asp. Accessed 25 August 2008.

Canadian Press. 2004a. "Tax Sharing Gas Prices Plunge at N.B. First Nations Stations As Tax Dispute Heats Up." 10 December.

– 2004b. "N.B. Plans to Review Tax Rebate; Gaming Deals with First Nations Communities." 16 April.

Casey, Quentin Casey. 2007. "Erasing the Jurisdictional Divide: Talks Time to Stop Expecting Ottawa to Carry all Responsibility for Aboriginal Issues: Premier." *Telegraph-Journal,* 9 August: A1.

Chiarelli, Nina. 2005. "Prime Minister Feted by First Nations." *Telegraph Journal,* 1 January.

Chute, Janet E. 2002. "Algonquians/Eastern Woodlands." In *Aboriginal Peoples of Canada: A Short Introduction,* ed. Paul Magocsi, 38–81. Toronto: University of Toronto Press.

Cloney, Robert John. 1993. Doctor, Lawyer, Indian Chief ... : Dependency Among the Maliseet and the Impact of the *Indian Act.* Master's thesis, Saint Mary's University.

Coates, Kenneth. 2000. *The Marshall Decision and Native Rights.* Montreal: McGill-Queen's University Press.

Constitution Act. 1982.

Dominion of Canada. 1889. *Annual Report of the Department of Indian Affairs for the Year Ended 31 December 1889.*

Dominion of Canada. 1891. *Annual Report of the Department of Indian Affairs for the Year Ended 31 December 1891.*

Dominion of Canada. 1912. *Annual Report of the Department of Indian Affairs for the Year Ended 31 December 1912.*

Duplessis, Antoinette Mary. 1995. "The 'Civilization' Program of the Department of Indian Affairs on New Brunswick Native Reserves, 1867–1932." Master's thesis, University of New Brunswick.

Fort Folly First Nation. n.d. Fort Folly First Nation Land Claim. Available: http://www.fortfolly.nb.ca/landclaim.html. Accessed 17 September 2008.

Foucault, Michel. 1978. *The History of Sexuality. An Introduction. Volume 1.* New York: Vintage Books.

Francis, Vera. 2008. "Defending the Rights of the Passamoquoddy." Public lecture delivered at the New Brunswick Social Forum, The New Brunswick Sports Hall of Fame, Fredericton. Video recording available at: http://nbsf-fsnb.org/?q=node/14.

Fredericton Native Friendship Centre. n.d. "Fredericton Native Friendship Centre: Respect, Honesty, Caring, Sharing." Available: http://www.fnfcnb.ca/. Accessed 25 August 2008.

Gould, Gary P. and A. J. Semple. 1980. *Our Land: the Maritimes: The Basis of the Indian Claim in the Maritime Provinces of Canada.* Fredericton: Saint Anne's Point Press.

Graham, Katherine A. H. 1999. "Urban Aboriginal Governance in Canada: Paradigms and Prospects." In *Aboriginal Self-Government in Canada: Paradigms and Prospects* 2nd edition, ed. John Hylton, 377–91. Saskatoon: Purich Publishing.

Graham, Katherine A.H. and Evelyn J. Peters. 2002. *Aboriginal Communities and Urban Sustainability*. Ottawa: Canadian Policy Research Networks.

Green, Joyce, ed. 2007. *Making Space for Aboriginal Feminism*. Halifax: Fernwood Press.

Hamilton, W. D. 1986. *The Federal Indian Day Schools of the Maritimes.* Fredericton: Micmac-Maliseet Institute, University of New Brunswick.

Hanselmann, Calvin. 2001. *Urban Aboriginal People in Western Canada: Realities and Policies*. Calgary: Canada West Foundation.

Harring, Sidney L. 1998. *White Man's Law: Native People in Nineteenth-Century Canadian Jurisprudence*. Toronto: University of Toronto Press for the Osgoode Society for Canadian Legal History.

Hawthorne, H.B., ed. 1966. *A Survey of the Contemporary Indians of Canada Economic, Political, Educational Needs and Policies*. Ottawa: DIAND. Available: http://www.ainc-inac.gc.ca/ai/arp/ls/phi-eng.asp. Accessed 22 August 2009.

Indian Act. 1876. Part 1, Chapter 81, 15 (2).

Isaac, Thomas. 1994. Case Commentary: Corbiere *v.* Canada. *Canadian Native Law Reporter* 1.

Klodawsky, F. 1999. "'Housing Need,' 'Neighbourhood Improvement', and the Contributions of 'Experts' in North Point Douglas, Winnipeg, 1971–1981: A Gender and 'Race' Sensitive Analysis." *Research in Community Sociology* 9: 255–83.

Knockwood, Isabelle and Gillian Thomas. 1992. *Out of the Depths: The Experiences of Mi'kmaw Children at the Indian Residential School at Shubenacadie, Nova Scotia*, 2nd edition. Lockeport: Roseway.

Krueger, R. R. 1975. "Changes in the Political Geography of New Brunswick." *The Canadian Geographer*, 19 (2): 121–34.

La Forest, Gerard and Graydon Nicholas. 1999. *Report of The Task Force on Aboriginal Issues*. Available: http://www.gnb.ca/0016/task/task.htm. Accessed 21 August 2008.

La Forest, Marie W. 1980. "Native Fishing and Hunting Rights in New Brunswick." *University of New Brunswick Law Journal* 29: 111–22.

La Nation Autochtone du Québec. 2006. East-West Official Statement, 11 October. Available: http://www.autochtones.ca/documents/20061011_east_west_official_statement.pdf. Accessed 16 January 2009.

Lawrence, Bonita. 2004. *"Real" Indians and Others: Mixed-Blood Urban Native Peoples and Indigenous Nationhood*. Vancouver: UBC Press.

Leavitt, Robert M. 2000. *Mi'kmaq of the East Coast*. Markham: Fitzhenry & Whiteside Ltd.

– 1996. *Passamaquoddy-Maliseet*. *Munich*. Newcastle LINCOM Europa Materials. Series: Languages of the World 27.

– 1995. *Maliseet and Micmac First Nations of the Maritimes*. Fredericton: New Ireland Press.

MacCormac, Dan. 1999. "Native Friendship Centre Needs New Board to Reopen: Official." *The New Brunswick Telegraph Journal*, 3 February.

Maritime Regional Office. 1958. "Memorandum to Indian Affairs Branch, 16 June." Subject: Carleton Ward (St Mary's Reserve, Fredericton). Library and Archives Canada RG 10, File 8565.

Mawani, Renasi. 2009. *Colonial Proximities: Crossracial Encounters and Juridical Truths in British Columbia, 1871–1921*. Vancouver: UBC Press.

McGee, H. F. 1983. *The Native People of Atlantic Canada: A History of Indian-European Relations*. Ottawa: Carleton University Press

McGraw, Rick. 2003. "Aboriginal Fisheries Policy in Atlantic Canada." *Marine Policy* 27 (5): 417–24.

McNabb, David. 1983. "Herman Merivale and Colonial Indian Policy in the Mid-nineteenth Century." In *As Long as the Sun Shines and Water Flows: A Reader in Canadian Native Studies*, eds. Ian A. L. Getty and Antoine S. Lussier, 277–302. Vancouver: UBC Press. Available: http://www.brandonu.ca/Library/CJNS/1.2/mcnab.pdf. Accessed 25 August 2008.

McNutt, W.S. 1984. *New Brunswick: A History, 1784–1867*. 2nd ed. Toronto: MacMillan of Canada.

Mi'kmaq and Maliseet – New Brunswick. 2007. "Relationship Building/ Bilateral Agreement." Available: http://www.gnb.ca/legis/education/070622program.pdf. Accessed 25 August 2008.

Miller, J. R. 2004. "History, the Courts, and Treaty Policy: Lessons from Marshall and Nisga'a." In *Aboriginal Policy Research*. Vol. 1: *Setting the Agenda for Change*, eds. Jerry P. White, Paul Maxim and Dan Beavon, chapter 2. Toronto: Thompson Educational Publishing.

Miller, Virginia P. 2004. "The Mi'kmaq: A Maritime Woodland Group." In *Native Peoples: The Canadian Experience*, eds. R. Bruce Morrison and C. Roderick Wilson, 248–67. Don Mills: Oxford University Press.

Milne, David. 1994. "The Case of New Brunswick-Aboriginal Relations." Research Report. Royal Commission on Aboriginal Peoples.

Moore, Dorothy E. 1983. *Micmac Culture and the Multiculturalism Policy*. Halifax, International Education Centre, Saint Mary's University.

Moss, Wendy and Elaine O'Toole-Gardner. 1991. *Aboriginal People: History of Discriminatory Laws*. Ottawa: Depository Services Program, Law and Government Division.

Murray, Karen Bridget. 2011. "The Early Years of the Shubenacadie Residential School." Unpublished draft paper.

New Brunswick Aboriginal Peoples Council. n.d.a. Post Powley. Available: http://post-powley.nbapc.org/main.asp?pid=1. Accessed 21 September 2008.

– n.d.b. *Who We Are*. Fredericton: New Brunswick.

– n.d.c. Constitution and by-Laws. Available: http://www.nbapc.org/pages.asp?pid=300&deptid=0&lid=0. Accessed 16 January 2009.

New Brunswick. 2006. "Supreme Court Upholds New Brunswick Courts' Position on Aboriginal Rights." Media Release 7 December. Available: http://www.gnb.ca/cnb/news/ag/2006e1529ag.htm. Accessed 25 August 2008.

– 1997. Select Committee on Demographics, Final Report. Fifty-third Legislature, 2nd Session. *The Report on the Select Committee on Demographics* Available: http://www.gnb.ca/legis/business/pastsessions/53/53–2/journals-e/970226-e.asp. Accessed 22 April 2011.

– 1996. *New Brunswick at the Dawn of a New Century: A Discussion Paper on Demographic Issues Affecting New Brunswick* (Fredericton: Province of New Brunswick). Available: http://www.gnb.ca/legis/business/committees/previous/reports-e/demog/nbdemoge.pdf. Accessed 22 April 2011.

Nicholas, Andrea Bear. 2005. "Our History: A Summary History of St Mary's to 1950." Draft Version No. 3. Available: http://www.stmarysfirstnation.ca/pages.asp?pid=86. Accessed 7 March 2009.

– 1986. "Maliseet Aboriginal Rights and Mascarene's Treaty, not Drummer's Treaty." In *Actes du dix-septième congrès des algonquinistes*, ed. William Cowan, 215–29. Ottawa: Carleton University.

Nicholas, Andrew. 1970. "New Brunswick Indians-Conservative Militants." In *The Only Good Indian: Essays by Canadian Indians*, ed. Waubageshig, 42–50. Toronto: New Press.

Nurse, Andrew. 2004. "History, Law, and the Mi'kmaq." *Acadiensis* 33 (2): 126–33.

Office of the Ombudsman and Child and Youth Advocate. 2010.

Oliver, Bruce and Linda-Ann Sturgeon. 1983. *Dwellers by the Beautiful River: Fredericton's Indian Legacy*. Fredericton: Fredericton Historical Research Project, Department of History, University of New Brunswick.

Pal, Leslie. 1992. *Public Policy Analysis: An Introduction.* 2nd ed. Toronto: Nelson.

Parenteau, Bill. 1998. "Care, Control, and Supervision: Native People in the Canadian Atlantic Fishery, 1867–1900." *Canadian Historical Review* 79 (1): 1–35.

Parenteau, Bill and James Kenny. 2002. "Survival, Resistance, and the Canadian State: The Transformation of New Brunswick's Native Economy, 1867–1930." *Journal of the Canadian Historical Association/ Revue de la société historique du Canada* 13 (1): 49–71.

Parker, Simon. 2004. *Urban Theory and the Urban Experience: Encountering the City.* New York: Routledge.

Paul, Daniel N. 2006. *We Were Not the Savages: Collision Between European and Native American Civilizations.* 3rd edition. Halifax: Fernwood.

Perley, Moses. 1843. "H.E. Perley's Report on the Indians of New Brunswick." In *The Native People of Atlantic Canada: A History of Indian-European Relations,* ed. Harold F. McGee, 81–9. Ottawa: Carleton University Press (1983).

– 1841. Report of Moses H. Perley on the Maliseet/Wulustukieg population of the St John River Valley. Excerpt from *Report on Indian Settlements. Journal of the House of Assembly of New Brunswick* 1842. Available: http://www.upperstjohn.com/madawaska/perley.htm. Accessed 25 August 2008.

Peters, Evelyn J. 2007. *Urban Reserves.* Research paper for the National Centre for First Nations Governance, Ottawa. Available: http://www.fngovernance.org/research/e_peters.pdf. Accessed 5 March 2009.

– 2002. "'Our City Indians': Negotiating the Meaning of First Nations Urbanization in Canada, 1945–1975." *Historical Geography* 30: 75–92.

– 2000. "Aboriginal People in Urban Areas." In *Visions of the Heart: Canadian Aboriginal Issues,* eds. David A. Long and Olivia P. Dickason, 305–34. Toronto: Harcourt Brace & Company.

– 1998. "Subversive Spaces: First Nations Women and the City." *Environment and Planning D: Society and Space* 16 (6): 665–85.

Prins, Harold. 1996. *The Mi'kmaq: Resistance, Accommodation, and Cultural Survival.* Orlando: Harcourt Brace.

Proctor, Steve. 2001. "Indian Brook to develop large parcel of land; Natives Take Over Former DND Property Oct. 29." *The Chronicle-Herald,* 6 April: A8.

R. v. Lavigne, 2005, NBPC 8.

R. v. Powley, 2003, 2 SCR 207.

Redmond, Theresa. 1998. "'We Cannot Work Without Food': Nova Scotian Indian Policy and Mi'kmaq Agriculture, 1783–1867." In *Earth, Water, Air, and Fire: Studies in Canadian Ethnohistory*, ed. David McNab, 95–113. Waterloo: Wilfrid Laurier University Press.

Sappier, Harold. 1969. "Statement of New Brunswick Indians by Harold Sappier, President, to the Government of Canada Indian Policy, 1969." Anglican Church of Canada, 1970.

Saunders, Douglas. 1970. "Native Rights." *Report of Discussions: Legal Status of Indians in the Maritimes*. Toronto: Indian-Eskimo Association of Canada.

Shewell, Hugh. 2004. *"Enough to Keep Them Alive": Indian Welfare in Canada, 1873–1965*. Toronto: University of Toronto Press.

Silman, Janet, ed. 1987. *Enough is Enough: Aboriginal Women Speak Out*. Toronto: The Women's Press.

Speck, Frank G. and Wendell S. Hadlock. 1946. "A Report on Tribal Boundaries and Hunting Areas of the Malecite Indian of New Brunswick." *American Anthropologist*, 48 (3): 355–75.

Squires, W. Austin. 1980. *History of Fredericton: the Last 200 Years*. Fredericton: Centennial Print and Litho Ltd.

St Mary's First Nation Wolastoqiyik. n.d. Child and Family Services. Available: http://www.stmarysfirstnation.ca/pages.asp?pid=82. Accessed 21 August 2008.

Statistics Canada. 2006a. *Census Tract Profiles, 2006*. Catalogue number 92–597-XWE. Online. Available: http://www12.statcan.ca/census-recensement/2006/dp-pd/prof/92–597/index.cfm?lang=E. Accessed 22 January 2009.

Telegraph Journal. 2002. "Deal Gives First Nation Land for Project", 25 October: A4.

Thomas, Isaac. 2003. "The Crown's Duty to Consult and Accommodate Aboriginal People." *The Advocate* 63 (5): 671–90.

Tobias, John L. 1991. "Protection, Civilization, Assimilation: An Outline History of Canada's Indian Policy." In *Sweet Promises: A Reader on Indian-White Relations in Canada*, ed. J.R. Miller, 127–44. Toronto: University of Toronto Press.

Tully, J. 1995. *Strange Multiplicity: Constitutionalism in an Age of Diversity*. Cambridge: Cambridge University Press.

Upton, L.F.S. 1979. *Micmacs and Colonists: Indian-White Relations in the Maritimes*. Vancouver: UBC Press.

– 1974. "Indian Affairs in Colonial New Brunswick." *Acadiensis* 3 (2): 3–26.

– 1973. "The Origins of Canadian Indian Policy." *Journal of Canadian Studies* 8 (4): 51–60.

Valverde, Mariana. 1991. *The Age of Light, Soap and Water: Moral Reform in English Canada, 1885–1925*. Toronto: McClelland & Stewart Inc.

Walker, R. C. 2006. "Interweaving Aboriginal/Indigenous Rights with Urban Citizenship: A View from the Winnipeg Low-cost Housing Sector, Canada." *Citizenship Studies* 10 (4): 391–411.

Wallis, Wilson and Ruth Wallis. 1957. *Malecite Indians of New Brunswick*. Ottawa: Northern Affairs and Natural Resources.

Walls, Martha. 2008. "Countering the 'Kingsclear blunder': Maliseet Resistance to the Kingsclear Relocation Plan, 1945–1949." *Acadiensis* 38 (1): 3–30.

Weaver, Sally M. 1981. *Making Canadian Indian Policy: The Hidden Agenda, 1968–1970*. Toronto: University of Toronto Press.

West, John. 1827. *Journal of a Mission to the Indians in the British Provinces of New Brunswick, Nova Scotia, and the Mohawks, on the Ouse, or Grand River, Upper Canada*. London: L. B. Seeley and Son.

Wicken, William C. 2002. *Mi'kmaq Treaties on Trial: History, Land and Donald Marshall Junior*. Toronto: University of Toronto Press.

– 1995. "'Heard it from our Grandfathers': Mi'kmaq Treaty Tradition and the Syliboy Case of 1928." *University of New Brunswick Law Journal/Revue de droit de l'Université du Nouveau-Brunswick* 44: 145–62.

– 1994. "The Mi'Kmaq and Wuastukwiuk Treaties". *University of New Brunswick Law Journal/Revue de droit de l'Université du Nouveau-Brunswick* 43: 241–53.

Wildsmith, Bruce. 1995. "The Mi'Kmaq and the Fishery: Beyond Food Requirements." *Dalhousie Law Journal* 18 (1): 116–40.

Wiseman, Frederick M. 2005. *Reclaiming the Ancestors: Decolonizing a Taken Prehistory of the Far Northeast*. London: University Press of New England.

Woodstock First Nation. n.d. "Welcome to Woodstock First Nation's History." Available: http://www.woodstockfirstnation.com/wfnhistory.htm. Accessed 17 September 2008.

4

Aboriginal People and Public Policy in Four Ontario Cities

FRANCES ABELE, RUSSELL LAPOINTE,
DAVID J. LEECH, AND MICHAEL MCCROSSAN

Along with constitutional provisions, governmental institutions, and the attitudinal legacy of Aboriginal-settler relations in Canada, the demographic realities of cities in Ontario play a significant role in shaping urban Aboriginal policy. At just 2 per cent of the total population of Ontario, Aboriginal people comprise a small proportion of Canada's most populous province.[1] Most of them (62 per cent) live in urban areas, but due to their small numbers and their sparse distribution throughout residential city neighbourhoods, they are rarely an identifiable or very visible group, especially in southern cities.[2] By contrast, in the northern parts of the province, Aboriginal people are a substantial proportion of both rural and urban populations – but they reside in a part of the province where overall population density lowers immediate political salience in the provincial capital. These demographic and geographic realities shape the policies and practices of all levels of government with regard to urban Aboriginal affairs.

The literature and the interviews conducted during the authors' research point to the vacuum created by the lack of capacity and perceived need for Aboriginal policy making at a municipal level. Into this vacuum step local Aboriginal organizations and service providers, which create networks of service and raise the profile of issues of importance to Aboriginal people in their communities. Local issues often become surrogates for larger issues that affect Aboriginal populations. For example, conflicts between Aboriginal people and cities over land use engage larger unresolved issues of Crown-

Aboriginal relations. Municipalities can be seen as a microcosm of larger Aboriginal issues, and the response of municipal governments to various issues is very instructive regarding the role of non-governmental organizations and coalitions in policy making. Indeed, in the absence of explicit policies focusing on urban Aboriginal peoples, strong pro-active urban Aboriginal organizations and coalitions of organizations have had the most pronounced effect in shaping municipal responses to urban Aboriginal issues.

The research presented here is based on interviews and research conducted in four cities – Kingston, Ottawa, Thunder Bay, and Toronto – and focuses on the relationships and patterns of interaction between municipal governments, policies, and urban Aboriginal people.[3] After an overview of the literature and the evolving policy context for Aboriginal people in Ontario, we provide a brief description of the salient characteristics of each of the four cities we visited. This section is followed by a comparative analysis of the patterns of interactions between city governments and Aboriginal residents, which is organized by the linked themes of visibility, jurisdiction, and community organization. Each of these themes is conditioned in locally specific ways by the diversity of the Aboriginal population and by the class differences therein.

THE URBAN ABORIGINAL EXPERIENCE IN THE LITERATURE

Cities face significant challenges in making good public policy in Aboriginal affairs. For many city governments, policy development is more an occasional practice (or an incidental outcome) than a systemic capacity: the political structure and fiscal position of municipal government often hamper orderly policy development. In the policy area of urban Aboriginal affairs, this problem is exacerbated because of the diversity of urban Aboriginal populations and issues, and because of the overarching responsibilities of federal and provincial governments. In addition, Canadian city governments are profoundly affected by North American and global economic forces, but they mostly lack the resources needed to influence them (Andrew and Goldsmith 1998). Cities are buffeted by the large forces of the global economy, but they remain collections of neighbourhoods – above all, homes to the people who live in them; residents require their municipal governments to ensure that the preconditions of a healthy and safe city life be maintained. This is true for the Aboriginal residents as it is for all others.

Canadian cities are increasingly complex, multicultural, and multinational Aboriginal landscapes. There are particular analytical challenges arising from this reality. First, Aboriginal people are found in all social classes and most neighbourhoods of Canadian cities, though they are disproportionately unemployed and, on the whole, poorer than the general population (Peters 2006, 2007; Mendelson 2004; Graham and Peters 2002; Cooke and Bélanger 2006). In some poor urban areas, they make up a large proportion of the population; they are both ignored and stereotyped (Culhane 2003; Andersen and Denis 2003). This combination of diversity and invisibility creates a special requirement for researchers to listen well, look carefully, and respect the specific socio-economic conditions of each city.

There is also the problem of jurisdictional ambiguity and de facto exclusion. Although Hanselmann and Gibbins document some notable exceptions with respect to cities in western provinces, they still find "that the challenges confronting many urban Aboriginal people in fields such as income support, family violence, childcare, addictions, suicide, and human rights appeared to be ignored *in terms of explicit policies*" (2002, 81; see also Graham and Peters 2002). With very few exceptions, urban Aboriginal people are not only invisible to policy makers but also invisible in policy making. Where they do appear in policy making and in the academic literature too, there is a tendency towards overgeneralization or stereotyping.[4]

The political activism and forms of social organization of urban Aboriginal people has been documented in a number of studies. Culhane (2003) describes the Valentine's Day Women's Memorial March, organized and attended by Aboriginal women and others, to remember the invisibly missing women of the Downtown Eastside in Vancouver. Suzanne Lenon's study (2000) of homelessness confirms that economic-based power relations are at the heart of understanding the disparities between urban Aboriginal and non-Aboriginal residents. In conversation with Aboriginal and non-Aboriginal women living in Vancouver's downtown eastside, Robertson and Culhane (2005) broaden conventional understandings of urban poverty, homelessness, and violence by recounting life experiences which have been ignored, excluded, and, often, simply unnoticed by the larger society. Fran Klodawsky, Tim Aubry, and Susan Farrell (2006) examine the issue of youth homelessness (including

Aboriginal youth) as a function of the lack of 'care' included in policy-making decisions about homelessness. Heather Howard-Bobiwash's account of the strategies of Aboriginal women in Toronto between 1950 and 1975 describes how Aboriginal women in the emergent "Native 'middle class'" did not "equate their relative economic success with assimilation," but rather "utilized their class mobility to support the structural development of Native community organizations and promote positive pride in Native cultural identity in the city" (2003, 567). Howard-Bobiwash identifies and illustrates what might be called the "social forms of agency" and the emergence of networks of social relations that mimic or replace traditional community structures.[5]

In summary, the academic literature documents urban Aboriginal communities that are self-organized and self-aware. It draws our attention to the problems of the relative *invisibility* of urban Aboriginal people to city officials and politicians; to the *jurisdictional maze* that makes development of an adequate array of services difficult; to the *diversity* of the urban population and the reality that Aboriginal people largely do not live in separate communities; and to the problems of *urban poverty* – though the urban poor are by no means all Aboriginal, urban Aboriginal people are disproportionately poor. As we shall argue below, these themes did emerge in our research in four Ontario cities, but to different degrees according to each city's particular circumstances.

THE PROVINCIAL POLICY CONTEXT

Municipal governments in Ontario are junior governmental partners in most areas of responsibility; their scope, financial means, and even their choice of initiatives are shaped by federal and provincial policies. This relationship of inequality is certainly prevalent in the area of Aboriginal affairs. Understanding how federal and provincial Aboriginal policy has evolved is central to understanding what has happened, and can happen, in Ontario cities. Federal policy is treated in another chapter in this volume, but it is important to recount here, in summary form, the evolution of Ontario's urban Aboriginal policy, with attention to how it has affected cities.

From the beginning, Ontario governments have focused on securing provincial constitutional jurisdiction over lands and resources, often over and against the rights of Aboriginal people; they have continually resisted the accepting of responsibility for service provision (Teillet 2005). This situation has a constitutional source. Under section 109 of the Constitution, all lands and resources contained within provincial borders fall under the jurisdictional authority of provincial governments. Section 91(24) of the Constitution gives the federal government legislative authority for "Indians, and Lands reserved for the Indians." Provincial governments have not only invoked section 91(24) as evidence that they have no jurisdictional responsibility for Aboriginal affairs but have also harnessed section 109 of the Constitution in a manner that denies Indigenous rights to land and resources. An early and consequential expression of these tensions was the *St Catherine's Milling* case of 1888, which laid the legal groundwork for provincial neglect of, and resistance to, Indigenous claims to land and resources in Ontario (see Christie 2005, 24–5).

Initially, federal and provincial governments regarded Status Indians as the sole responsibility of the Crown due to its authority under section 91(24) of the Constitution, while Non-Status and Métis were not recognized as populations having any particular rights at all. From the perspective of the Ontario government, not only were Aboriginal people perceived as being outside its jurisdictional purview but they were also seen as barriers to the exploitation of provincial land and resources (Cameron and Wherrett 1995; see also Sampson 1992, 14).

The extent of provincial involvement in Aboriginal affairs began to change after the Second World War in response to the mobilization and self-organization of Aboriginal people. Concurrent demographic changes were also important. Even as Aboriginal people became more visible through political mobilization, the number of First Nations people living off-reserve grew, and so did provincial involvement in service provision (Cameron and Wherrett 1995). By the 1990s, the role of provincial governments in Aboriginal affairs was taken for granted and even identified by some as being as important as the federal role. For example, the Royal Commission on Aboriginal Peoples (RCAP) argued that provinces, like the federal government, had an "in right of the Crown" fiduciary responsibility to Aboriginal peoples (RCAP Volume 2, Part One, Sections 5, 7; Volume 4, Section 7).[6]

Early provincial responses neither recognized nor attempted to accommodate the historic entitlements and cultural differences of Aboriginal people (Cameron and Wherrett 1995; Malloy 2003, 113). Instead, the government of Ontario tended to view the interests of

Aboriginal people living in cities as being no different from those of any other citizens. This provincial understanding gradually shifted as the national and Ontario Aboriginal movements affected changes in federal law and in federal policy, especially during and after the 1970s. In 1976, the Ontario government appointed its first minister responsible for Aboriginal affairs, though this minister was without a portfolio and was originally assigned only a single policy advisor to provide support (Sampson 1992, 18). In the same year, the Ontario government created an office for administering Indian land claims that was housed in the Ministry of Natural Resources – an institutional arrangement that reflects the decades-long provincial perspective on Aboriginal land rights (Cameron and Wherrett 1995; Malloy 2003, 118).

The Liberal and New Democratic governments that came to power after 1985 took a different approach to Aboriginal affairs. For instance, when the Liberal government was elected in 1985, it increased the size and internal visibility of the Office of Native Affairs Policy; in 1988, it centralized the administration of Aboriginal affairs by transferring the Office of Indian Resource Policy from the Ministry of Natural Resources to the (renamed) Ontario Native Affairs Directorate (ONAD) (Malloy 2003, 119). This change can be seen as a de facto recognition of the importance of control over land to the relations between the province and First Nation, as well as an attempt to organize for the resolution of outstanding disputes. There is little evidence during this period of significant provincial engagement in urban Aboriginal affairs or matters of specific concern to Métis and Non-Status Indians.

The 1990 election of a New Democratic government brought further changes.[7] Under the NDP, ONAD was renamed the Ontario Native Affairs Secretariat (ONAS) and given responsibility for implementing the Ontario government's Aboriginal agenda, investigating land claims, negotiating land settlements, and monitoring Aboriginal policy development across various ministries (Cameron and Wherrett 1995). Perhaps the most significant change was the NDP government's assertion that Aboriginal people had inherent political rights. Milloy et al. (1992) note that within weeks of assuming office, Premier Bob Rae demonstrated the priority granted to Aboriginal affairs by outlining his government's support of "inherent" Aboriginal rights as follows: "We believe there is an inherent right to self-government, that the inherent right stems from powers, and if you will, sovereignty, which existed prior to 1763, certainly existed prior to 1867 and certainly prior to 1982" (Cited in Milloy et al. 1992, 2).

This embrace of both the concept of inherent rights and its foundation within Aboriginal sovereignty is broader than previous discussions of self-government that occurred within the province. For example, in their 1989 assessment of the Liberal government's policy discourse, Abele and Graham noted that the provincial government had merely embraced the concept of self-government without actually defining its terms. This led the authors to suggest that "the evolution of self-government towards some form of municipal model is implicit in the province's acceptance of this term" (1989, 152).

The NDP Throne Speech in 1990 made self-government negotiations with First Nations a priority, and the government committed itself that year to improving financial resources and provincial programs for First Nations communities. An early example of this new approach was a meeting between First Nations Chiefs and Premier Bob Rae in August of 1991 at Mount McKay, which was located south of Thunder Bay on the lands of the Fort William First Nation. They signed a Statement of Political Relationship (SPR) at this meeting. The SPR both recognized that First Nations held an inherent right to self-government under the Canadian constitution and acknowledged that First Nations "exist in Ontario as distinct nations, with their governments, cultures, languages, traditions, customs, and territories" (quoted in Milloy et. al 1992, 1).

Along with these measures, the NDP developed a number of policies and programs specific to Aboriginal people in the areas of health and social services, and housing – all of them important for Aboriginal people living in the cities. During the early 1990s, the Ministry of Health provided funding for community consultations and developed partnerships with Aboriginal organizations in an effort to formulate an Aboriginal-specific health policy. As well, in 1992 and 1993, the Ministry of Housing consulted with Aboriginal organizations in order to determine how its non-profit housing programs could better serve the urban Aboriginal community in Ontario (Cameron and Wherrett 1995).

All this progress halted with the election of the Conservative government led by Mike Harris. Under the Harris government, a number of organizational and structural changes occurred, such as a reduction in the size of ONAS and the demotion of its deputy minister to the status of assistant deputy minister. As well, self-government and land claims negotiations entered into by the previous NDP government "slowed or stopped entirely under Harris' conservatives" (Malloy 2003, 123). The new Conservative government emphasized increasing the economic self-reliance of Aboriginal people and backed away from discussions premised on inherent rights.[8] Probably the most notorious initiative of the Harris Conservatives in Aboriginal affairs was its handling of the Ipperwash reoccupation by the Stoney Point First Nation, a calamitous confrontation that resulted in the death of Dudley George, a member of the Stoney Point First Nation.[9]

The Harris years had a pronounced impact on Aboriginal people living in Ontario cities, particularly those who were poor. The Harris Conservatives cut social assistance rates for single recipients, closed secondary women's shelters, and "downloaded" to city administration a number of social services, including public housing. These measures, along with top-down city amalgamations, put new pressures on all Ontario cities, and at once increased their social welfare responsibilities and reduced their financial means (Marquardt 2007).

The Liberal government elected in 2003, led by Dalton McGuinty, reversed many of these measures. In 2005, the government released *A New Approach to Aboriginal Affairs*, a document that outlined the organizing principles and values that would guide its relations with Aboriginal people. *New Approach* stressed the need to build constructive "partnerships" and "co-operative" relations with Aboriginal people through "mutual respect" and "goodwill" (ONAS 2005, 4). The Ministry of Aboriginal Affairs was re-established and equipped with an experienced minister (Michael Bryant, a former attorney-general who represents an urban Toronto riding), a deputy minister, and an assistant deputy minister. The department was also organized into the following branches and directorates: Policy and Relationships Branch (charged with coordination and political support); Ipperwash Response Team; Negotiations Branch (charged with representing Ontario in federally-led governance negotiations); Legal Services Branch (advising the Minister on legal affairs); as well as Communications and Business Services Branches. While none of these offices have a specific brief to deal with urban affairs, most engage urban Aboriginal issues from time to time.

Recognizing that the number of Aboriginal people living off-reserve was increasing rapidly, the McGuinty government offered to build partnerships with both the federal government and Indian Friendship Centres. In December 2005, the government announced a partnership with the Ontario Federation of Indian Friendship Centres to help support urban Aboriginal children. The program, known as "Akwe:go," would provide culturally appropriate education and health resources to Aboriginal children and youth (OSAA 2005). There was also a commitment of funds in 2006 to support renovations of Indian Friendship Centre buildings across the province (OSAA 2006).

At the same time, land issues continued to dominate the headlines, with instances of civil disobedience and effective stalemates concerning land use near Patagonia, Belleville, and the Ardoch territories north of Kingston. These difficult and multilevel disputes are long-standing and will likely be a feature of provincial-Aboriginal relations for decades. Provincial policies of consequence to urban Aboriginal people are a much newer development. After a long period in which provincial governments ignored the needs of Métis, Non-Status, and urban Aboriginal people, policy and programs now recognize the importance of providing targeted services and funding to Aboriginal people who live in the cities. These policies and the shifting approaches to social provision in Ontario, characteristic of the successive provincial governments, have had a major effect on municipal-Aboriginal relations.

FOUR CITIES IN OVERVIEW

There are fifty-one cities in Ontario, and no selection of four can hope to provide a representative picture of urban Aboriginal affairs in the province. Such a selection, however, can highlight some patterns of interaction between urban Aboriginal residents and city governments. To the extent that these patterns can be traced back to common features of colonial history, socio-economic and structural factors, and to provincial policies, they may advance our general understanding of Aboriginal affairs in Ontario (Pal 1995).

These four cities were chosen because the situations of their Aboriginal residents can easily be compared and contrasted with one another. However, they were also chosen because they have significant Aboriginal populations. Toronto and Ottawa are the two largest cities in Ontario; between them they are home to over 30,000 Aboriginal people. Kingston and Thunder Bay share relatively small size and locations outside the Golden Horseshoe of southern

Table 1
Comparison of Four Cities

	Thunder Bay	*Kingston*	*Toronto*	*Ottawa*
Size	Small	Small	Large	Large
Proportion of Aboriginal Residents	8.3%, growing rapidly, fourth largest per capita	Less than 2.2%	Less than 1%, but more than 25,000 Aboriginal residents in the city	Less than 2%
Economic Base	Regional centre; resource base	Regional service centre; many public institutions	Mixed economic base; very large	Mixed economic base; many public institutions
Treaty History	Subject to Robinson Treaty, contested	Originally used and occupied by a number of peoples	Crown land purchase contested by Mississaugas of New Credit	Subject to Algonquin land claim
UAS	Yes	No	Yes	Yes
Other Aboriginal Organization Network or Coalition	Aboriginal Interagency Council	Kingston Aboriginal Community Information Network	Toronto Aboriginal Support Services Association	Ottawa Aboriginal Coalition
Aboriginal-Specific Institutions in City Government	No	No	Aboriginal Affairs Advisory Committee	Aboriginal Working Committee
Aboriginal Policies of City Government?	No formal policy	No formal policy	No formal policy	No formal policy

Ontario; they have more specialized (though contrasting) economic bases. All four cities are located in Aboriginal territory that was once a crossroads or trading centre. In all cases, Aboriginal people make up a very small proportion of the population of the city. In 2002, Thunder Bay had the largest proportion of Aboriginal people (officially, 8.3 per cent) followed by Kingston (2.2 per cent), Ottawa (1.6 per cent), and Toronto (less than 1 per cent). Despite these small proportions, the absolute number of Aboriginal people in each city is significant.

THUNDER BAY

Thunder Bay is a relatively small city (121,055 people) in the Ojibway territory of northern Ontario. The area around Thunder Bay is subject to the Robinson Treaty (1850), Treaty 3 (1873), and Treaty 9 (1905, 1906).[10] All three treaty areas have been known disputes over land and resources between First Nations and the Crown.

The Aboriginal population in Thunder Bay has been steadily increasing over the past number of years because the impoverished conditions of Aboriginal communities in northern Ontario have caused many Aboriginal people to relocate to the city in search of health care, employment, and education. Although the Census identified 10,055 Aboriginal residents in 2006, this figure is probably an underestimate. During the initial planning for Thunder Bay's Urban Aboriginal Strategy, consultations and meetings with service providers and Aboriginal elders within the community suggested that the Aboriginal population in Thunder Bay was likely closer to 20,000 people (Thunder Bay UAS 2004).

The city and surrounding area are in a period of relative economic hardship brought on by declines in the forestry industry (HRSDC 2005, 2; 2006, 3). Thunder Bay's labour force continues to be dominated by its educational sector, manufacturing industries, health and social services, and municipal government. Thunder Bay's municipal government, in particular, is the largest single employer in the area followed by the Thunder Bay regional health sciences centre and the Lakehead district school board.

There has been significant public discussion about issues of interest to Aboriginal people in Thunder Bay, which focused in recent years on racism, poverty, homelessness, and unsettled land claims in the area. In March 2002, a coalition of Aboriginal and non-Aboriginal service providers, and municipal government officials (known as "Diversity Thunder Bay") released a report on race relations in the city of Thunder Bay. Discrimination based on race was a significant problem for Aboriginal peoples and minority groups within the city. In particular, a substantial number of Aboriginal respondents (75 per cent) revealed that they had observed incidents of racial discrimination in the city (Diversity Thunder Bay 2002, 35).[11] One year later, a meeting was organized to discuss the federal government's Urban Aboriginal Strategy (UAS). Thunder Bay was chosen as one of the UAS pilot sites due to the large size of its Aboriginal population. After a number of consultations and forums, which involved members of the urban Aboriginal community, Aboriginal child poverty was identified as a priority (Thunder Bay UAS 2004, 5). Consequently, the overall strategic objectives were to "reduce the socio-economic disparity" and differences in "life-chances" between Aboriginal and non-Aboriginal people (Thunder Bay UAS 2004, 10).

Public life in Thunder Bay is likely also affected by disputes over land that have occurred near Thunder Bay, since the resources on these lands are the foundation of the city's prosperity; one such dispute was the constitutional claim by the Kitchenuhmaykoosib Inninuwug (KI) First Nation that challenged the legitimacy of the *Ontario Mining Act*. The protests launched by the KI First Nation against mining incursions on their traditional lands demonstrate the continuing contestation over territorial rights and jurisdiction between the provincial government, First Nations, and third parties in the region (Platinex Inc. 2006).

While the City of Thunder Bay formally recognizes the inherent cultural diversity of its community members, it does not have corporate policies directed solely towards its urban Aboriginal population. Instead, the municipal government of Thunder Bay recognizes its urban Aboriginal component through policies on race relations and multiculturalism that apply to all ethnic groups without differentiation (City of Thunder Bay 1996). In an effort to respond to Diversity Thunder Bay's report on systemic discrimination, the Human Resources Division distributed an employment equity survey in 2005 to all its employees. The survey was designed to measure the fairness of its hiring practices in relation to the following groups: men, women, Aboriginal peoples, visible minorities, and persons with disabilities. The report concluded that because the percentage of the corporation's Aboriginal population was commensurate with the percentage of Aboriginal people residing within Thunder Bay, "the Corporation's hiring practices allow for fair and equitable employment opportunities" (City of Thunder Bay 2005). The city has implemented outreach strategies in relation to Aboriginal people, such as sponsoring Aboriginal Day, participating in Diversity Thunder Bay meetings, and partnering with the Aboriginal Employment Resource Committee (AERC) to improve employment opportunities for Aboriginal people (City of Thunder Bay 2005).[12]

The municipal government of Thunder Bay has not yet established an institutional mechanism for Aboriginal people to provide input

Table 2
Aboriginal Service Organizations in Thunder Bay in 2007

ANISHNAWBE MUSHKIKI is an Aboriginal Community Health Centre that provides a holistic approach to health care by combining western, traditional, and alternative approaches to medicine.

KA-NA-CHI-HIH is a solvent abuse treatment centre for First Nation youth who are between 16 and 25 years of age. Ka-Na-Chi-Hih employs holistic approaches that emphasize "traditional and contemporary teachings, skills, and values."

BEENDIGEN INC. is an agency established by the Thunder Bay Anishnawbequek, which provides a Crisis Home for Aboriginal women and children in cases of domestic violence.

DILICO OJIBWA Child and Family Services provides health and welfare services to Anishinabek children and their families.

OSHKI-PIMACHE-O-WIN provides post-secondary education and training to members of the Nishnawbe Aski Nation and other First Nation communities.

THUNDER BAY INDIAN FRIENDSHIP CENTRE, established in 1964, assists Aboriginal people in making the transition within the urban environment through such programs as employment and training; family support; healing and wellness; and women's awareness.

---

into policy making. While the corporation of Thunder Bay's strategic plan for 2004 stated that the Mayor would "provide a forum for Aboriginal and Municipal leaders to work cooperatively and develop strategies that best meet the needs of our communities" (City of Thunder Bay 2004, 13), service providers expressed disappointment with the lack of meaningful interaction that has occurred with the municipality. Nevertheless, the agencies serving Aboriginal people in Thunder Bay have organized themselves into an interagency council, which meets once every month to discuss and address issues facing the urban Aboriginal community. The Aboriginal Interagency Council is composed of over twenty Aboriginal service providers in Thunder Bay and functions as a forum for service providers not only to identify gaps in existing programs and services but to ensure that these needs are addressed within the urban Aboriginal community.

PATTERNS AND ISSUES

By virtue of numbers alone, Aboriginal people in Thunder Bay are a visible presence, but visibility does not always entail understanding. A number of service providers told us during interviews that the city does not reach out to them. While there was talk of establishing a new cooperative relationship between the municipal government and Aboriginal people through the creation of an Aboriginal/Municipal "forum," Aboriginal service providers told us that this forum never materialized. They suggested that the city often interacts and consults with the Nishnawbe Aski Nation (NAN), a political organization rooted in the First Nations territories around Thunder Bay, at the expense of broader forms of consultation. While NAN itself does have a substantial presence within the city and has established its administrative offices mere blocks from Thunder Bay's City Hall, some Aboriginal service providers stressed that the city often forgets that other nations exist within the urban Aboriginal community.[13]

The matter is complex. Though Aboriginal organizations said on multiple occasions that the municipality does not reach out to them, some also expressed uneasiness at the notion of interacting with the municipality in the first place, fearing a diminution of federal fiduciary responsibilities and of their own sovereignty.

For their part, municipal government officials were puzzled by the very notion of "urban Aboriginal policy." According to one city official, the role of the municipal government is to deal with community relations and to serve the entire Thunder Bay community. As such, the municipality does not want to develop policies that might discriminate among members of its community. Another city official stressed that the municipality has neither the jurisdiction nor the legislative drivers for developing specific policies in relation to urban Aboriginal people. This official objected to the phrase "urban Aboriginal policy" itself and argued that the term "'urban Aboriginal' is nebulous. I don't understand what that term means. How would middle-class Aboriginal people connect [to an urban Aboriginal policy]? The city government tries to help people move upwards" (Interview 12). What the city does do in relation to Aboriginal people, however, is to "ensure that the community is welcoming to everyone" and therefore works on recognizing its Aboriginal population by sponsoring Aboriginal Day, participating in an Aboriginal career fair, and committing itself to ensuring that its own recruitment and selection practices are free of racial discrimination of any kind.

Federal funding under the Urban Aboriginal Strategy has enabled Aboriginal organizations to build partnerships with non-Aboriginal service providers, though there is concern about continuity. As one

Aboriginal service provider succinctly put it, "the federal government's Urban Aboriginal Strategy is not a strategy. To call it a strategy is false. There are only 'pilot sites'" (Interview 14). This lack of continuity constrains efforts to build infrastructure and make longer term plans. Furthermore, with greater interaction comes even greater transaction costs: the smaller Aboriginal organizations found it exhausting to navigate and engage with the entrenched organizational structures of each relevant federal department. According to one health care provider, his/her organization continues to create separate proposals and deal with different reporting requirements unique to each department. To complicate matters, this organization is often forced to educate new project managers about itself and the program due to high turnover rates within each department. In the words of one service provider, "the UAS can have an impact, but it is too short a time frame. There is no time to work on larger issues facing the community. We are so overworked and understaffed; we are always going project to project. Why are Aboriginal programs always fighting for funding and survival?" (Interview 13)

However, a sense of the future came from one of the individuals who was interviewed: "The city needs to understand what is happening here. Our population is very young and it is growing; by 2010 we will be roughly fifty per cent of Thunder Bay's population. There are also very lucrative resources on our reserve lands. We will be the economic drivers of this region; they will have to come to us" (Interview 14).

KINGSTON

Kingston, the other small city in our study, is located in the distinctive "Loyalist" region of southeastern Ontario. The city's image appears to be dominated by a well-established Anglophone majority with few traces of its origins as a meeting place of Aboriginal peoples and (later) a French colony. Public institutions (prisons, hospitals, two universities, a community college, and major military institutions) shape the economy, which has a small manufacturing sector and a growing tourism industry. A significant portion of the Aboriginal population is transient, drawn from many parts of Ontario and northern Canada. Many individuals and family members relocate there in order to be closer to relatives who are seeking post-secondary education, receiving medical care, or being held in prison.

Kingston is built on lands that have long been a meeting place and a crossroads for the Aboriginal nations of the Great Lakes basin and indeed for the settler societies as well. Before they had extensive contact with Europeans, Iroquoian-speaking peoples followed, for the most part, an agriculturally based lifestyle in the lands around the Great Lakes, and Algonquian-speaking peoples lived by hunting, fishing, and gathering in the lands of the Canadian Shield just to the north.[14] Both Iroquoian-speaking Huron and Algonquin-speaking Mississaugas made use of the area where Kingston now stands, although it is likely that the Mississaugas were the permanent occupiers of the territory. In the general disruptions that followed the arrival of European weapons and trade goods – and later, European armies and settlers – both the Huron and Mississaugas moved out of the area. The Iroquoian-speaking Mohawks settled in the Tyendenaga territory (located on Lake Ontario between Kingston and Belleville) after the American Revolution on the invitation of British authorities. A large area immediately to the north of Kingston that extended as far as Golden Lake is the traditional territory of several of the Algonquin-speaking Anishnabe nations including the Ardoch, who are nearest to the city.[15]

Today, the Aboriginal population of the City of Kingston is small and markedly heterogeneous. In 2006, the total population of Kingston was 148,475; of these, just over two per cent were Aboriginal people.[16] This community is predominantly comprised of those who identify themselves as North American Indian, with Métis comprising a quarter of the Aboriginal population, and Inuit, a much smaller fraction. In each category of Aboriginal people, men outnumber women, and in all cases, the Aboriginal population is younger than the non-Aboriginal population.

PATTERNS AND ISSUES

At the time of our research in 2006–07, the city government of Kingston had no specialized units for dealing with Aboriginal peoples in either the legislative or the administrative branch. Neither the mayor nor particular members of council are known for their particular interest in Aboriginal matters. Staff in the Arts and Recreation offices, however, have dealt with the Mohawks of the Bay of Quinte on the Bell Island issue (discussed later). Additionally, Aboriginal residents of Kingston encounter city officials as they use

Table 3
Aboriginal Service Organizations in Kingston in 2007

KINGSTON ABORIGINAL COMMUNITY INFORMATION NETWORK (KACIN) is a network of the Aboriginally-focused institutions in Kingston.

KATAROKWI NATIVE FRIENDSHIP CENTRE assists Aboriginal people who are new to Kingston and provides supportive programs for all in the areas of adult and child health; literacy; social and cultural events; and recreation.

KINGSTON INTERVAL HOUSE (KIH) provides services for women and children in need but with a specific focus on women who are physically and mentally abused and/or threatened.

RED CEDARS SHELTER, located on the Tyendinaga Mohawk Territory, provides shelter, counselling, advocacy, referrals, information, and access to traditional healing for abused women and children.

KAGITA MIKAM ABORIGINAL EMPLOYMENT AND TRAINING SERVICES delivers employment and training programs and services to Aboriginal people in eastern Ontario.

WEENEEBAYKO PATIENT SERVICES AND GEAGANANO RESIDENCE are services at Hotel Dieu Hospital for Aboriginal patients and their families from northern Ontario.

ONTARIO ABORIGINAL HIV/AIDS STRATEGY office for eastern Ontario, established to provide information, education, services, and support to both urban and rural (off-reserve) Aboriginal peoples.

city services as a matter of course. Some municipal funding, which is channelled through programs at the Katarokwi Native Friendship Centre, supports day care services. Another important target of municipal funding is Tipi Moza (Iron Homes), a public housing service originally funded by the Canada Mortgage and Housing Corporation (CMHC). CMHC funding was dramatically reduced in the late 1980s and 1990s, and was eventually transferred to the province as part of the changes resulting from the 1995 Program Review. Almost immediately, the province downloaded this responsibility to the City of Kingston. The city inherited seventeen houses and a residence, all of which suffered from over a decade of underfunding.

Aboriginal people are not very visible in Kingston. They are a small proportion of the total population, and many are sojourners who live in the city temporarily in order to be near relatives who are there for medical care, education, or are in prison. There is some symbolic recognition of the Aboriginal population, but such recognition is limited: for example, Aboriginal representatives are invited to civic celebrations to fill a ceremonial role, but their presence is not acknowledged in the city's "self-presentation," whether in tourist brochures or economic development information. City officials indicated that a higher profile could be given to the city's Aboriginal history as an item of local touristic interest.

The relative invisibility of Aboriginal people in Kingston's official communications is mirrored in the lack of working or formal relationships between the city's Aboriginal residents and its politicians and officials. In fact, it appears that city officials have developed better (if limited) relationships with representatives of the Tyendanaga Mohawk territory, which is nearly an hour's drive from Kingston. Interestingly, other public institutions, such as the Royal Military College and the hospitals, do have stronger and even multifaceted relations with the urban Aboriginal community as is evidenced by their membership in the Kingston Aboriginal Community Information Network (KACIN). It is not surprising then, that a major force behind the formation of KACIN was a desire to make the needs of the resident Aboriginal population in Kingston more visible to city officials. Unlike Toronto, Ottawa, and Thunder Bay, Kingston was not chosen as an Urban Aboriginal Strategy site.

There is no formal statement of the priorities of either the Kingston Aboriginal community or the City of Kingston with regard to Aboriginal affairs in general and land use within and outside the city in particular. City officials were aware of the obstacles to city development that might be posed by historically significant Aboriginal sites (such as burial sites) within the city boundaries. It is evident that in Kingston, as in other cities, the city's assumption of public housing responsibilities had been onerous. On the other side, land use issues did not seem to be a priority for the existing urban Aboriginal organizations. Each of these of course have their own area of interest and focus; they are united in their interest in developing a functional working relationship with those levels of government (or other institutions) whose support they require in fulfilling their mandates. Finally, several respondents mentioned the problem of urban poverty and the relative invisibility of the poor Aboriginal people who live within city limits. Furthermore, the Ardoch First Nation opposition to uranium mining in the Sharbot Lake area, just north of Kingston, has not emerged as an important issue in the City of Kingston itself. That this lack of attention exists in Kingston is evidenced by the fact that a Queen's University professor's involvement and arrest in the Sharbot Lake protests went virtually unnoticed at City Hall.

TORONTO

Toronto is the largest city in Canada, the provincial capital, and the metropolis for the densely-populated social and economic powerhouse referred to as the "Golden Horseshoe," which hugs the western shores of Lake Ontario. It has the largest urban population of Aboriginal people in Ontario, one of the smallest proportions of Aboriginal people among larger Ontario cities, and – as a major destination for immigrants to Canada – the greatest degree of ethnic heterogeneity overall.

While much of the large area now occupied by Toronto is traditional Mississauga territory, the Aboriginal population of Toronto is heterogeneous.[17] According to the 2006 Census, there were 26,575 Aboriginal people in Toronto, less than one per cent of the population. Aboriginal service providers argue that this estimate is significantly low, estimating instead between 65,000 and 90,000 people. While this last estimate would still be small in the context of the overall population of Toronto, it is large in the context of the local Aboriginal community. The impact of size is attenuated, perhaps, by the reality that Aboriginal people in Toronto are dispersed in various parts of the city. While there are identifiable districts for many ethnic groups in Toronto, there is no "Aboriginal" neighbourhood.

One fact that gives credence to the comment that the Census underestimates the number of Aboriginal people in Toronto is that the Aboriginal community is known to comprise about 25 per cent of the city's homeless population, a group quite likely to be underrepresented in the Census (City of Toronto AAC 2006). As a group, Aboriginal people in Toronto earn less and are less likely to be employed than other city residents.

Like the other cities in this study, Toronto has no policy statement or permanent agency directed towards its Aboriginal residents. There would appear to be two reasons for this situation: a perceived lack of constitutional jurisdiction and a recognition that Aboriginal people form a small proportion of an ethnically diverse city. Such statements as have been made by the city exhibit a certain ambivalence. The government of Toronto vacillates between publicly affirming

Aboriginal "uniqueness" and the principle of Aboriginal self-determination while simultaneously pursuing policies grounded in "equality" (see City of Toronto 2002).

Yet Toronto has taken a number of concrete steps to recognize its Aboriginal residents. In 1989, the City of Toronto endowed two scholarships for Aboriginal students studying in health professional programs at the University of Toronto.[18] In 1999, Toronto's City Council approved the creation of a number of advisory committees that would address issues of access, equity, and human rights across the city. One of the committees that developed out of this process was given a mandate for urban Aboriginal affairs. Chaired by a member of Council, the Aboriginal Affairs Committee has focused in the past on establishing an Aboriginal monument in the City of Toronto, creating an Aboriginal cultural centre, streamlining permit applications for Aboriginal ceremonies, building relations between Aboriginal agencies and Toronto police officers, and responding to housing concerns. It is particularly in the area of housing where much interaction has occurred between the city and the Aboriginal community through the city's Affordable Housing Office and its Shelter, Support, and Housing Administration. The city has subsequently approved the purchase and renovation of a sixty-two unit property by Nishnawbe Homes in order to provide permanent affordable housing for Aboriginal residents in Toronto's downtown core; this project has received funding from the city, provincial, and federal governments (City of Toronto 2007).

Since taking office in 2003, Toronto's then mayor, David Miller, made numerous references to the historical entitlements of the city's urban Aboriginal community. In December of 2003 and 2004, Miller stressed the city's "proud" history of promoting equal rights for all of its citizens and also acknowledged that Toronto's history has not been completely honourable towards its Aboriginal community (Miller 2004; 2003). Beginning in 2003, the City of Toronto has honoured individuals and organizations whose efforts had made a "significant contribution" to the urban Aboriginal community.[19]

PATTERNS AND ISSUES

In the mid-1980s and early 1990s, the urban Aboriginal community in Toronto faced hostility from its non-Aboriginal neighbours when attempts were made to establish non-profit homes for Aboriginal people. Zoning applications for Toronto's first non-profit housing

Table 4
Aboriginal Service Organizations in Toronto in 2007

GABRIEL DUMONT NON-PROFIT HOMES provides subsidized housing to urban Aboriginal families in Scarborough.

NISHNAWBE HOMES provides affordable housing to Aboriginal people throughout Toronto's downtown core.

NA-MA-RES provides shelter and services to homeless Aboriginal men as well as outreach programs to Toronto's homeless population.

WIGWAMEN offers affordable housing to urban Aboriginal individuals, families, and seniors in Toronto.

NATIVE CHILD AND FAMILY SERVICES is the only off-reserve Aboriginal Children's Aid Society in the province of Ontario, providing culturally appropriate care and support programs.

ANISHNAWBE HEALTH TORONTO is a community health centre that provides traditional healing and mental health programs to Toronto's urban Aboriginal community based upon Aboriginal traditions and values.

ABORIGINAL LEGAL SERVICES OF TORONTO provides legal support and services to Toronto's Aboriginal community such as a court worker program that enables Aboriginal clients to know their rights, secure legal counsel, and receive assistance with pre-sentence reports; a legal aid clinic for low income Aboriginal people; and a community council program for Aboriginal offenders.

TORONTO COUNCIL FIRE is an Aboriginal cultural centre which provides culturally specific services and programs to Toronto's Aboriginal community.

NATIVE CANADIAN CENTRE of Toronto is a friendship centre that provides a range of practical assistance to Aboriginal residents and newcomers.

project for Aboriginal people were initially rejected amidst vigorous citizen opposition (James 1986, A6). Furthermore, Aboriginal people in Toronto garnered national attention in the mid-1990s when about thirty Aboriginal people took over an entire wing of the Revenue Canada Taxation Centre in downtown Toronto (Chidley 1995, 14; Platiel 1995, A1). Commonly referred to as "Revenue Rez," the occupation lasted twenty-nine days; it was carried out in protest of the elimination of income tax exemptions for Status Indians who lived and worked off-reserve.[20]

While Aboriginal people have staged symbolic protests within urban centres against discrimination (such as "Revenue Rez"), they have also used legal methods to achieve measures of self-determination within the City of Toronto. For instance, in 2001, Native Child and Family Services issued a Charter suit against the Ontario government for refusing to recognize the organization as a children's aid society despite the fact that they permitted the operation of such agencies for Catholic and Jewish children (see Calleja 2001). Native Child and Family Services was ultimately successful and attained the designation of a children's aid society in 2004. This designation provides a measure of institutional control and enables the urban Aboriginal community in Toronto to direct the development of its own members.

In the face of limited institutional support, the urban Aboriginal community has organized itself into an interagency body, which oversees a network composed of twelve Aboriginal service providers throughout Toronto. Known as the "Toronto Aboriginal Support Services Association" (TASSA), this interagency body meets once every month to discuss the issues facing the urban Aboriginal community in Toronto and to work out ways of providing services to its community. Federal and provincial budgetary decisions have forced increased interaction among the municipality, Aboriginal organizations, and other levels of government. As was the case in other cities, the devolution of housing responsibilities in the 1990s from the federal, to the provincial, to the municipal governments forced Aboriginal service providers into a continual process of re-educating project officers.[21]

Aside from TASSA, the Urban Aboriginal Strategy (UAS) has also brought people together. The City of Toronto's UAS is overseen by the Toronto Urban Aboriginal Strategy Management Committee (TUMC), whose mandate is to identify and advance opportunities for Aboriginal people so that social and economic gaps between urban Aboriginal people and the larger Toronto community are eliminated. It has identified priority areas and dispersed funds.[22] In December 2005, the Aboriginal Task Force released a preliminary report that focused on the middle-class urban Aboriginal community in Toronto and described a community marked by social isolation, cultural diversity, community fragmentation, and a disparate sense of identity (Service Canada 2005).

Our interviews revealed some problems with present arrangements.[23] Although the city interacts with representatives from the urban Aboriginal community through its Aboriginal Affairs Advisory Committee (AAC), its ability to effectively serve the interests of Aboriginal people is constrained by both the municipal government's institutional framework and the advisory status of the committee. Aboriginal service providers expressed frustration with this situation as well as with the pointlessness of "planning in a vacuum." Since the municipality does not have jurisdiction for developing Aboriginal policy, it was very difficult for substantive discussions to occur within the committee on issues and concerns facing the urban Aboriginal community. In the view of some, emphasis on recognizing the community primarily through historical monuments (mentioned above as one of AAC's aims) fails to represent the urban Aboriginal community as a living reality.[24] Appreciation was expressed, however, by other members for the role of the committee in giving a voice to Aboriginal housing concerns and affording them the opportunity to provide input into the city's homelessness survey.

From the city's perspective, on the other hand, the emphasis on symbolic forms of recognition is consistent with its governing principles and underlying values. Municipal officials stress that the city engages in "positive" forms of recognition, such as sponsoring Aboriginal Day, holding youth powwows, and recognizing the archaeological components of the city's Aboriginal history. These "positive" forms of recognition are consonant with the principles of multiculturalism and "equality" espoused by the city. As one senior official put it, "the city [of Toronto] is an open, transparent government; when we write policy we don't want to provoke a response from the larger community" (Interview 6). As such, by recognizing and acknowledging the multiplicity of cultural distinctions and identities that exist throughout its urban population, the city is able to ensure that its governing framework remains coherent with the larger goals of respecting multiculturalism and equality rights of all its citizens.

City officials were puzzled by our questions concerning "urban Aboriginal policy." One official situated urban Aboriginal people outside the boundaries of municipal governance: "The City of Toronto has no jurisdiction and/or requirement in this area" (Interview 6). In other words, because the municipality does not have constitutional authority for Aboriginal affairs, city officials do not perceive the development of an Aboriginal-specific policy as either a municipal necessity, or even, a possibility. Moreover, according to this city official, even if one were to set jurisdictional constraints aside, a fundamental problem for the city would be to define or frame the policy itself. From this city official's perspective, what matters most in the formulation of policy are jurisdiction and demographics, rather than rights based in "past history."

However, from the perspective of Aboriginal service providers, it is this very history that not only informs present conditions within the urban Aboriginal community but also calls for municipal responses that are not based on conventional delivery models. According to one Aboriginal service provider, "the city does not want to look at setting aside resources or expenditures for our community; it is still trying to fit the urban Aboriginal community into its own generic model" (Interview 3). On a number of different occasions, Aboriginal service providers noted that they felt it was necessary for the municipality to create an Aboriginal department and "recognize that Aboriginal solutions will be different." As one Aboriginal service provider stated, "one of the most problematic aspects of dealing with the municipality is that there is no recognition that the community is organized. We have a way to govern ourselves" (Interview 4).

Aboriginal organizations objected to the downloading of responsibility for public housing from the "senior" levels of government because this transfer of responsibility required Aboriginal housing providers to compete with non-Aboriginal providers for subsidies and continually re-educate project managers as to why urban Aboriginal organizations are unique. One person described this downloading as a violation of the federal government's fiduciary responsibilities; some providers have refused to sign operating agreements with the municipality on this basis: they argue that the federal government has a better understanding of their concerns and their cultural uniqueness.

OTTAWA

The second largest city in Ontario is Ottawa,[25] site of a large concentration of federal government offices and location of the head offices of all the national Aboriginal organizations and numerous advocacy and non-governmental organizations. As the second largest city in Ontario and a "destination" city for Aboriginal people relocating from northern Canada, Ottawa provides an interesting comparative case to Toronto.

Ottawa shares some of the economic characteristics of Kingston because it has a stable economic base that is created by the presence of the federal government and many other national institutions and organizations. With a much larger population and more diversified

Table 5
Aboriginal Service Organizations in Ottawa in 2007

ODAWA NATIVE FRIENDSHIP CENTRE provides a variety of programs for children, parents, youth, elders, and the general population. Popular cultural events are the annual Odawa Festival of Aboriginal Culture and Pow Wow.

SHAWENJEAGAMIK provides services for those who are homeless or at the risk of being homeless in an area of the city where there are many Aboriginal newcomers.

WABANO CENTRE FOR ABORIGINAL HEALTH provides a very wide range of education, health, and wellness services.

MINIWAASHIN LODGE – ABORIGINAL WOMEN'S SUPPORT CENTRE provides services and programs for Aboriginal women, children, and youth who are direct and inter-generational survivors of family violence and the residential school system.

GIGNUL NON-PROFIT HOUSING CORPORATION provides services and shelter to Aboriginal people who are at risk of losing their housing and those who are currently homeless.

PINGANODIN LODGE addresses the needs of Aboriginal males who require transitional housing or a safe place to help them nurse back to health from the effects of alcohol and drug abuse.

TUNGASUVVINGAT INUIT provides culturally specific employment, health, and children's programs for the Inuit community in Ontario from the City of Ottawa.

INUIT NON-PROFIT HOUSING CORPORATION provides housing, new arrival orientation, and meeting rooms to Inuit.

INUIT CHILDREN CENTRE is a child care centre that provides programs for children and youth.

INUIT FAMILY RESOURCE CENTRE provides pre- and post-natal care, and employment training.

MAMUSARVIN HEALING CENTRE supports people who are recovering from trauma, addiction, or homelessness.

PIGIARVIK HOUSE is a residential home for Mamusarvin Healing Centre.

---

economy than Kingston, Ottawa is a second-tier destination for new immigrants. The national institutions have attracted people from all over Canada, and so have the Aboriginal organizations. Built on Algonquin territory,[26] Ottawa boasts Aboriginal people from virtually every nation and every part of Canada. In 2006, Aboriginal residents numbered 12,970, about 1.5 per cent of Ottawa's total population. Although most of them were First Nation or Métis, Ottawa does have a substantial Inuit population, large enough to support the creation of a number of Inuit-specific service organizations.

PATTERNS AND ISSUES

In 2000, the Odawa Native Friendship Centre, the Wabano Centre for Aboriginal Health, Minwaashin Lodge, and the Inuit Children Centre formed the Ottawa Aboriginal Coalition (OAC) with the goal of developing priorities and communicating with all three levels of government with a united voice. The OAC responded to the Supporting Communities Partnership Initiative (SCPI) of the 1999 National Homelessness Initiative, which tied funding to collaboration among community organizations and collaboration between community organizations and governments. In the initial phase, there was some tension within the OAC concerning the allocation of funding, but the group has been effective, notably in establishing a strong working relationship with the City of Ottawa. In a report to Ottawa's City Council and Community and Protective Services Committee, city officials applauded the role that OAC has played in creating a better relationship with the city. The report proposed the creation of an Aboriginal Working Committee in city government in order to "provide opportunities to develop better service delivery systems to maximize the effectiveness of services provided to the Aboriginal community" (City of Ottawa 2007). Such a committee was created, finally, in 2006.

The OAC helped to alter the community's relationship with the City of Ottawa, at least at the level of city officials. To date, no elected representatives have made Aboriginal relations a priority, and the current mayor (Larry O'Brien) has shown general support for a responsive city administration, but little interest in seeing such responsiveness established. The catalyst in the evolution of the city's stance on Aboriginal matters was a 2004 report, *The Silent Crisis*.[27] The report responded to the City of Ottawa 20/20 Growth Management Strategy and particularly the Strategy's examination of mental illness and mental health services. *The Silent Crisis* documented the problems of homelessness, poverty, unemployment, substance abuse, mental illness, the lack of cultural options, and the problems faced by Aboriginal youth (City of Ottawa 2007). It demonstrated that the city had no policy to provide appropriate services to Aboriginal residents.

A second, nearly concurrent initiative added momentum to the policy change. The Urban Aboriginal Task Force was a project of the Ontario Federation of Indian Friendship Centres (OFIFC), the

Ontario Native Women's Association (ONWA), and the Ontario Métis Aboriginal Association (OMAA). A number of provincial government ministries and provincial Aboriginal organizations funded the Task Force's[28] examination of five research sites, of which Ottawa was one.[29] The Task Force created Community Advisory Committees (CACs) for each study site to advise on research priorities and directions. The Ottawa CAC provided a valuable forum for the exchange of ideas among organizations. Not coincidentally, the membership of the CAC and the leadership of the OAC were the same.[30] Together, these groups became a powerful source of information and collective motivation in the development of means for inter-organizational co-operation and for building beneficial relations with the city.

A third source of change came from the designation of Ottawa as an Urban Aboriginal Strategy (UAS) city in 2006. The designation provided funding for consultations and meetings, and provided the reasons for both sides to engage in them. It strengthened and supported developing lines of communication among organizations as well as between the organizations and the city.

One immediate result of changes in community organization was the formation, by City Council, of the Aboriginal Working Committee, a group of city staff, in November 2006. The AWC planned a series of surveys to gather information, an Information Fair to disseminate it, and a Consultation Forum that relied upon "listening circles." The surveys revealed that the Ottawa Aboriginal community was concerned about employment and training (62.5%); housing and homelessness (61.72%); culture and language (60.94%); health issues (49.22%); access to services (49.22%); and addiction, mental health, and life skills (49.22%). Service providers identified similar issues, though they ranked them slightly differently; 30% of service providers also mentioned poverty as an overarching concern of the Aboriginal community.

CONCLUDING THOUGHTS

Even infrequent readers of daily newspapers would expect that there would be two large issues underlying most of the interaction between Aboriginal people and city governments: (1) potential disputes over land use, ownership, and disposition; and (2) poverty and associated forms of economic social disadvantage for a large proportion of urban Aboriginal residents. These issues certainly dominate news coverage of Aboriginal issues in most provinces, including Ontario. In fact, in the four cities chosen for study here, we found that relatively little interaction had to do with land; land ownership and control did not emerge as a major issue. Most political interaction concerned the adequacy of employment opportunities, coordination of service delivery among multiple agencies and governments, housing, and various forms of social provision. Poverty was indeed important in this discussion, as were issues of invisibility, exclusion, and non-recognition of cultural specificity.

For reasons having to do with city demographics and, we suspect, with historical legacies, the city governments can be seen to have taken quite different approaches to their Aboriginal citizenry. All of the cities wrestled with questions of jurisdiction and responsibility but reached different resolutions. Where Ottawa has been responsive and, once roused, even proactive, Toronto seems to have struggled to distinguish Aboriginal citizens from the general, very vibrant and challenging multicultural city population. Kingston seems barely to have recognized the existence of Aboriginal residents, while Thunder Bay is coming to terms with a burgeoning Aboriginal population of great importance to the city and its region, and it is still seeking a way to conceptualize its relationship with it. Beneath these broad general impressions are the all-important details of accommodation and action, important factors at the operational, if not at the general, policy level.

Cities and municipalities do not govern with practices that recognize special attributes of citizens in a way that the federal or even the provincial government have come to do. Cities deal with residents and with neighbourhoods. Aboriginal rights and entitlements, whatever their legal bearing in cities, do not form part of the taken-for-granted governance framework of municipal governments. In this regard, we may learn from our case studies something about the importance of community organization in creating local visibility. City governments respond to community organizations, and when Aboriginal service providers come together, they make it easier for cities to "see" needs and respond to them.

To create this effect, Aboriginal organizations in all four cities had to learn how to engage the municipal level of government. In other words, they had to learn to deal with politicians who have different concerns and different preoccupations than federal politicians and with bureaucracies who may have much less experience with

Aboriginal issues. Aboriginal organizations in all of the cities face a significant task of education and relationship development.

The importance of the federal role is evident in all four cases. The 1990s withdrawal of the federal government from the provision of housing had a negative effect in all four cities, exacerbated by provincial downloading to city governments, which did not necessarily have all the resources needed to provide an adequate level of service. On the other hand, federal funding provided through the Urban Aboriginal Strategy was important in every city where it was available, for it stimulated community organization and provided the means for coalitions to act.

Changing provincial preoccupations are very important to the circumstances of Aboriginal people living in Ontario's cities. While the attention of the provincial government seemed often to be captured by the land disputes that are a product of unresolved federal-Aboriginal relations and the province's complex history of settlement, a large constituency of urban Aboriginal people has been forming. Some provincial governments, including the current one, have looked beyond crisis politics and have begun to consider provincial responsibilities and capacities in the cities.

Although there have been no constitutional changes to drive the evolution of new relationships between Aboriginal people and their city governments, it is evident that these are developing; they are a product of provincial downloading of services and the organizational development described in this paper. These changes forced new responsibilities on cities and forced municipal governments to develop new relationships with citizen groups with which they have had limited or no contact.

Finally, we would like to note one last interesting feature of all of the coalitions and networks in our study: most of them involved not only Aboriginal organizations and service providers but also Aboriginal and non-Aboriginal people in governments and other public institutions. The urban Aboriginal coalitions cut across jurisdictional and ethnic lines, or rather, built bridges across them. It is these organizations, service providers, and coalitions that are the drivers of municipal actions with respect to Aboriginal issues. In its absence, these grassroots organizations serve as the policy-making conscience of Ontario municipalities, countering, often without resources and support, invisibility, poverty, jurisdictional mazes, and the challenges of diversity (cultural, linguistic, and – due to the "focusing" effect of municipalities – geographical) on behalf of their constituents. The self-organization of urban Aboriginal people in all its diversity – along with reasonably receptive and attentive city governments – seems to be a major element in the making of good public policy in this area. The rest is discussion, experimentation, and negotiation.

NOTES

1 For comparison, Aboriginal people are 4 per cent of the population of Canada, 15 per cent of the population of Saskatchewan, and 5 per cent of the population of British Columbia. See Statistics Canada (2006a).
2 Of those living in urban areas, 69,525 live within urban Census Metropolitan Areas (CMAS). Statistics Canada defines a CMA as an "(a)rea consisting of one or more neighbouring municipalities situated around a major urban core. A census metropolitan area must have a total population of at least 100,000 of which 50,000 or more live in the urban core." See http://www12.statcan.ca/english/census06/reference/dictionary/geo009.cfm.
3 The analysis is based upon internet and documentary research, monitoring of media reports, historical research, and on-site interviews in each city. Attempts were made to interview city staff and elected officials, and staff of every Aboriginal organization in each city. All were offered confidentiality. In the event it was possible to interview elected officials in only one city (Thunder Bay), staff in all four city administrations were nevertheless interviewed. In each city, staff from over three quarters of the Aboriginal organizations were interviewed.
4 Razack argues that the marginalization of urban Aboriginal people is a product of the same "nearly absolute geographical separation of the colonizer and the colonized" that was produced by the reserve system. This physical separation is reinforced by the misrepresentation of and ignorance about urban Aboriginal people. Indeed, their experience is presented as "exotic and spectacular," hiding the "mundane brutality of everyday existence" (Razack 2002, 129; see also Culhane 2003; Silver, Keeper, and MacKenzie 2005; Silver 2006).
5 An American study uncovers similar patterns. Susan Lobo (2003) identifies and analyzes a "network of relations" within the urban Indian community of San Francisco that serves as a network of urban Clan Mothers. This network replaces the traditional expectation of geographically proximate dwellings as the basis for community with a series of "nodes" in a network that serve as anchors around which the network is formed.

These "nodes" serve as stable reference points in the ebb and flow of urban Aboriginal community life.

6 Leonard Rotman (1994) argues that the provincial governments hold fiduciary obligations to Aboriginal people. While lower courts have engaged this issue (see *Haida Nation* 2001, para. 23), the Supreme Court of Canada has not specifically issued a ruling on this matter. For instance, the Supreme Court argued in *Haida Nation* that while the provincial government has a duty to consult with First Nations, which derives from the "honour of the Crown," this requirement does not arise out of a fiduciary duty, since "Aboriginal rights and title have been asserted but have not been defined or proven" in the case under dispute (see *Haida Nation* 2004, para. 18).

7 General works on the Rae government include White (1997); Walkom (2002).

8 General assessments of the Harris years may be found in Marquardt (2007); White (1997); and Ralph (1997).

9 In 1995, members from the First Nations community took possession of Ipperwash Provincial Park, once part of their reserve. Eventually, the Ontario Provincial Police (OPP) attempted to forcibly remove the First Nations members, a decision that resulted in the death of Dudley George who was a member of the Stoney Point community. In 2003, a public inquiry was called to investigate the circumstances surrounding George's death in an effort to determine the culpability of the provincial government in the decision to use violence against the First Nations protestors. The Inquiry's report, released in 2007, provides a searching analysis of the specific events that led to Dudley George's death as well as an analysis of the circumstances that led to those events; it concludes, in part, that resolution of the land issue was a top priority.

10 See copy of the Robinson Treaty at http://www.ainc-inac.gc.ca/pr/trts/rbt2_e.html; see also Lytwyn (1995, 16).

11 The study relied upon three hundred and ninety-two distributed surveys and forty-five interviews with members of the Thunder Bay community. Similar comments in relation to systemic forms of racism were also expressed during our interviews with service providers in Thunder Bay.

12 The AERC was established in 2002. It is a body composed of a number of Aboriginal employment agencies located in Thunder Bay in order to help promote employment opportunities for Aboriginal peoples through the sharing of resources between the various agencies.

13 Five confidential interviews were conducted with officials in Thunder Bay during 29 January — 2 February 2007.

14 For more detail, see Harris and Matthews (1987), and Gentilcore and Matthews (1993).

15 The vast Anishnabe (Algonquin) territories extend north of the Ottawa River into northern Quebec. Today, there are a number of nations in this vast area, some with outstanding land claims. See http://www.aafna.ca/history.html, (accessed 30 November 2007).

16 See Statistics Canada (2007).

17 In 1999, the Mississaugas of the New Credit filed a land claim with the Indian Claims Commission, which implicated the territorial boundaries of Toronto, including Toronto Island. A 1787 land cession agreement, known as "The Toronto Purchase" between the British Crown and the Mississaugas, is alleged to have ceded lands now occupied by Toronto. In 1805, a second land cession agreement was made with the Mississaugas in an effort to legally ratify the 1787 purchase. The Mississaugas of the New Credit claim that the Crown breached its fiduciary obligations by not informing them of the invalidity of the initial purchase and that the 1805 ratification agreement contained more land than they agreed to surrender to the Crown. See http://indianclaims.ca/claimsmap/completed_claims_8-en.asp?id=73.

18 See City of Toronto Scholarships for Aboriginal Students at <http://www.icah.ca/content/en/scholarships/detail/index.php?sid=1674&scol=ps>

19 For an outline of the City of Toronto's Aboriginal Affairs Award and past recipients, see <http://www.toronto.ca/civicawards/aboriginal_award.htm>.

20 Though the occupation was sparked by changes to the federal *Income Tax Act*, the protest was about much more than the issue of taxation. The broader issue at stake concerned the transferability of treaty rights beyond the boundaries of Aboriginal reserves. For Aboriginal people, the issue of off-reserve taxation was perceived as a direct breach of the rights guaranteed to Aboriginal people under treaty rights which they continued to possess within urban centres. See Sumi (1995, A11).

21 Aboriginal health care providers have been affected by the provincial government's creation of Local Health Integration Networks (LHINs). While the legislation aimed to devolve decision-making power to local communities, its emphasis on particular geographic areas served to limit the ability of Aboriginal health care providers to effectively reach dispersed urban communities.

22 For a list of funded projects, see http://www.ainc-inac.gc.ca/ai/ofi/uas/prj/index-eng.asp.

23 Seven confidential interviews were conducted in Toronto between 10 January and 25 January 2007.

24 On the other hand, city officials have stated in correspondence that they understood the monument's purpose as a way to recognize the role of Aboriginal history in the city's development. As well, they state that this recognition was something that the Aboriginal community wanted.

25 Because of the organization of this research project in terms first of provinces, we choose not to study Ottawa-Gatineau, though for many purposes the two cities on either side of the Ottawa River should be understood as a single community. In spite of being located in two different provinces – and being served by two municipal governments – the cities are both home to many federal government offices and thousands of residents who live in one province and work in the other.

26 The Algonquins of Golden Lake (Pikwàkanagàn) filed a land claim in 1983 with the federal government for territory; they did likewise with the provincial government in 1985. The claim states that the "Algonquins have continuing ownership of 8.9 million acres of land (14,000 square miles) on the basis that they never ceded their rights through treaty or sold or lost their territory through war. This claim was linked to a series of petitions to the Crown by the Algonquins dating back to 1772." The negotiations over the claim are still proceeding. See Ministry of Aboriginal Affairs (2007).

27 The report was by Allison Fisher of the Wabano Centre. See City of Ottawa (2007).

28 It was funded by the following organizations: Ontario Ministry of Children and Youth Services, the Ontario Ministry of Community and Social Services, the Ontario Ministry of Health and Long Term Care, the Ministry for Aboriginal Affairs, the Office of the Federal Interlocutor for Métis and Non-Status Indians, the Ontario Federation of Indian Friendship Centres, and the Ontario Native Women's Association. In addition, Statistics Canada provided in-kind contributions of the 2001 Census data for each research site.

29 The other four were Thunder Bay, Barrie/Midland/Orillia, Sudbury, and Kenora. All final reports can be found on the Ontario Federation of Indian Friendship Centres at www.ofifc.org.

30 Members of the CAC: Lorraine Augustine, Makonsag Aboriginal Head Start; Gary Lafontaine, Odawa Native Friendship Centre; Jerry Lanouette, Tewegan Transition House; Marc Maracle, Gignul Housing; Pamela Tabobundung Washington, Tabobundung and Association; Alison Fisher, Wabano Centre for Aboriginal Health; Castille Troy, Minwaashin Lodge Aboriginal Women's Support Centre; Verna McGregor, National Aboriginal Circle Against Family Violence; and Tina Slauven-White, Tewegan Transition House.

INTERVIEWS

Interview 1, Aboriginal organization official, 14 December 2006
Interview 2, municipal official, 15 December 2006
Interview 3, Aboriginal service provider, 10 January 2007
Interview 4, Aboriginal service provider, 11 January 2007
Interview 5, Aboriginal service provider, 24 January 2007
Interview 6, Aboriginal service provider, 25 January 2007
Interview 7, Aboriginal service provider, 25 January 2007
Interview 8, municipal official, 25 January 2007
Interview 9, municipal official, 25 January 2007
Interview 10, Aboriginal service provider, 29 January 2007
Interview 11, municipal official, 30 January 2007
Interview 12, municipal official, 31 January 2007
Interview 13, Aboriginal service provider, 1 February 2007
Interview 14, Aboriginal service provider, 2 February 2007
Interview 15, municipal official, 10 February 2007
Interview 16, municipal official, 19 January 2007
Interview 17, Aboriginal organization official, 9 February 2007
Interviews 18 and 19, Aboriginal organization official, 15 February
     and 20 June 2007
Interviews 20–25, Group interview with five municipal officials, 16
     February 2007
Interview 26, Aboriginal organization official, 16 February 2007
Interview 27, Aboriginal organization official, 26 February 2007
Interview 28, Aboriginal organization official, 12 March 2007
Interview 29, Aboriginal organization official, 13 March 2007
Interview 30, Aboriginal organization official, 13 March 2007
Interview 31, Aboriginal organization official, 15 March 2007
Interview 32, Aboriginal organization official, 23 August 2007
Interview 33, Aboriginal organization official, 12 September 2007
Interview 34, Aboriginal organization official, 7 March 2008

REFERENCES

Abele, Frances and Katherine A.H. Graham. 1989. "High Politics Is
     Not Enough." In *Aboriginal Peoples and Government Responsibility:
     Exploring Federal and Provincial Roles*, ed. David C. Hawkes, 141–71.
     Ottawa: Carleton University Press.

Andrew, Caroline and Michael Goldsmith. 1998. "From Local Government to Local Governance and Beyond." *International Political Science Review* 19 (2): 101–17.

Andersen, Chris and Claude Denis. 2003. "Urban Natives and the Nation: Before and After the Royal Commission on Aboriginal Peoples." *The Canadian Review of Sociology and Anthropology* 4 (40): 373–90.

Calleja, Frank. 2001. "Native Children's Aid Plan Headed for Court Fight." *The Toronto Star.* 22 November: 34.

Cameron, David and Jill Wherrett. 1995. "New Relationship, New Challenges: Aboriginal Peoples and the Province of Ontario." In *For Seven Generations. An Information Legacy of the Royal Commission on Aboriginal Peoples, RCAP Research Reports. Governance. Project Area 8: Domestic Government Case Studies [CD-ROM].* Ottawa: Libraxus.

Chidley, Joe. 1995. "Under Occupation." *Maclean's,* 16 January: 14.

Christie, Gordon. 2005. "A Colonial Reading of Recent Jurisprudence: Sparrow, Delgamuukw, and Haida Nation." *Windsor Yearbook of Access to Justice* 23 (1): 17–53.

City of Thunder Bay. Corporate Report. 2005. *Employment Equity Report.* Report No. 2005.298. [Report on file with authors].

City of Thunder Bay. Strategic Plan. 2004. *New Foundation – A Living Strategic Plan To Build a New Foundation for a Better Future.* Available: http://www.thunderbay.ca/docs/news%5C848.pdf.

City of Thunder Bay. Corporate Policy. 1996. *Race Relations.* Policy No. 06–01–04. [Report on file with authors]

City of Toronto. 2007. Staff Report – Aboriginal Affordable Housing Opportunity. Available: http://www.toronto.ca/affordablehousing/pdf/backgroundf_aboriginal.pdf.

– *Aboriginal Affairs Committee (AAC) Meeting Report.* 18 January, 2006. [Report on file with authors].

– *Aboriginal Affairs Committee (AAC) Decision Document.* Meeting No. 1. 14 February 2005. [Report on file with authors].

– 2002. *Report of the Community Consultations on the Plan of Action for the Elimination of Racism and Discrimination.* [Report on file with authors].

City of Ottawa. 2007. "Report to Community and Protective Services Committee and Council," 22 February.

– The Road Travelled. Available: http://www.ottawa.ca/residents/aboriginal/listening_circles/road_travelled_en.html. Accessed 3 October 2008.

Cooke, Martin and Daniele Bélanger. 2006. "Migration Theories and First Nations Mobility: Towards a Systems Perspective." *The Canadian Review of Sociology and Anthropology* 43 (2): 141–64.

Culhane, Dara. 2003. "Their Spirits Live Within Us: Aboriginal Women in Downtown Eastside Vancouver Emerging into Visibility." *American Indian Quarterly* 27 (3–4): 593–606.

Diversity Thunder Bay. 2002. *A Community of Acceptance: Respect for Thunder Bay's Diversity.* Thunder Bay: CSOP Research & Consulting. Available: http://edocs.lib.sfu.ca/ccrc/html/CCRC_PDF/CommunityOfAcceptance(Walid).pdf.

Graham, Katherine A.H. and Evelyn J. Peters. 2002. *Aboriginal Communities and Urban Sustainability.* Ottawa: Canadian Policy Research Networks Inc.

Gentilcore, Louis and Geoffrey J. Matthews, eds. 1993. *Historical Atlas of Canada Volume II.* Toronto: University of Toronto Press.

Goldie, Terry. 1989. *Fear and Temptation: The Image of the Indigene in Canadian, Australian, and New Zealand Literatures.* Kingston and Montreal: McGill-Queen's University Press.

Haida Nation v. British Columbia (Minister of Forests), [2004] 3 S.C.R. 511.

Haida Nation v. British Columbia (Minister of Forests), [2001] 2 C.N.L.R. 83.

Hanselmann, Calvin and Roger Gibbins. 2002. "Another Voice is Needed: Intergovernmentalism in the Urban Aboriginal Context." Paper presented at the conference *Reconfiguring Aboriginal-State Relations: Canada State of the Federation*, 1–2 November, at Queen's University.

Harris, R. Cole and Geoffrey J. Matthews, eds. 1987. *Historical Atlas of Canada: Volume I: From the Beginning to 1800.* Toronto: University of Toronto Press.

Howard-Bobiwash, Heather. 2003. "Women's Class Strategies as Activism in Native Community Building in Toronto, 1950–75." *American Indian Quarterly* 27 (3–4): 566–82.

Human Resources and Skills Development Canada. 2006. "Labour Market Bulletin:" Human Resource Centre of Canada, Thunder Bay.

– 2005. "Labour Market Bulletin:" Human Resource Centre of Canada, Thunder Bay.

Indian Affairs and Northern Development. Copy of the Robinson Treaty made in the Year 1850 with the Ojibewa Indians of Lake Superior Conveying Certain Lands to the Crown – Indian and Northern Affairs

Canada. Available: http://www.ainc-inac.gc.ca/pr/trts/rbt2_e.html.
Accessed 3 October 2008.

James, Royson. 1986. "Residents Fight Native Indians' Housing Project."
The Toronto Star, 29 April: A6.

Klodawsky, Fran, Tim Aubry, and Susan Farell. 2006. "Care and the Lives
of Homeless Youth in Neoliberal Times in Canada." *Gender, Place, &
Culture* 13 (4): 419–36.

Lenon, Suzanne. 2000. "Living on the Edge: Women, Poverty, and Homelessness in Canada." *Canadian Woman Studies* 20 (3): 123–27.

Lobo, Susan. 2003. "Urban Clan Mothers: Key Households in Cities."
American Indian Quarterly 27 (3–4): 505–22.

Lytwyn, Victor. 1995. "The Anishinawbeg and the Fur Trade." In *Thunder Bay: From Rivalry to Unity*, eds. Thorold Tronrud and Ernest Epp,
16–32. Thunder Bay: Thunder Bay Historical Museum Society.

Malloy, Jonathan. 2003. *Between Colliding Worlds: The Ambiguous
Existence of Government Agencies For Aboriginal and Women's Policy.*
Toronto: University of Toronto Press.

– 2001. "Double Identities: Aboriginal Policy Agencies in Ontario
and British Columbia." *Canadian Journal of Political Science* 34 (1):
131–55.

Marquardt, Richard. 2007. *The Progressive Potential of Municipal Social
Policy: A Case Study of the Struggle over Welfare Reform in Ottawa
during the Common Sense Revolution.* Doctoral diss., School of Public
Policy and Administration, Carleton University.

Mendelson, Michael. 2004. *Aboriginal People in Canada's Labour Market: Work and Unemployment, Today and Tomorrow.* Ottawa: The
Caledon Institute of Social Policy.

Miller, David. 2004. *Human Rights Day.* Human Rights Day Address,
City Hall, Toronto, 9 December 2004. Available: http://www.toronto.ca/
mayor_miller/speeches/human_rights.htm.

– 2003. *Human Rights Day Program.* Human Rights Day Address, City
Hall, Toronto, 10 December 2003. Available: http://www.toronto.ca/
mayor_miller/speeches/human_rights_day_121003.htm.

Milloy, John S., Shawn Heard, and Bruce W. Hodgins. 1992. "Introduction." In *Coexistence?: Studies in Ontario-First Nations Relations*, eds.
Bruce W. Hodgins, Shawn Heard, and John S. Milloy, 1–5. Peterborough: Frost Centre for Canadian Heritage and Development Studies.

Ministry of Aboriginal Affairs. 2007. *Algonquin Land Claim. Ontario
Secretariat for Aboriginal Affairs.* Available: www.aboriginalaffairs.

osaa.gov.on.ca/english/negotiate/algonquin/algonquin.htm. Accessed 13 February 2006.

Ontario Native Affairs Secretariat (ONAS). 2005. *A New Approach to Aboriginal Affairs*. Toronto: Queen's Printer for Ontario. Available: http://www.aboriginalaffairs.gov.on.ca/english/news/aboriginalaffairs. pdf.

Ontario Secretariat for Aboriginal Affairs (OSAA). 2006. *Ontario Promotes Prosperity and Well-Being Among Urban Aboriginal Peoples.* 28 April 2006. Available: www.aboriginalaffairs.gov.on.ca/english/news/ news_060428.pdf.

– 2005. *Ontario Government Launches New Program To Help At-Risk Urban Aboriginal Children.* 12 December 2005. Available: www. aboriginalaffairs.gov.on.ca/english/news/news_051212.htm.

Pal, Leslie A. 1995. *Interests of State: The Politics of Language, Multiculturalism, and Feminism in Canada.* Kingston and Montreal: McGill Queen's University Press.

Peters, Evelyn J. 2007. "First Nations and Métis People and Diversity in Canadian Cities." In *Belonging? Diversity, Recognition, and Shared Citizenship in Canada*, eds. Keith Banting, Tom J. Courchene, and F. Leslie Seidle, 207–46. Ottawa: Institute for Research on Public Policy.

– 2006. [W]e do not lose our treaty rights outside the ... reserve: Challenging the Scales of Social Service Provision for First Nations Women in Canadian Cities. *Geojournal*. 65 (4): 315–327.

Platiel, Rudy. 1995. "Celebration Greets Native Tax Protesters." *The Globe and Mail*, 14 January: A1.

Platinex Inc. v. Kitchenuhmaykoosib Inninuwug First Nation, [2006] 4 C.N.L.R. 152.

Razack, Sherene H. ed. 2002. *Race, Space, and the Law: Unmapping a White Settler Society.* Toronto: Between the Lines.

Robertson, Leslie and Dara Culhane. 2005. *In Plain Sight: Reflections on Life in Downtown Eastside Vancouver.* Vancouver: Talonbooks.

Rotman, Leonard I. 1994. "Provincial Fiduciary Obligations to First Nations: the Nexus between Governmental Power and Responsibility." *Osgoode Hall Law Journal* 32 (4): 735–83.

Royal Commission on Aboriginal Peoples. 1996. *Restructuring the Relationship*. Vol. 2 of the *Report of the Royal Commission on Aboriginal Peoples.* Ottawa: Minister of Supply and Services Canada.

Royal Commission on Aboriginal Peoples. 1996. *Perspectives and Realities*. Part 1, Vol. 4 of the *Report of the Royal Commission on Aboriginal Peoples.* Ottawa: Minister of Supply and Services Canada.

Sampson, Fiona. A. 1992. "An Historical Consideration of Ontario Aboriginal Policy." In *Coexistence?: Studies in Ontario-First Nations Relations*, eds. Bruce W. Hodgins, Shawn Heard, and John S. Milloy, 11–26. Peterborough: Frost Centre for Canadian Heritage and Development Studies.

Service Canada. 2005. Urban Aboriginal Task Force – Progress Report Phase 1. Available: http://www.servicecanada.gc.ca/eng/on/epb/uas/reports/uatfphase1.pdf.

Silver, Jim. 2006. *In Their Own Voices, Building Aboriginal Communities*. Halifax: Fernwood.

Silver, Jim, Cyril Keeper, and Michael MacKenzie. 2005. '*A Very Hostile System in Which to Live*': Aboriginal Electoral Participation in Winnipeg's Inner City. Winnipeg: Canadian Centre for Policy Alternatives.

Sumi, Craig. 1995. "Natives End Tax Protest." *The Spectator*, 14 January: A11.

St Catherine's Milling & Lumber Co. v. The Queen (1888), 14 App. Cas. 46.

Statistics Canada. 2003. *2001 Census: Analysis Series Aboriginal Peoples of Canada: A Demographic Profile*. Ottawa, Minister of Industry. Catalogue No. 96F0030XIE2001007. Available: www12.statcan.ca/english/census01/products/analytic/companion/abor/contents.cfm.

Statistics Canada, 2006a. *Census of Population*, Statistics Canada catalogue no. 97–558-XCB2006010. Available: http://www12.statcan.ca/english/census06/data/topics/RetrieveProductTable.cfm?Temporal=2006&PID=89126&GID=614141&METH=1&APATH=3&PTYPE=88971&THEME=73&AID=&FREE=0&FOCUS=&VID=0&GC=99&GK=NA&RL=0&d1=3&d2=0&d3=0.

Statistics Canada. 2006b. Aboriginal Peoples in Canada in 2006: Inuit, Metis, and First Nations. Catalogue No. 97–558-XIE.

Statistics Canada. 2007. *Kingston, Ontario* (table). *2006 Community Profiles*. 2006 Census. Statistics Canada Catalogue no. 92–591-XWE. Released March 13, 2007. Available: http://www12.statcan.ca/english/census06/data/profiles/community/Index.cfm?Lang=E. Accessed 12 March 2008.

Thunder Bay Urban Aboriginal Strategy (UAS). 2004. *A Strategic Community Action Plan: 'Circle of Certainty.'* [Report on file with authors].

Teillet, Jean. 2005. "The Role of the Natural Resources Regulatory Regime in Aboriginal Rights Disputes in Ontario." *Final Report for the Ipperwash Inquiry*, 31 March. Available: http://www.attorneygeneral.jus.gov.on.ca/inquiries/ipperwash/policy_part/research/pdf/Teillet.pdf.

Walkom, Thomas. 2002. *Rae Days: The Rise and Follies of the* NDP. Toronto: Key Porter Books.

White, Graham. 1997. *The Government and Politics of Ontario.* Toronto: University of Toronto Press.

5

Urban Aboriginal Programming in a Coordination Vacuum: The Alberta (Dis)Advantage

CHRIS ANDERSEN AND JENNA STRACHAN

According to the most recently available numbers from Statistics Canada, in the last decade Canada's Aboriginal population has grown by nearly 50 per cent. Alberta has experienced its fair share of this growth; it is now home to about 190,000 Aboriginal people, a 20 per cent increase in the last five years alone. Alberta's Aboriginal community constitutes the largest aboriginal population among the Prairie provinces,[1] more than half of whom live in cities. Edmonton's Census Metropolitan Area (CMA) has the second largest urban Aboriginal population in Canada (behind Winnipeg) and the largest urban Métis community in the country.[2] Although on a smaller scale, Calgary has also experienced considerable population growth over the past decade.[3] As with most provinces, Alberta's current urban Aboriginal policy field[4] – as much as it can be said to have one – is struggling to keep pace with the powerful demographic shifts that continue to ripple through its social, economic, and cultural fabric.

This chapter's argument is that the lack of urban Aboriginal-specific policy in Alberta over the past four decades has both occurred in and produced a *jurisdictional maze* (Graham and Peters 2002) that in turn has cemented a current patchwork of short-term, overlapping, and inefficient urban Aboriginal programs and policies. This inefficiency and lack of coordination has produced what we term the "Alberta Disadvantage," an ironic play on the province's "Alberta Advantage" marketing campaign.[5] However, we would like to point out that this disadvantage is neither the result of a lack of provincially based activity nor is it the result of the province's lack of goodwill or sympathy. Rather, it is a manifestation of the lack of *coordinating* leadership displayed by the Government of Canada over the past four decades. The power of this legacy remains in place today, we argue, despite the potential of more recent inter-jurisdictional, Federal-lead initiatives such as the Urban Aboriginal Strategy[6] (UAS), which purports to assist in the coordination of policies, programs, and services between government and social forces actors within an urban context (by "social forces actors," we mean non-governmental actors such as businesses and religious or social service delivery organizations).

In service of this argument, the chapter is divided into four parts and a conclusion. Part one introduces the notion of a jurisdictional maze, highlighting its negative consequences for urban Aboriginal policy making, particularly with respect to individual provincial departments, which are responsible for the bulk of policy and programming funding, but work in relative isolation from other provincial departments (not to mention departments at other levels of government or social forces actors). Part two then positions urban Aboriginal policy in Alberta and its place in Alberta's social "order of things." Here, we use Calvin Hanselmann's (2002; 2001) still valuable discussion of policy and programming and the impact of "policies of general application" (discussed later) on the specific situation of urban Aboriginal policy and programming, and trace the broad provincial policy statements and initiatives (such as the Aboriginal Policy Framework of 2000) under which urban Aboriginal programming is (said to be) carried out.

Part three lays out the conceptual parameters of the urban Aboriginal policy field and presents the major sets of policy actors that comprise the field, including federal, provincial, and municipal actors; non-governmental social forces (in particular, but not only, service delivery organizations); and Aboriginal constitutive/ representative organizations. Part four, which forms the bulk of the chapter, argues that these structural features have cemented three themes and associated tensions in Alberta's urban Aboriginal policy field. These cluster around: 1) distinctiveness of policy-making structures and programming by city (which has produced tensions between larger and smaller cities); 2) the character of intergovernmental policy making (which has produced tensions around appropriate policy relations); and 3) feelings of marginalization among social forces actors involved in the actual production of policy avenues (often manifested in tensions around government requirements for fulfilling policy auditing requirements). The chapter concludes with a discussion of the remarkable stability of (now intergenerational) urban Aboriginal policy and programming created in what amounts to a policy coordination vacuum marked by the absence of a federally coordinated leadership mechanism. We begin, however, more conceptually with a broad discussion of jurisdiction.

PART I: THE "JURISDICTIONAL MAZE" AND ITS EFFECTS

In the introduction to this edited collection, Evelyn Peters discusses the problems of jurisdiction in the context of urban Aboriginal policy and programming. We have no wish to repeat her analysis, except to agree that Canadian urban Aboriginal policies and policy-making practices have more generally been shaped by the particularities of Canada's legislative jurisdictional spheres. The federal government has long interpreted section 91(24) of the *British North America Act* – the Act through which Britain accorded Canada the right to govern "Indians" – to refer to Indians residing on reserves (with several notable exceptions around health care and post-secondary education funding). It is certainly still fair to say that provinces have become responsible – with various degrees of reluctance – for the bulk of urban Aboriginal policy and programming funding as well as some of the direct delivery mechanisms. Indeed, existing federal interpretation of the legislation has effectively forced provincial governments to act for all urban Aboriginal peoples ("Indians" or not) as part of their general mandate for improving the overall quality of life of their residents (Graham and Peters 2002, 9).

It needs to be emphasized, however, that a jurisdictional maze should not be conflated with a vacuum. Indeed, Alberta's urban Aboriginal policy field is distinctive for the sheer volume of programming that takes place in the absence of inter-jurisdictionally coordinated, urban-specific Aboriginal policy. The idea of a jurisdictional maze does, however, capture several peculiar features of urban Aboriginal programming in Alberta (to be explored in more depth later). First is the sheer number of actors involved in the creation, implementation, and/or evaluation of programming. In part three we provide two examples (one federal and one provincial –

though both are intergovernmental) of this complexity. Second, and related, is the lack of coordination that manifests itself in inefficient and overlapping programming and policy. Given that provincial programs and policies are geared not towards "urban Aboriginals" as a specific object of governance but rather as members of a provincial constituency (that is, they are aimed at, for example, improving the socio-economic conditions or health of Aboriginal residents, whether urban or not), policy has tended to take a piecemeal, sector by sector approach in which each ministry attempts to improve the areas under its aegis, whether health, justice, employment, or education, to name but a few.

Policy and programming not based in rights must often rely on the goodwill and sympathy of social actors invested in the issues at hand, whose goodwill and sympathy – and the funding that accompanies it – can be cut with little or no notice and with little potential for redress by social forces actors. Alberta possesses this goodwill and sympathy in abundance, which has led to a situation in which a vast constellation of uncoordinated policy and programming structures deals with large amounts of financial and social capital from numerous government departments, interested service-delivery organizations, representative governments, and, in some cases, religious and business-oriented organizations. Perhaps more importantly, it has produced a policy climate marked by short-term, project-based funding, announced by governments with great aplomb and publicity in one period and quietly retracted, retrenched, or re-coordinated in another.

The intergenerational impacts of this lack of inter-jurisdictional coordination have played themselves out in various ways and at various levels in the policy-to-programming circuit. For example, a non-Aboriginal organization in one of the smaller cities accessed program funding for urban Aboriginal project development, yet delivered the project solely on reserves. In another case, a municipal official who approached a First Nations band council to seek assistance for an urban Aboriginal resident was turned away on the grounds that the urban resident was no longer considered to be the responsibility of the First Nations band. Aboriginal residents who live in the smaller municipalities and wish to access culturally relevant services are frequently directed to nearby reserves or Métis settlements. Residents without a "home community" are thus left under-serviced. Interviewees discussed how the current jurisdictional impasse even produced tensions between *clients* of urban services. A pair of executive directors recalled situations in which their staff was forced to address waiting room hostilities between First Nations and Métis clients over matters directly related to unsettled jurisdiction and the portability of treaty rights. Interviewees also argued that Métis clients were often considered "roadside": that is, despite a high level of service needs, they were left un-serviced, at the side of the road (Interviews 1 and 2). On the opposite side of the issue, an Aboriginal program manager expressed frustration that organizations couldn't "fund on-reserve women's programs but [could] fund urban programs. They have to send reserve women to INAC. They should be dealing with the issue and not where the issue is taking place. Jurisdictional issues hinder interrelations among groups" (Interview 5).

Ideological complexities regarding culturally specific policies tended to affect government responses as well. A senior official cogently explained these stances in his reflection that: "jurisdiction is a concept that is so engrained within Aboriginal issues that it is difficult to get away from. The jurisdictional issue is part of overall rhetoric but it is peripheral to what needs to be done. Those who take a rights-based approach tend to champion jurisdictional issues. But second and third generation urban Aboriginal peoples, while retaining their culture, are less concerned with jurisdictional issues because they are farther removed from home community politics" (Interview 15).

On the one hand, the "poverty is poverty" paradigm aligns with a needs-based approach and thus elides the jurisdictional issues discussed earlier. However, as played out in programs, it tends to naturalize the structural racism that undergirds the current lack of respect for treaty and Aboriginal rights. At the opposite end of the spectrum, rights-based approaches are based on the argument that the federal government is responsible for Status Indians (or more radically, for *all* Aboriginal people) regardless of place of residence. Most policy actors viewed this position as a conversation stopper in that rights-based approaches tended to hinder, rather than expedite, policy action. On a practical policy-making level, in some cases this jurisdictional division necessitated a form of "doublespeak." One interviewee in a smaller city explained that policy discussions often occurred twice: once with the province and then again with the federal government. This process makes it difficult to provide services in an amalgamated area that is characterized by a high degree of mobility and service interdependence in overlapping rural, reserve, urban, and worksite areas.

Situations precipitated by this jurisdictional maze are very different from the "wrap-around services" models that exist in other countries – for example, such a model is used by the indigenous peoples' urban authorities in New Zealand through *Te Whanau O Waipareira Trust*.[7] Though we have more to say about this lack of coordination in the conclusion, suffice it to say for now that these jurisdictional issues are not the result of an absence of sincerity or goodwill on the part of urban Aboriginal policy field actors; they exist *because* of their sincerity and goodwill (acting when official federal policy did not). As we explain in part two, urban Aboriginal policy and programming need to be understood in the context of the "un-coordination" in which both exist and the numerous service delivery agencies through which they are manifested. We turn to this now.

PART 2: PROGRAMMING IN AN ORGANIZATIONAL VACUUM[8]

In his still useful foray into examining urban Aboriginal policy in western Canada, Calvin Hanselmann, then a policy analyst for the Canada West Foundation (a non-profit think tank based in western Canada) defined *policy* as a statement of expected behaviour that "provides guidance to public servants in performing their duties; it also delineates the extent to which public servants have discretion in an area" (2001, 10). Additionally, he highlighted the symbolic dimensions of policy and argued that they signalled "statements of responsibility" between government and the public insofar as the existence of policies presupposes the importance of a particular issue to government and produces (in a best-case scenario) lines of government responsibility for dealing with that issue in a clear and responsible manner (Hanselmann 2001, 10). Here, we use the term "policy" to refer to both general principles and statements of intent presented by government agencies to guide the development and application of the more specific, technical elements involved in the actual business of on-the-ground programming.

As we explain a little later, the lack of both coordination and urban-Aboriginal-specific policies or initiatives has, over the past four decades, made differentiating between policy and programming far less important than it might otherwise be. As numerous actors, acting in a project-based atmosphere, apply for numerous funds to undertake often disparate programs that use the same social-service delivery mechanism, policies become more local and programming more broadly conceived. The one distinction we retain is to see policy as more concerned with abstraction and intent while programming deals with locality and deliverability, but even this distinction is often more apparent than real. Indeed, service delivery organizations can be stable and long-lived, despite the fact that the policy intent under which they deliver programming can change from government to government or even year to year (for example, the change to a Conservative government changed the policy prerogatives for UAS without actually changing the programs propped up by the policies). This isn't to say that urban Aboriginal programming isn't shaped along various policy lines, merely that four decades of jurisdictional vacuity have produced a vast cacophony of programs – often in competition – developed under the aegis of ostensibly similar policy.

Hanselmann (2002) differentiates three tracks of policy/programming: policies of general application; specific or "enhanced" Aboriginal-specific programming; and, as a subset of the latter, *urban* Aboriginal-specific programming. General application policies are those that accord programming and services to Aboriginal clientele as members of a larger population (for example, financial assistance programming). Specific and enhanced programming, by contrast, targets specific (often disadvantaged) members of the population, such as Aboriginal people (without targeting urban Aboriginal residents exclusively). An example of this type of programming might be provincially generated anti-bullying or anti-gang programs such as those produced inter-ministerially through Alberta Youth and Child Services. As a subset of this targeted programming, Hanselmann (2002) identifies a third track: Aboriginal-specific programming geared exclusively towards the urban Aboriginal population and its needs. Examples of programs included in this subset are those of the federal government's Urban Aboriginal Strategy (UAS) or, municipally, Edmonton's Aboriginal Youth Aquatic Leadership Program.

More important for our purposes is Hanselmann's observation that a lack of specific enhanced programming does not necessarily indicate a government's failure to think about or act on urban

Aboriginal issues. He argues not only that urban Aboriginal residents benefit from programs of general application but also that "in many jurisdictions, service provision is almost *exclusively* through programs of general application that, by definition, are intended to address the needs of urban Aboriginal people as members of the larger society. Indeed, urban Aboriginal people often utilize programs in such fields as health care, social services, education, and justice at higher rates than the general population" (Hanselmann 2002, 4, emphasis added). Indeed, the presence of "enhanced," urban-specific Aboriginal policies that produced easily traceable links to their eventual manifestation as programs and services within government or non-governmental organizations would have made this chapter far more conceptually straightforward. However (in Alberta as elsewhere), the situation is far more complex precisely because so much of the programming landscape in Alberta is grounded in policies of general application or in specialized policies meant for all Aboriginal people, regardless of geographical residence. One official we talked to guessed that as little as 10 per cent of the programming utilized by urban Aboriginals is specifically earmarked for urban Aboriginal issues (Interview 31). While others doubted that such calculations could be made with any accuracy (and indeed, the first interviewee suggested it was just a guess), they agreed that the number of urban-specific programs paled in comparison to those aimed at general application or general Aboriginal use.

Currently, the province of Alberta has no formal urban Aboriginal policy statement, although in 2000 it produced a broad document outlining its stance on Aboriginal relations more generally. Titled *Strengthening Relationships* (Government of Alberta, 2000), this document set out principles to address emerging social and economic issues for all Aboriginal residents of Alberta, including those who live off reserve or outside Métis settlements "in villages, towns, cities, specialized/regional municipalities [and] municipal districts" and makes a specific (though again, vague) commitment to "address the needs of Aboriginal persons living in urban areas" (2000, 10). Perhaps not surprisingly, the Aboriginal Policy Framework is geared principally towards two goals: to "address improving socio-economic opportunities for Aboriginal peoples and communities and clarifying roles and responsibilities of federal, provincial, and Aboriginal governments and communities" (2000, 1). Perhaps equally relevant to this discussion, the Framework explicitly emphasizes the need to include not only all government ministries but also any relevant cross-government initiatives (listing several in existence at the time of its inception). As we address in the chapter's third part, although the Aboriginal Policy Framework makes only sparse reference to urban Aboriginal residents, its intention to "close the gap" in the quality of life in the province between non-Aboriginals and Aboriginals and its emphasis on clarifying jurisdictionally the place of Aboriginal peoples in the Canadian federal system have exerted an enormous influence on urban Aboriginal policy and programming in Alberta.

PART 3: UNTANGLING THE URBAN ABORIGINAL POLICY FIELD IN ALBERTA – THE MAJOR PLAYERS

This chapter employs the phrase "policy field" with some regularity. In this section we outline the broad characteristics of a policy field, including its methodological value and major actors. A *policy field* is a heuristic device that allows the conceptualization of the policy and programming process and the actors involved in terms of their *relationality*: those involved in the field, who believe deeply in the field's values (in this case, delivering urban-Aboriginal programming), possess specific, learned technical competencies and operate according to specific rules and conventions in the context of longstanding collaborative relationships, regardless of the numerous tensions that threaten to disrupt the field's stability (see Bourdieu and Wacquant 1992). However, like all social fields, the urban Aboriginal policy field does not operate on a level playing field – existing tensions are often the result of sets of social actors competing (often unconsciously) to modify and monopolize the relations within the field; they compete in the context of occupying (dis)positions of greater or lesser power within the field's parameters.

Like all social fields, the Aboriginal urban policy field is characterized by a specific history and set of relations between its actors. In the context of an uncoordinated jurisdictional quagmire and an enormous volume of policy and programming activity largely funded by provincial actors, government departments control a bulk of the power and decision-making resources; Aboriginal-centered social forces occupy the more dominated positions within the field. This power asymmetry manifests itself in various tensions between, for example, government auditing requirements around program effectiveness and Aboriginal social forces' emphasis on cultural appropriateness and the need for long-term benefits from programming: the latter may fail to fit neatly into short-term, project-based funding timelines. The urban Aboriginal policy field's dynamics must be understood in light of the relations of conflict and coordination, of *struggle,* between the social actors that animate it. This section explores the contours of the urban Aboriginal policy field in the specific context of the five major classes of players involved in its dynamics: 1) provincial actors; 2) federal actors; 3) municipal actors; 4) social forces (including service delivery organizations); and 5) national and provincial Aboriginal political/representative organizations.

1 Provincial Government Actors

It has become commonplace to note that provincial governments have, by necessity, become a major player in the conception and delivery of urban Aboriginal policy and programming. This is certainly the case in Alberta. Despite the lack of coordination between government departments, Alberta has produced an enormous volume of Aboriginal policy and programming used in an urban context. The Alberta government is currently comprised of twenty-four ministries, and while only two of them refer specifically to Aboriginal people in their statements of ministerial responsibility (the Ministry of Aboriginal Relations and the Ministry of Education), numerous other government departments possess Aboriginal-specific policies and programs. For example, Children and Youth Services, Advanced Education and Technology, Sustainable Resource Development, Employment and Immigration, Housing and Urban Affairs and Tourism, and Parks and Recreation all contain programs and initiatives that focus on Aboriginal people. Though not specifically directed towards cities, many of these ministries contain an urban component within their purview, whether through the funding of urban Aboriginal service-delivery organizations or through the programs delivered by the provincial government itself.

2 Federal Government Actors

Although *urban* Aboriginal issues have a relatively low policy priority as a distinct object of governance for the federal government – a situation similar to that of the province of Alberta – the government does fund (or directly deliver) programs accessed by urban Aboriginal policy makers and program delivery agencies. The government of Canada has hundreds of departments, agencies, and crown corporations, many of which directly or indirectly fund Aboriginal programming utilized by urban Aboriginal residents. Possibly the most well-known of these programs (at least in recent years) is the Urban Aboriginal Strategy (UAS), administered by Indian and Northern Affairs Canada (INAC). The UAS has been in existence for about a decade and was, most recently, carried out under the auspices of the Office of the Federal Interlocutor, part of INAC. The stated basis of UAS is to improve the social and economic opportunities of urban Aboriginals in targeted cities (the number of which has been expanded over the past decade). Through partnerships with provincial and municipal governments, and community and Aboriginal organizations, the UAS focuses specifically on the improvement of life, job, and entrepreneurial skills with a specific emphasis on supporting Aboriginal women, children, and families (Urban Aboriginal Strategy 2005).

As we detail further a little later on, both Edmonton and Calgary are "UAS cities" and this status has had an impact on their urban Aboriginal policy relations. However, in reality, UAS exists as a small, albeit urban-specific program alongside programs of policies of general application and Aboriginal-specific policy (per Hanselmann's earlier discussion) in the form of Aboriginal Human Resources and Development Agreements (AHRDAS). These agreements are part of Human Resources and Skills Development Canada and are delivered through Service Canada. AHRDAS are part of the federal government's attempt "to assist Aboriginal people to prepare for, find, and keep jobs. All Aboriginal people, regardless of status or location, may access its programs and services. These include: labour market interventions; programs for youth, urban, and Aboriginal persons living with disabilities; creation and maintenance of child care spaces (First Nations and Inuit Child Care); and capacity building for Agreement holders."[9]

Currently, more than eighty AHRDAS exist across Canada, monitored through numerous regional offices – these offices are presently being phased out in favour of the subsequent Aboriginal Skills and Training Strategic Investment Fund program.[10] Service Canada suggests that these agreements provide Aboriginal organizations with the flexibility and "the authority to make decisions that will meet the needs of their communities"[11] provided that these same organizations, the major deliverers of AHRDAS, meet the funding and accountability requirements set out in the AHRDA agreements. ·

3 Municipal Government Actors

Until the 1990s, municipal actors in Alberta played virtually no role in urban Aboriginal policy or programming with respect to planning, production, implementation, or coordination. This lack of participation remains the case for the smaller cities in our study, but it can no longer be said to be the case in Edmonton or Calgary (or at least, certainly not to the same extent). While neither of these cities has much in the way of funding or delivery of urban Aboriginal programming, they have begun to play a more prominent role in policy coordination and capacity building through the creation of explicit coordination structures. The Urban Aboriginal Strategy has assisted in the development and implementation of municipal coordinating structures whose aim is to produce more efficient (if not necessarily more inclusive) urban policy and programming. Calgary has a longer municipal history of involvement in such coordination than Edmonton, although the Edmonton Urban Aboriginal Initiative is now creating processes similar to those created under the longer-standing Calgary Urban Aboriginal Initiative. (We explain this change in more detail in part four of this chapter.)

4 Social Forces

We define social forces here to include *non-governmental* policy actors involved in either the creation, production, or implementation of urban Aboriginal policy: service delivery organizations comprise an important component of these social forces and include cultural and non-cultural social service delivery agencies, churches, business organizations, sports organizations, etc. One of the many ironies of the urban Aboriginal policy field in Alberta is that virtually all non-governmental social forces actors capable of operating, at least in part, because of provincial, federal, and (sometimes) municipal funding or social capital (i.e. social networks, contacts, etc.). Importantly, these organizations may self-identify as Aboriginal organizations (for example, Nechi Training, Research and Health Promotion Institute in Edmonton or the Awo Taan Family Wellness Center in Calgary) or they may deliver services for individuals or families in need without an explicit focus on Aboriginal people (for example, the Bissell Centre in Edmonton or the Boys and Girls Club Community Services in Calgary).

One effect of nearly four decades of jurisdictional maze is that urban Aboriginal programming is almost always organized around short-term, project-based funding. On this fiscal structure, although an organization may receive very little in the way of base funding, it may, through successful applications for project funding, leverage this initial funding into considerably larger program and service delivery dollars. However, the flipside of this arrangement is that organizations that offer services to an Aboriginal urban clientele are almost always propped up by a patchwork of funding networks; they access funding and offer programs under a number of different policies – or, through project applications, they attempt to access program funding under simultaneous (yet widely divergent) federal and/or provincial policies of general application or Aboriginal specific. For example, Edmonton's Bissell Centre (a multi-service agency that provides various types of support for low income clients) receives funding and other support from: Alberta Health, Boyle Street Community Services, Boyle McCauley Health Centre, E4C, Edmonton Inner City Housing Society, Family Shelter Network, Fort Saskatchewan Correction Centre, Inner City Youth Housing Project, Operation Friendship Senior's Society, People In Need Shelter Society (PIN), University of Alberta, and Youth Emergency Shelter Services (YESS), Inner City Pastoral Ministry (ICPM), Alberta Employment and Immigration, AADAC, Edmonton Public Health, Edmonton Coalition on Housing and Homelessness, Skills, Grant MacEwan College, and the Elizabeth Fry Society.[12]

5 Representative Organizations

A final class of major players in the urban Aboriginal policy field is the group of national and provincial representative organizations (that is, organizations whose leaders are voted in by constituents). In Alberta, these organizations include the Assembly of First Nations regional affiliates (including Treaty 6, Treaty 7, and Treaty 8 Offices); the Métis National Council and its regional affiliate – the

Métis Nation of Alberta; and the Métis Settlements General Council. As we discuss further in the next section, the lack of jurisdictional coordination has produced enduring tensions between representative organizations such as these and service delivery organizations with respect to who urban Aboriginal individuals "belong to" in terms of policy and program implementation dollars; who has the right to deliver these programs; and under what policy aegis (that is, needs versus rights/treaty-based) these programs are to be delivered. Indeed, political organizations felt marginalized by UAS's decision to bypass them (and in doing so, downgrade their legitimacy) by placing the funding for their UAS-sponsored programs in the hands of regional affiliates of federal departments. This "bypassing" remains a particular issue in Edmonton, where the Métis Nation of Alberta remains outside the UAS-sponsored policy coordination structures in that city.

Part three of this chapter was meant to provide an overview of the major players involved in the creation, production, and implementation of urban Aboriginal policy. By way of summarizing this lengthier section, we wish to reiterate two points. First, given the historical absence of coordinated and inter-jurisdictionally clear policy structures, and the Alberta government's emphasis on inter-ministerial collaboration, this policy field is notable for the sheer number of players and organizations involved in it. Second, when analyzing urban Aboriginal policy in Alberta, we must contextualize it by noting that more than a generation of jurisdictional vagueness and unpredictability has produced short-term funding pockets. These pockets have in turn produced a policy delivery ethos in which viable service delivery requires the coupling of an organizational focus on the pragmatics of programming with a flexible and creatively interpreted stance towards Aboriginal policy (which is usually not specifically urban in focus). That is to say, urban Aboriginal organizations have, as a means of survival, become catchment areas for numerous (and sometimes conflicting) policy logics which they (must) successfully stitch into a stable patchwork of year-to-year program funding – it is this funding scheme that ensures the continuation of their organization. However stable, this funding relationship between Aboriginal organizations and the Alberta government has produced several long-standing and distinctive features and tensions. In the final substantive part of this chapter, we explore these features and tensions in greater depth.

PART 4: THEMES AND TENSIONS IN ALBERTA'S URBAN
ABORIGINAL POLICY FIELD

So far, this chapter has highlighted the impact of an absence of urban-specific, inter-jurisdictionally coordinated Aboriginal policy on Alberta's urban Aboriginal policy field. As noted by many of our interviewees, the effects of this absence, though wide ranging, have particularly effected the ways in which policy is produced and programs are delivered, resulting in a patchwork of short-term funding pockets that often overlap with programs delivered by other agencies and within which social actors feel marginalized from the policy-making stage and, more importantly, lack a voice in the policy *evaluation* standards. This state of affairs produces and maintains a certain level of inefficiency in the policy field. In this final section, we highlight the results of our interviews with thirty agents involved in the urban Aboriginal policy field in Alberta by identifying three major themes and associated tensions: 1) the distinctiveness of urban Aboriginal policy making by city; 2) the character of intergovernmental policy making; and 3) the feelings of marginalization of social actors.

1 Distinctiveness of Urban Aboriginal Policy Making by City

Four cities – Edmonton, Calgary, Cold Lake, and the Regional Municipality of Wood Buffalo – comprised our research foci; given the distinctiveness of policy relations in each of these cities, extrapolating on city-specific policy relations is particularly important. These particular cities were chosen for two reasons: first, to reflect the diversity between so-called "large city" (like Edmonton and Calgary) and "small city" (Cold Lake and Municipality of Wood Buffalo) milieus, and second, to reflect the diversity of socio-economic realities and opportunities. Cities are often said to possess their own distinctive personalities; the distinctiveness of urban Aboriginal policy and programming, therefore, might often be written off as a reflection of a city's particular size, demography (both Aboriginal and non-Aboriginal), or personality. However, we argue that the lack of coordination of urban Aboriginal policy making over the past four decades has fostered a policy climate within which city-distinctiveness rose to the fore more often and more intensely than it might otherwise have.

COLD LAKE

Located near the eastern border of the province of Alberta and adjacent to First Nations, Métis settlements, and a Canadian Air Forces base, Cold Lake is the smallest city included in our study. In 2006, the Aboriginal population of Cold Lake was about 1,000 people, just under 10 per cent of the total population of about 12,000. Participants in this city warned, however, that such official figures were misleading with respect to the Aboriginal population because they failed to capture what Mary Jane Norris and others have referred to as "churn" – movement from cities to surrounding small town and rural areas (Norris and Clatworthy 2003). This is particularly important for a city like Cold Lake, which is surrounded by half of the Métis settlements[13] in the province (with thousands of Métis residents), as well as several large First Nations communities. From a policy standpoint, the Aboriginal population comprises up to 85 per cent of the clientele who use social services within the city. Current funding formulas make long-term planning difficult because demographic information is calculated inconsistently; sometimes Cold Lake is considered to be an isolated municipality and sometimes it is defined as an area that includes reserves, Métis settlements, and municipal districts. Cold Lake's policy environment, such that it is, is shaped by the proximity of both First Nations and Métis settlements, a point we will develop further.

The relative dearth of specific urban Aboriginal policy in Cold Lake, whether generated by federal, provincial, municipal, or Aboriginal policy makers, makes it clear that the municipality does not emphasize urban Aboriginal issues as an "enhanced" policy priority. What general policies Cold Lake does have tend to be tied into broader categories related to employment and job training, and even these categories reflect a complex mélange of provincial and federal funding. Interviewees maintained that access to Aboriginal programs was usually restricted to rural-based programs in the communities surrounding the municipality. A Native Friendship Center operates in Cold Lake, but low levels of funding make it difficult for it to provide the level of service delivery that urban Aboriginal people require. Indeed, the Friendship Center is as much a referral agency to other social service venues as it is a deliverer of social services.

REGIONAL MUNICIPALITY OF WOOD BUFFALO

Located adjacent to the massive Tar Sands Oil project in northern Alberta, which fuels much of Alberta's economic growth, the

Municipality of Wood Buffalo comprises the urban centre of Fort McMurray, five First Nations reserves, several small rural communities, and a Métis organization (also referred to as a "local") that represents the local Métis population. In 2006, the total population was 52,555 and the Aboriginal population was 6,465, or about 12 per cent.[14] The Athabasca Tribal Council is the primary representative organization of the five First Nations in the area, while the Métis local represents the Métis Nation of Alberta. As in Cold Lake, the Friendship Centre in Fort McMurray operates as much as a drop-in centre/referral agency as it does a locus of urban Aboriginal policy formation or delivery. The policy milieu of this municipality overlaps closely with that of Cold Lake with regard to the challenges of delivering policy within a relatively small and isolated city. Much like Cold Lake, the primary policies that apply specifically to Aboriginal people in the city are employment and hiring policies. However, due to an overwhelming amount of natural resource development in the area and well-publicized labour shortages, the policy environment is shaped in a distinct manner that is not comparable with that in the other cities in this study. Although the lure of employment draws people from across the country into Fort McMurray, it is a difficult city within which to access the basic services necessary to successfully *sustain* employment opportunities – services that include housing, childcare, and transportation, to name but a few.

EDMONTON

The City of Edmonton was historically a major trading depot in the transcontinental fur trading system operated most prominently by the Hudson's Bay Company. All of the Indigenous nations who reside in Alberta have names in their own language for the area known as "Edmonton" (see Goyette 2004, 19–37). This Aboriginal presence continues today: Edmonton's CMA Aboriginal population of 52,100 people represents the second largest urban Aboriginal population in Canada, comprising about 5 per cent of the total population of the CMA of Edmonton, which numbers just over 1,000,000 people.

More than any other city in our study, Edmonton can be characterized as possessing a literal avalanche of organizations, programs, and services, all of which exist within a broader set of policies of general application and policies geared towards Aboriginal residents of Alberta in general. Edmonton publishes a helpful (and annual)

"Guide to Aboriginal Edmonton" (City of Edmonton, 2008). This guide includes the names, addresses, and contact information of Edmonton's nearly 400 Aboriginal organizations, revealing a morass of programs and services relating to such diverse fields as arts and crafts, business and economic development, communications, education, employment, Friendship Centres and related organizations, housing, political representation organizations, social/health services, women's groups, regional tribal organizations, and miscellaneous organizations involved with prisons, justice, Aboriginal relations, Aboriginal war veterans, sports, recreation, consultation, youth and senior citizens. While this list is not exhaustive, it does give some indication of the breadth and depth of Aboriginal programming in the city of Edmonton.

Edmonton is currently in the process of formalizing a number of mechanisms aimed at improving inclusion and communication among its numerous and varied Aboriginal programming and service actors. In conjunction with all three levels of government and coordinators funded through the Urban Aboriginal Strategy (which paralleled and partly funded a "Dialogue" process), the Edmonton Aboriginal Urban Affairs Committee (an Aboriginal and non-Aboriginal volunteer committee selected by City Council) has helped produce an "Urban Aboriginal Accord," which involved development of a declaration to guide the working relationships of municipal decision makers and the urban Aboriginal community. The accord is an encouraging example of a new policy ethos in that the process included seeking out the opinions of not only political organizations and community leaders but also individual citizens, aboriginal youth, elders, men, and women: stakeholders normally on the periphery of such decision-making spheres. The eventual declaration promised to "build relationships with Aboriginal Peoples that are rooted in trust and respect. All of our partnerships must involve shared responsibility and ensure that Aboriginal Peoples take their rightful place in building a strong Aboriginal presence and voice in the cultural, social, and economic future of Edmonton."[15] Though policy produced through these processes is approaching the three to four year mark, how effective these processes will be in future practice remains to be seen. Moreover, given that the Métis political representatives remain formally outside this process, celebrating the inclusive success of this model is premature.

CALGARY

Calgary is Alberta's largest city and, like Edmonton, has a long Aboriginal history that predates its existence as a city. Calgary is often seen as more "white collar" and corporate and Edmonton more "blue collar"; the two cities hold a long-standing "friendly" rivalry, manifested not least in their competing professional hockey and football teams. Founded as a fort in the late 1800s by North West Mounted Police as a base from which to disrupt the region's illegal whiskey trade, Calgary remains home to Aboriginal people. In 2006, the population of the CMA of Calgary was just over 1,00000, of which 26,000 were Aboriginal (about 2.5 per cent). Like Edmonton, Calgary has several First Nations within easy commuting distance as well as a First Nation (the T'suu Tina) within its municipal boundaries.

Calgary lacks Edmonton's sheer volume of organizations, programs, and services. This lack is not surprising, given that the city's Aboriginal population is less than half that of Edmonton. Its urban Aboriginal programming and services landscape is nevertheless marked by considerable activity. Calgary possesses organizations and policies in the same areas as Edmonton: economic/business activity, education, employment, Native Friendship Centres, social/health services, tribally affiliated organizations, justice, and human rights, to name but a few (City of Calgary, 2008). Presently, however, what separates Calgary's from Edmonton's policy landscape – both of which operate according to the same policies of general application – is not a lack of volume, but rather a difference in the overall *coordination* of programming activities, especially with respect to the role of the municipality. Although Calgary has not produced an accord like Edmonton's per se, in practice its municipal prioritization of urban Aboriginal issues has existed for a longer period (including a Calgary Aboriginal Urban Affairs Committee, in existence since 1979)[16] and it has a significantly larger (relative to the size of its Aboriginal population) municipal infrastructure dedicated to urban Aboriginal issues.

The major coordinating body for urban Aboriginal policy in Calgary is the Calgary Urban Aboriginal Initiative (CAUI – paralleling and partly funded through the Urban Aboriginal Strategy and in existence since 2003), whose membership includes representatives from both the government of Canada and the government of

Alberta, the city of Calgary, the Calgary Aboriginal Urban Affairs Committee, two Aboriginal political organizations, eight seats for the various "domain" groups, an elder, youth, and two Aboriginal community "members at large," and a seat for the local Chamber of Commerce.[17] The domain groups (that is, those dealing with mutually agreed upon policy and programming areas) included in this process are the following: 1) services, 2) justice, 3) human rights, 4) housing, 5) health, 6) employment, 7) education, and 8) funding. Despite this coordination, however, there are still gaps in the education of non-Aboriginal Calgary residents – even among those, like the Community and Neighbourhood Services workers, who might be expected to be better informed. For example, the City of Calgary's guide to Aboriginal agencies and services notes in its introduction that it "values its many residents who are of Aboriginal, Inuit, or Métis descent"[18] (City of Calgary 2008). This misstep does not necessarily indicate a lack of respect between Aboriginal residents and others in the city of Calgary, but it does speak to a lack of knowledge about basic terminology.

Certainly, part of the distinctiveness in policy and programming by city is a function of scale. We would not, for example, expect small cities like Cold Lake and Municipality of Wood Buffalo to possess urban Aboriginal policy and programming relations like those of Edmonton and Calgary – these cities possess nowhere near the density or diversity of Aboriginal population, nor, for that matter, the critical mass required to produce the volume of Aboriginal policy present in these larger cities. However, policy actors in smaller cities nonetheless expressed feelings of marginalization in the policy-making process both in terms of perceived formal policy-making arrangements and in terms of more informal kinds of relations – chance meetings at building or agency openings, the unveiling of government initiatives, or even Christmas parties: on more than one occasion, policy actors in smaller cities felt as if they were on the outside looking in and saw little opportunity to affect the policy processes they inherited through their local service delivery agencies.

2 Character of Intergovernmental Policy Making

Intergovernmental policy making reflects the longstanding lack of coordination between various levels of government and social forces actors. The Bissell Centre example, which demonstrates the patchwork of funding networks through which much programming is produced and sustained, is not an anomaly. In Alberta, in fact, intergovernmental cooperation (both between levels of government and within government departments themselves) has become a programmatic emphasis.

Because of this lack of coordination, Alberta urban Aboriginal programming almost always takes place in the context of a wide array of intermediary interests, which include Aboriginal representative organizations, service delivery organizations with a large Aboriginal clientele, and various levels of government; largely working according to policies of general application or Aboriginal-specific policies that fail to discriminate by geographical residence. This state of affairs has the effect of making it nearly impossible to say with any confidence (except in several relatively small, exceptional circumstances) that Policy A leads to Program and/or Service B or perhaps more accurately, that Policy A has an isolatable *impact* on Program or Service B, since the very viability of most service delivery agencies in Alberta requires that they access funding from numerous initiatives, regardless of their specific policy orientations.

Generally, Alberta funds and delivers programming and services through the following process: legislation → Aboriginal Policy Framework → initiative → program or service. However, any link between policy and program in such an explicitly interdepartmental atmosphere can never be so neat, particularly in the context of urban Aboriginal policy. Provincially-directed Aboriginal policy making (including that accessed by urban Aboriginal residents) takes place under the aegis of the Aboriginal Policy Framework and the Aboriginal Policy Initiative, which represents a concrete operationalization of the latter's policies. The Initiative is explicitly cross-ministerial and includes monthly meetings between various senior policy advisors and deputy ministers from most of the different ministries. As one interviewee pointed out, however, even though such meetings are important, they do not necessarily remove the "silo thinking" that might exist within any given ministry (Interview 29).

As one example of the effect of this cross-ministry emphasis, we can look at the policies of Alberta's Child and Youth Services ministry (ACYS). ACYS works in the context of policies of general application with the goal of supporting "families and communities, helping them to provide nurturing, safe environments for their children." It strives "to break the cycles of family violence, abuse, and poverty that prevent some children from becoming strong, sound individuals."[19] Its programs deal with: adoption and guardianship, bullying, child care, child welfare (for abused children), child exploitation, children with disabilities, family and community support, family violence, fetal alcohol spectrum disorder, foster care and kinship care, internet safety, parenting, and youth programs. While these are policies of general application, they are utilized by Aboriginal program and service delivery agencies (and include Aboriginal-specific programming).

Moreover, even within this single ministry, the actual facilitation of these programs is enormously complicated by intervening initiatives that not only form policies in their own right but also put meat on the bones of broader policies (like that of the Aboriginal Policy Framework). For example, in the context of the Province of Alberta's Ministry of Child and Youth Services, programs are carried out not only under the framework of various pieces of legislation – the *Child Care Licensing Act*; the *Child, Youth and Family Enhancement Act*; the *Drug-endangered Children Act*; the *Family and Community Support Services Act*; and the *Family Support for Children with Disabilities Act* – but also under the guidance of two dovetailing initiatives: the Aboriginal Policy Initiative (already noted above) and the Alberta Child and Youth Initiative (ACYI). These two initiatives in turn give way to more specific Aboriginal initiatives, which currently include Aboriginal Youth Suicide Prevention Strategies, Bullying Prevention Strategy, Children and Youth with Complex Needs, Fetal Alcohol Spectrum Disorder, and Review of Speech-Language Services.

Furthermore, within these more specific initiatives, the Alberta government's cross-ministry focus relies on partnerships between Alberta Child and Youth Services, Alberta Education, Alberta Health and Wellness, Alberta Advanced Education and Technology, Alberta Aboriginal Relations, Alberta Employment and Immigration, Alberta Justice and Attorney General, Alberta Seniors and Community Support, Alberta Solicitor General and Public Security, Alberta Alcohol and Drug Abuse Commission, and the Alberta Mental Health Board.[20] All these partnerships involve the provincial government's policy and programming alone! If these various initiatives, programs, and services merely indicated lines to sub-departments within Alberta Child and Youth Services, that might be one thing. But they don't. Each of these entities brings along with it various pieces of financial and social capital, which are then manifested in numerous Aboriginal social service delivery organizations. Thus, while one might examine a policy of "bullying" and trace it provincially from ACYS through to the Alberta Native Friendship Centre Association's Provincial Youth Council,[21] it would make little sense to understand this link outside the enormously complex set of structures just described, just as it would make little sense to understand the Alberta Native Friendship Centre Association in terms of its youth policies and programs. Program delivery organizations operate only due to their continued ability to successfully secure funding to deliver programming existing under numerous policies.

Federally, this inter-jurisdictional cooperation works in much the same way. Take, for example, Aboriginal employment and training programs, each of which has various missions, goals, and policies. Oteenow Employment and Training Society in Edmonton, for example, has been in existence for more than a decade and has a mandate to improve employment and job training skills for First Nations People in the Greater Edmonton area. It offers holistic and culturally specific approaches to employment services with a focus on career decision-making, skills enhancement, job search assistance, and employment maintenance.[22] However, the realities of short-term, project-based funding means that Oteenow operates under the auspices of numerous stakeholders, including the Aboriginal Relations Office of Service Canada, the Confederacy of Treaty 6 First Nations, Treaty 8 First Nations of Alberta, the Assembly of First Nations, Indian and Northern Affairs Canada, Alberta Learning and Information Services, Human Resources and Social Development Canada, and Alberta Employment, Immigration, and Industry.[23] AHRDAS remain a particularly important part of Oteenow's ability to offer its services, although federally these agreements are themselves part of a larger, initiative-based strategy that includes the Aboriginal Skills and Employment Partnership Program.[24] These AHRDAS are also supplemented by Labour Market Agreements between the federal government and the Province of Alberta through the latter's Ministry of Employment and Immigration.

3 The Marginalization of Social Forces Actors

In the Alberta urban Aboriginal programming landscape, social forces constitute a linchpin for developing a community able to respond to the complexities of urban Aboriginal life: "[w]ithout the policy community's special capabilities for studying alternative courses of action, for debating their rival merits, and for securing administrative arrangements for implementation, governments would have great difficulties discerning and choosing between policy options" (Pross 1986, 207). The input from social forces to the policy field is critical to the development of flexible and efficient policy action that ensures balanced representative processes and policy advocacy that is considerate of the local and cultural contexts of urban Aboriginal people in cities.

In Alberta, the majority of urban Aboriginal programming activity comes about in response to initiatives from Aboriginal and non-Aboriginal organizations and public service agencies. However, although intergovernmental policy discussion tables provide seats for urban Aboriginal organizations, the latter experience barriers that preclude their full participation in policy and programming. As Hanselmann has pointed out, the emerging policy community will have to renegotiate the misguided policies of the past, which "will take more than one generation, [and, therefore], governments should commit to long term objectives" (Hanselmann in Chalifoux 2003, n.p). However, as previously noted, project-based, short-term strategies trump core operations funding. This makes long-term, proactive planning difficult and encourages short-term solutions to deeply rooted issues (Berdhal 2002). Little room exists for the failure and experimentation necessary to produce the seeds of successful policy activity (Landry and Bianchini 1995).

Perhaps more pressing is the fact that current funding arrangements appear to limit the ability of social forces to form partnerships. Project funding opportunities in both small and large cities create a competitive atmosphere between service agencies, which can (in some cases severely) impair the development of a collaborative environment (Johns et al. 2006). A respondent from a small city mentioned that "rather than working together to use funding more effectively, they are too busy protecting themselves, they are worried that they will lose their money if they don't protect it from others" (Interview 3). Another respondent mentioned that the Urban Aboriginal Strategy (seen as a potential panacea for bringing together policy actors) has also become a source of funding competition: some among the more frustrated service delivery agents have argued that it has become "another funding agency," with funds "delivered by a non-Aboriginal organization ... [it] is a way to

control the Aboriginal community, and it has its favourites, organizations that it will give millions to, and others have to fight for fifteen
thousand dollars, and then they micro manage you on that fifteen
thousand dollars, it's crazy" (Interview 8).

An additional barrier to the advocacy of urban Aboriginal
people's policy imperatives is the fact that the founding charters of
local service providers incorporated as charities limit their ability
to advocate on behalf of their clientele (Graham and Peters 2002,
20). Indeed, many organizations deliberately avoid overt "political"
lobbying or advocacy work; as one interviewee explained, "lobbying absolutely has an advantage, but you have to be careful with
the wording because if there is any hint of that in project applications, you won't qualify" (Interview 3). Similarly, despite their commitment to Aboriginal protocol and their high levels of Aboriginal
clientele, some organizations have strategically avoided incorpor-
ating themselves as "Aboriginal" to avoid limitations on the types
of funds accessible with such a designation. A service coordinator
with a seventy-five per cent Aboriginal clientele explained that the
organization is "not registered as an Aboriginal agency because once
you do, you have to partner up with certain organizations, and we
strategically stayed out of that game" (Interview 21). Informants felt
that non-Aboriginal funding provided maximum flexibility to serve
their Aboriginal clients' interests.

Some informants located in non-governmental organizations felt
excluded from the policy-making process. Although current intergovernmental strategies such as the Urban Aboriginal Strategy are
encouraging formalized participation spaces for all actors in the
policy field, informants feel that these strategies remain unproduct-
ive in a policy and programming context. In fact, having attended
many of these meetings, the coordinator of a housing and homelessness service mentioned that attending consultation meetings often
left her wondering "what for?" Developing an inclusive policy community requires that forums go beyond mere invitations. Another
informant stated: "we are an Aboriginal organization but we are
doing project by project funding, so to run this organization you
are meeting someone else's eligibility and criteria all the time. We
have calculated that 78 per cent of administration time is spent on
meeting criteria of these different level government projects so, who
is really running the agenda then of these organizations?" (Interview
25). Exclusion of some of those implicated in program delivery from

agenda setting, proposing alternatives, and program design produces a policy field that is perceived to be less amenable to urban policy actor input and, therefore, one that may produce policies that lack ground level practicality, functionality, and legitimacy.

In the absence of genuine participation and input from all actors at the early stages of policy design, the socio-economic disparities experienced by urban Aboriginal peoples are doomed to be simplistically constructed as the inevitable circumstances of poverty, a mindset that positions urban Aboriginal residents as simply another segment of the disenfranchised urban underclass (Abelson and Gauvin 2006). The resulting policy environment will create an urban milieu characterized by cultural crisis management and the "homogenizing forces" (Johns et al. 2006) of economic rationalities.

CONCLUSION

In conclusion, we wish to reiterate that the current state of the urban Aboriginal policy field in Alberta, with its emphasis on patch-worked, short-term, project-based funding that leads to overlapping and ultimately inefficient results, is the result of four decades of goodwill and program production in a federal coordination vacuum. Moreover, the jurisdictional maze has produced service delivery organizations that produce relatively stable relationships with numerous policy and programming agents as a way of maintaining their long-term viability to deliver a wide range of programs and services instead of operating according to specific policy or programming lines. Given this situation, we think it's more helpful to think about this policy field in Alberta in terms of the organizational dynamics between its actors rather than through a fruitless effort to link policy to programming; even if we were to emphasize the latter, we would also have to emphasize the organizational dynamic through which these links take place.

Although it is far too soon to tell conclusively, urban Aboriginal *policy relations* appear to be improving, despite the fact that the policies themselves have yet to show any progress. Jurisdictional issues notwithstanding, the federal government is slowly becoming more involved in urban Aboriginal policy creation (through the advent of the Urban Aboriginal Strategy), and it appears that the voices and frustrations of Aboriginal policy actors are being taken more seriously – although the implementation of UAS caused deep consternation by circumventing representation-based Aboriginal political organizations in implementing policy funding. However, the gulf between municipal and federal actors remains wide and, though it does not seem to be widening, the provincial government remains the monitor, advocate, broker, regulator, and major partner in the design, implementation, and evaluation of urban Aboriginal programming. Those actors involved in this field remain divided over jurisdictional issues and issues of cultural difference: one major tension we identified is that between needs- and rights-based approaches, which is played out amidst tension between economic efficiency and cultural appropriateness.

At least in the Alberta urban Aboriginal policy field, the hierarchy between government and social forces appears to be correlated with the hierarchy between non-Aboriginal and Aboriginal policy actors, respectively. The latter are increasingly engaged as stakeholders in the policy process but their brand of expertise is (at least until recently) disregarded in the early stages of policy development. Though they possess the closest view of the issues and imperatives that are to be framed for policy interventions, they lack a provincially and federally audible voice. Their constant struggle to maintain operations on a day-to-day basis makes it nearly impossible to organize the resources required to seek private funding contributions from business or to exert political pressure through lobbying and general advocacy activities. Ultimately, in the current situation, the financial barriers to partnership between social forces remain a significant stumbling block to the horizontalization of urban Aboriginal policy relations in Alberta.

Similarly, hierarchies *within* the ranks of social forces actors hamper their ability to influence policy. This hierarchy is reproduced and solidified whenever funding is provided to a city. Well-established, proven service delivery agents and organizations (especially those in the biggest cities) tend to be awarded the bulk of funding and thus the opportunity to maintain staff, deliver services, and engage in policy participation forums, advocacy, proposal writing, and program development. One interviewee suggested that in the early stages of policy field development, "there is need for Aboriginal organizations to partner with non-Aboriginal organizations, learn from them, and move on. Native Counselling services of Alberta is an excellent example of partnerships and collaborations with Aboriginal and non-Aboriginal organizations. While there may be jealousy directed toward them, they are the ones that are doing business and doing it well" (Interview 13).

The notable growth in municipal and general public awareness of Aboriginality in Alberta's big cities is by no means spontaneous; it has been led by the social forces most connected to urban Aboriginal peoples. In Alberta, social forces play a critical role in bringing urban Aboriginal policy to the attention of municipalities. The locally textured and culturally attuned social forces need to be involved in the policy process at the deepest levels of problem framing because, as we have argued throughout this paper, "problems that people care about are not defined or shaped in the same way that departments and agencies are, and when government reform focuses only on smooth administration, real problems fall between the gaps" (Peach 2004, 2). In the urban Aboriginal context, the environment is already long on "gap" and short on "foundation." Long-term investments in social forces and urban Aboriginal capacity building constitute a move toward a less reactive and more proactive, locally invested policy field. This move speaks to both a largely untapped creative potential located within social forces and the ability of governments to respond to these pressures. These positive trends now require intergovernmental (and intergenerational!) mechanisms to bring these positive developments into the broader policy-making ethos and the implementation of innovative solutions.

Due to the inefficacy of past policy approaches to urban Aboriginality and the potential consequences of implementing policy in a reactive environment, both innovative and long-term policy perspectives are necessary. The field is showing some innovative policy processes and creative approaches to policy at the grassroots level, which seem to be gaining federal and provincial departmental support. Although cities are currently working to create the mechanisms needed to build appropriate relationships and communication structures, they remain disconnected from the broader policy-making structures, and creative ideas tend to remain at the municipal level. The growing political acknowledgement of urban Aboriginal policy interests (as evidenced through the UAS, the Calgary Urban Aboriginal Accord Initiative, Edmonton's Accord Initiative, and the Strengthening Relationships document) are applauded by urban Aboriginal organizations. However, representatives from service delivery agencies recognize that there are "good intentions and individual goodwill, but these aren't getting moved past the discussion

table" (Interview 17). Acknowledgement of Aboriginal proto-
cols and priorities is growing, but as one interviewee pointed out,
"the owning that philosophy, the practicing that philosophy, and
the interpretation in action of what that philosophy means and the
impact is not there yet" (Interview 26).

NOTES

1 Aboriginal Peoples Highlight Tables, 2006. Accessed 20 June 2009 from
  http://www12.statcan.gc.ca/english/census06/data/highlights/Aboriginal/
  Index.cfm?Lang=E.
2 Aboriginal Peoples Highlight Tables, 2006. Accessed 20 June 2009 from
  http://www12.statcan.gc.ca/english/census06/data/highlights/Aboriginal/
  Index.cfm?Lang=E.
3 Aboriginal Peoples Highlight Tables, 2006. Accessed 20 June 2009 from
  http://www12.statcan.gc.ca/english/census06/data/highlights/Aboriginal/
  Index.cfm?Lang=E.
4 We define and explain the contours of a policy field in part three.
5 Alberta Advantage. Accessed 2 August 2009 from http://alberta.ca/home/
  43.cfm?. The "Alberta Advantage" refers to the various features of the
  province of Alberta that make its quality of life superior to that of residents of other provinces.
6 Part three describes this strategy in more detail.
7 Te Whanau O Waipareira Trust – Wai Whanau Social services – Wrap-
  around Services. Accessed 2 August 2009 from http://www.waipareira.
  com/socservices.html.
8 Methodologically, the research for this chapter was carried out over three
  years between 2006 and 2009 – the original research was carried out over
  the summer of 2007, with subsequent conversations (email, telephone,
  and in-person) carried out after that initial research period. The data
  is a combination of written notes, recorded interviews, and subsequent
  conversations. During this period, we interviewed thirty governmental
  and non-government based actors, including individuals from the federal,
  provincial, and municipal governments as well as those from the non-
  governmental social service delivery and business sector. The interviews
  were semi-structured with a set list of questions that every interviewee was
  asked. Two students (one male, one female) were sent to a majority of the
  interviews for safety purposes, to honour interviewees who subscribe to
  "traditional" beliefs, and, more mundanely, to allow a more seamless

asking of questions and writing of answers (in addition to the recorded interviews). The one exception to this practice was the primary investigator's trip to Calgary – to interview research informants individually – and subsequent follow-up conversations with Calgary interviewees. One thing that should be emphasized is the difficulty of gaining interviews during our research period. Alberta was undergoing an era of unprecedented economic growth (due to the skyrocketing price of oil in particular) and this situation posed two issues: first, students would often make appointments only to have the interviewee cancel in advance or, on other occasions, simply not show up for the interview. Second, the economic boom produced numerous employment opportunities such that several of our interviewees were extremely new to their position (so much so, in fact, that on several occasions we were forced to explain to the interviewees the current urban Aboriginal policy relations in Alberta and their organizations' role in it).

9   Human Resources and Skills Development, Canada – The Service. Accessed 2 August 2009 from http://www.hrsdc.gc.ca/eng/employment/ aboriginal_employment/strategy/index.shtml.

10 Aboriginal Skills and Training Strategic Investment Fund. Accessed 3 August 2009 from http://www.hrsdc.gc.ca/eng/employment/aboriginal_ employment/astsif/index.shtml.

11 Human Resources and Skills Development, Canada – The Service. Accessed 2 August 2009 from http://www.hrsdc.gc.ca/eng/employment/ aboriginal_employment/strategy/index.shtml.

12 Bissell Centre Annual Report, 2008. Accessed 20 June 2009 from http:// www.bissellcentre.org/documents/annualreport.pdf.

13 Métis settlements are a policy nexus peculiar to Alberta's policy landscape. Briefly, the settlements are the result of early twentieth century political leadership of Métis and First Nations leadership pushing for distinctive land bases for Indigenous people who "squatted" on Alberta-claimed territories and who fell outside of treaty. This led to a *Métis Betterment Act* in the 1930s, which in turn produced twelve distinct settlements, eight of which continue to exist today (see Sawchuk et al. 1981).

14 "Aboriginal identity population by age groups, median age and sex, percentage distribution (2006), for Canada, provinces and territories, and census metropolitan areas and census agglomerations – 20% sample data." Accessed 20 June 2009 from http://www12.statcan.gc.ca/english/ census06/data/highlights/Aboriginal/pages/Page.cfm?Lang=E&Geo=CMA &Code=48&Table=1&Data=Dist&Sex=1&Age=1&StartRec=1&Sort=2 &Display=Page.

15 Edmonton Urban Aboriginal Accord Declaration. Accessed 20
    June 2009 from http://www.edmonton.ca/CityGov/CommServices/
    EdmontonUrbanAboriginalAccordDeclaration.pdf, pg. 1 of 1.

16 Edmonton's has only been in existence since 1994. Edmonton Aborig-
    inal Urban Affairs Committee. Accessed 20 June 2008 from http://www.
    aboriginal-edmonton.com/committee.html.

17 Calgary Urban Aboriginal Initiative: Committee Model. Accessed 20 June
    2009 from http://tamarackcommunity.ca/downloads/learning_centre/cuai_
    structure.pdf, pg. 3 of 7.

18 "Aboriginal" is a constitutional term which includes "Indians", Inuit and
    Métis – hence, "Aboriginal" should not be separated from Métis. Calgary
    Aboriginal Agencies and Services Guided. Accessed 20 June 2008 from
    http://www.calgary.ca/docgallery/bu/cns/aboriginal_agencies_services_
    guide.pdf.

19 Government of Alberta Child and Youth Services – About Us. Accessed 20
    August 2009 from http://www.child.alberta.ca/home/about_us.cfm.

20 Government of Alberta Child and Youth Services Accessed 2 August 2009
    from http://www.child.alberta.ca/home/programs_services.cfm.

21 Alberta Native Friendship Centre Association – Youth. Accessed 2 August
    2009 from http://www.anfca.com/youth.html.

22 Oteenow Employment and Training Society. Accessed 3 August 2009 from
    http://www.oteenow.com/clients.html.

23 Oteenow Employment and Training Society. Accessed 3 August 2009 from
    http://www.oteenow.com/links.html#programs.

24 Aboriginal Skills and Employment Partnership (ASEP) Program. Accessed
    3 August 2009 from http://www.hrsdc.gc.ca/eng/employment/aboriginal_
    training/index.shtml.

INTERVIEWS

Interview 1, Edmonton, 19 July 2006
Interview 2, Edmonton, 19 July 2006
Interview 3, Edmonton, 19 July 2006
Interview 4, Edmonton, 19 July 2006
Interview 5, Edmonton, 19 July 2006
Interview 6, 20 July 2006
Interview 7, 20 July 2006
Interview 8, 20 July 2006
Interview 9, 27 July 2006

Interview 10, 27 July 2006
Interview 11, Edmonton, 26 July 2006
Interview 12, Edmonton, 31 July 2006
Interview 13, 1 August 2006
Interview 14, Edmonton, 10 August 2006
Interview 15, Calgary, 15 August 2006
Interview 16, Calgary, 15 August 2006
Interview 17, Calgary, 15 August 2006
Interview 18, Calgary, 16 August 2006
Interview 19, Edmonton, 16 August 2006
Interview 20, Calgary, 17 August 2006
Interview 21, Calgary, 17 August 2006
Interview 22, Edmonton, 17 August 2006
Interview 23, Calgary, 18 August 2006
Interview 24, Edmonton, 16 July 2007
Interview 25, Edmonton, 19 July 2007
Interview 26, Edmonton, 17 November 2008
Interview 27, Edmonton, 10 June 2009
Interview 28, Edmonton, 22 June 2009
Interview 29, Edmonton, 23 June 2009
Interview 30, Edmonton, 24 June 2009

REFERENCES

Abelson, Julia and François-Pierre Gauvin. 2006. "Assessing the Impacts of Public Participation: Concepts, Evidence, and Policy Implication." Ottawa: CPRN. Available: http://www.cprn.com/en/doc.cfm?doc=1403.

Berdhal, Loleen. 2002. *Structuring Federal Urban Engagement: A Principles Approach*. Calgary: Canada West Foundation.

Bourdieu, Pierre and Lois Wacquant, eds. 1992. *An Invitation to a Reflexive Sociology*. Chicago: University of Chicago Press.

Chalifoux, Thelma. 2003. *Urban Aboriginal Youth: An Action Plan for Change*. The Standing Senate Committee on Aboriginal Peoples – Sixth Report.

City of Calgary. 2008. *Calgary Aboriginal Agencies and Services Guide*. The City of Calgary: Community and Neighbourhood Services.

City of Edmonton. 2008. *Guide to Aboriginal Edmonton – 2008–2009 Edition*. City of Edmonton: Aboriginal Relations Office.

Government of Alberta. 2000. *Strengthening Relationships: The Government of Alberta's Aboriginal Policy Framework*. Edmonton: Government of Alberta.

Goyette, Linda. 2004. *Edmonton in our Own Words*. Edmonton: University of Alberta Press.

Graham, Katherine A.H. and Evelyn J. Peters. 2002. *Aboriginal Communities and Urban Sustainability*. Ottawa: Canadian Policy Research Network.

Hanselmann, Calvin. 2002. *Uncommon Sense: Promising Practices in Urban Aboriginal Policy Making and Programming*. Calgary: Canada West Foundation.

— 2001. *Urban Aboriginal People in Western Canada: Realities and Policies*. Calgary: Canada West Foundation.

Johns, Carolyn, Patricia O'Reilly, and Gregory Inwood. 2006. "Intergovernmental Innovation and the Administrative State in Canada." *Governance: An International Journal of Policy, Administration, and Institutions* 19 (4): 627–49.

Landry, Charles and Franco Bianchini. 1995. *The Creative City*. London: Demos in association with Comedia.

Norris, Mary Jane and Stewart Clatworthy. 2003. "Aboriginal Mobility and Migration within Urban Canada: Outcomes, Factors and Implications." In *Not Strangers in These Parts: Urban Aboriginal Peoples*, eds. David Newhouse and Evelyn J. Peters, 51–79. Ottawa: Policy Research Initiative.

Peach, Ian. 2004. "Managing Complexity: The Lessons of Horizontal Policy Making in the Provinces." Public Lecture at the Saskatchewan Institute of Public Policy, 8 June in Regina. Available: http://www.uregina.ca/sipp/documents/pdf/SS_Ian%20Peach_%20SpringSummer%2004.pdf.

Pross, Paul. 1986. *Group Politics and Public Policy*. Toronto: Oxford University Press.

Sawchuk, Joe, Patricia Sawchuk, and the Métis Association of Alberta. 1981. *Metis Land Rights in Alberta: A Political History*. Edmonton: Métis Association of Alberta.

Urban Aboriginal Strategy. 2005. *Urban Aboriginal Strategy Pilot Projects Formative Evaluation – Final Report*. Ottawa: Office of the Federal Interlocutor for Métis and Non-Status Indians, Indian and Northern Affairs Canada.

6

More than Stakeholders, Voices, and Tables: Towards Co-Production of Urban Aboriginal Policy in Manitoba[1]

RYAN WALKER, JAMES MOORE, AND
MAEENGAN LINKLATER

This chapter contributes to the debate about what combinations of multilevel governance and Aboriginal political and service organizations are most conducive to good Aboriginal affairs policy in Canadian municipalities. Using the concepts of policy and program co-production and "deep federalism" as normative principles for reviewing Aboriginal affairs policy, our conclusions provide ideas for improving the state of practice in Manitoba. These conclusions are context dependent but also have broader application in other parts of the country – although it will be up to the reader to determine the degree of transferability.

Policies and *programs* are not typically understood as meaning the same thing; nor are they always neatly divisible concepts. Following Calvin Hanselmann (2001), a policy can be understood as a guide for governments, for specific departments, and generally, for the public service in the performance of its duties. Programs, on the other hand, often serve to implement policies; they address conditions "on the ground" to realize the goals of broader policies. Programs can and often do exist, however, in the absence of policy frameworks. For our purposes in this chapter, we discuss policies and programs in conjunction because we believe that the principles for creating good urban Aboriginal policy and programs are similar. For simplicity, we sometimes refer to "policy" when we really mean policy and programs. Sometimes we distinguish between the two, if such a distinction helps us make a specific point.

Urban policy in Canada is a concern shared among municipal, provincial, and federal governments. With roughly 80 per cent of Canadians living in urban areas, every government is in effect an urban government. As Andrew Sancton (2007) observes, the Ontario provincial government was able to pass and implement ambitious smart-growth legislation that single municipalities and metropolitan areas would have had a difficult time carrying out. Neil Bradford (2004) summarizes the literature on the relevance of place-based approaches for undertaking multilevel governance in urban policy fields. He points to a well-known OECD (Organization for Economic Co-operation and Development) report that described Canada's "disjointed approach" to urban policy and a level of national engagement that is falling behind that of other countries. Bradford points out – in making sense of what is needed to improve the potential of urban places – that thriving cities will be places of innovation and inclusion. In cities where citizens who "are different or poor find themselves increasingly marginalized," governments will have a difficult time reversing urban decline and advancing ambitious urban agendas (Bradford 2004, 40).

Christopher Leo (2006) tackles the difficult question of how to build community aspirations and capacity at the local level into strong national policy. He introduces his idea of "deep federalism as process," suggesting that state and community actors work together to implement relevant local solutions. Such solutions can differ from place to place but are driven by a common national policy framework. He cites as an example the Neighbourhood Improvement Program in the 1970s, when the federal government implemented a scheme to renovate public facilities and infrastructure in declining neighbourhoods across the country. The program required that each participating community have a neighbourhood renewal plan derived from a public participation process. The Neighbourhood Improvement Program was structured, therefore, so that it could be implemented across the country in a way that respected differences between cities and between neighbourhoods within cities (Leo 2006). The same idea is applied on a provincial scale in the provincial government's recent Neighbourhoods Alive! Program, which requires that a local community planning process be used to match funding allocations to neighbourhood objectives (Walker 2006).

Leo draws on David Elkins' notion of "unbundled sovereignty" to have us imagine governance where governments are not stacked in a perfect hierarchy, jurisdiction in policy areas is shared, and a new political space is created (Magnusson 1996). Leo's (2006) concept of deep federalism relies on non-state actors at the local level as well, in a way that makes good sense when trying to understand the role of Aboriginal community aspirations in urban affairs. His inclusion of "other communities," with self-defined political boundaries is very important for understanding how urban Aboriginal political and social organizations fit into multilevel governance and deep federalism: "If we challenge ourselves to think in terms of unbundled sovereignty, and to emphasise process over hierarchy in our understanding of governance, our concept of community must extend beyond metropolitan areas and cities to neighbourhoods and other communities, defined according to the boundaries these communities implicitly draw by the way they understand themselves, not according to anybody's preconceived notion of how governance ought to look" (Leo 2006, 493).

Similar to Leo's idea about deep federalism as process, Katherine Graham and Evelyn Peters (2002) argue that a collaborative policy relationship between the federal government and local Aboriginal communities can contribute to better understanding and responsiveness in urban Aboriginal affairs. The current state of urban Aboriginal public policy is so complicated on the government side that it has created a jurisdictional maze, with all three levels of Canadian government, Aboriginal communities, and federal courts pointing in different directions on the question of policy and statutory responsibility for urban Aboriginal peoples (Graham and Peters 2002).[2] However, the need to make policy interventions in this field has led the three levels of Canadian government to engage in intergovernmental work in which jurisdictional issues are set aside in order to address issues of shared concern in practical ways (Hanselmann and Gibbins 2005).

According to Calvin Hanselmann and Roger Gibbins (2005), an effective urban Aboriginal "voice" is needed at the intergovernmental table in order to make effective policy. Their conclusions about how to create that voice are problematic because they centre on the notion of "a" self-defined urban Aboriginal voice that is broadly inclusive and can engage "authoritatively" with all levels of government "across a broad policy front." Such a (single) "voice" is neither likely nor desirable in our view: this chapter sheds light on why. However, we do agree that the general notion that intergovernmentalism in urban Aboriginal affairs requires greater Aboriginal community involvement than is occurring at present is accurate. Their work is also important for its identification of shortcomings in the present process of policy creation and its argument for the need to grapple with urban Aboriginal governance in the context of intergovernmentalism. This chapter builds upon the important work of Hanselmann and Gibbins and others in the field to get behind "voices" and "tables" to determine the suitability and effectiveness of different approaches to policy "co-production" with Aboriginal urban communities.

Co-production goes beyond co-operation (Nyland 1995); it goes beyond "voices at the table." It is a type of policy generation and implementation process where non-state actors are involved in the creation of policy instead of only its implementation (Brudney and England 1982; Casey and Dalton 2006). State and non-state actors work together from problem or issue identification, to priority setting, through to programs and services, and beyond. The state does not give away its responsibility for public policy making when it engages in co-production: instead, it proceeds on the basis that there is value in co-production and shared responsibility for defining issues and priorities accurately and in devoting public resources to the programs that result, which stand a high likelihood of achieving good outcomes. We use the principle of "policy co-production" as a normative principle for urban Aboriginal policy making. It may not always be quick and easy to identify the best co-production partners, however, and these partners will likely change from policy field to policy field in the same locale. Government officials have a responsibility to identify and engage appropriate Aboriginal leaders and experts in the policy process. The important question is to what extent the right *leadership* and *expertise* is present in the co-production of policy from agenda setting to problem definition, to production and decisions upon alternatives, to implementation.

The basis for arguing that urban Aboriginal policy needs to be co-produced with Aboriginal community leaders and experts is the principle of self-determination. Aboriginal communities and scholars have argued consistently that facilitating self-determination and forging relationships with meaningful outcomes based on mutual recognition and respect are central to strengthening relations between the state and Aboriginal society (Durie 2003; Green 2005; Hunter 2006; Maaka and Fleras 2005; Mercer 2003; Royal Commission on

Aboriginal Peoples 1996). The Aboriginal right to self-determination emanates from original occupancy, Treaties, and the constitutional arrangements made between settlers and Aboriginal peoples in order to create and reproduce the modern settler state. Self-determination in the Canadian context is not aimed at separation and isolation but rather is the right to the fulfillment of Aboriginal community aspirations in partnership with non-Aboriginal communities (and governments). The view of Frances Abele and Michael Prince (2006, 571) is important here: "To examine models of self-determination is to examine the beliefs of people who want it, the varying visions of those people regarding what it might be and should be, as well as the beliefs of those who reject or challenge a certain vision."

It is sufficiently well documented now that policy and programs co-produced with Aboriginal communities have better outcomes (for example, Minore and Katt 2007; Walker 2008a), largely because Aboriginal quality of life can be improved, arguably, only on Aboriginal peoples' own terms and not on pre-packaged Eurocentric terms (Salée, Newhouse, and Lévesque 2006). In our work, we have found that Aboriginal leaders and community members in urban areas are not focused on discovering ways to squeeze new urban *government structures* jurisdictionally into a territorial or juridical space somewhere between the municipal, provincial, and federal levels of the Canadian state. Rather, their interest seems to be in actively determining the course of affairs (for example, policy) as Aboriginal communities. Policy co-production at all stages of the policy process – if done with appropriate leaders and experts – can achieve this goal to a reasonable extent and has very little to do with territorially based jurisdictions of governance. In urban areas particularly, it becomes difficult and perhaps undesirable to try to fit the diversity of Aboriginal peoples into a territorial box (or boxes). Yet as Chris Andersen and Claude Denis (2003) point out, the land-based nation model – where a political community is delineated by drawing a territorial boundary around it – is the one that is privileged by settler governments in advancing Aboriginal political claims, even in urban areas.

Scholars have argued that the modern urban experience has created new "status-blind" multicultural Aboriginal political communities from which emanate aspirations for culturally appropriate policy and programming in urban areas (Barcham 2000; LaGrand 2002; Maaka 1994; Morgan 2006). It is also important to recognize, however, that in many cities in Canada Métis and First Nations groups wish to maintain specific political communities as well, based on shared history, culture, and land-bases in and around urban areas. For example, the Métis Nation and Treaty One Nations (Saulteaux Ojibwa, Swampy Cree, and others) were traditionally, that is, territorially, based in an area that included Winnipeg. Thus for many Aboriginal people the urban area is only part of the "homeplace" that also includes reserve and rural communities. It is important to add, however, the caution given by Evelyn Peters (2007) in her interpretation of how the Kelowna Accord might have been implemented, that urban First Nations and Métis organizations are not necessarily well linked to national Aboriginal organizations. This chapter, and some of our past work, shows that this caution applies to links with provincial First Nations and Métis organizations as well. For example, the urban strategy developed by the Assembly of Manitoba Chiefs in 2002 has not been implemented to any great extent, and research participants noted that it is low on the Assembly's list of priorities, given the higher priority of allocating scarce resources to reserve-based issues. National and provincial First Nations and Métis umbrella political organizations are not necessarily the most appropriate parties for policy co-production at the urban level.

Abele and Prince (2006, 588) make an interesting observation about discussions that occurred among the staff of the Royal Commission on Aboriginal Peoples (RCAP) concerning the nation-to-nation approach so prevalent in the final report, pointing out that for some, "at the level of *principle*, Commissioners were arguing for nation-to-nation; while at the level of *practicality*, they talked in terms of government-to-government." The concept of nation-to-nation relationships between Aboriginal peoples and the settler state is one that encompasses but is not strictly delineated by government structures. The idea of government-to-government is an instrumental and limiting approach to nation-to-nation relationships. It fixes the idea of Aboriginal peoples and communities as well as the aspirations of complex Aboriginal cultural identities that work through networks across space into well-bounded territorial and jurisdictional forms. This issue of principle versus practicality will be considered further in the conclusion but we suggest that the overarching principle of nation-to-nation and principles of mutual respect and recognition can comfortably guide practical approaches to urban Aboriginal policy that do not privilege land-bases or identities that are fixed in time and space.

This chapter argues that Aboriginal political and social organizations are being identified by governments as stakeholders for consultation on policy – usually late in the process – but are not really involved in co-production along all stages of the policy process. Aboriginal organizations are used heavily at the implementation stage, mainly to adjudicate proposals for funding. When included in consultations and in an advisory capacity during policy implementation, placation of many "voices" seems to be more important to governments than ensuring that there is some principled basis for including the right leaders and experts in the policy process at all stages.

Not all of the policies we examined in Manitoba are discussed in detail; however, their analysis has contributed to our conclusions. The policies (or policy sectors) discussed in detail are: 1) Aboriginal justice (Winnipeg), 2) municipal Aboriginal policy initiatives (Winnipeg, Brandon, Thompson), 3) multilevel urban policy (Winnipeg Partnership Agreement – Aboriginal Participation component), 4) Urban Aboriginal Strategy (Winnipeg, Thompson), 5) Winnipeg Housing and Homelessness Initiative (Aboriginal components from all levels of government), 6) Urban Multipurpose Aboriginal Youth Centre Initiative (Winnipeg, Thompson, Brandon), and 7) urban reserves (Thompson, Swan River). These policies were chosen because they allow us to best convey the main themes that were identified in the larger analysis.

The research methods employed in our study involve a combined analysis of policy-related documents and notes from one-to-one interviews with forty-two people across the four selected research sites in addition to notes from four group interviews. The general questions designed for comparability across policy fields in Canada were adapted so that the most applicable questions were asked of the following three types of participants: 1) those involved with Aboriginal political organizations, 2) those involved with Aboriginal service organizations, and 3) federal, provincial, and municipal officials and politicians. Several interviews were conducted with Aboriginal community leaders who have years of experience in a variety of policy fields in the province and are widely respected as mediums for community leadership.

After a discussion of our four research sites, the subsequent sections examine policy processes in seven fields and answer questions about who is making the policy, the nature of intergovernmental relations with Aboriginal political and service organizations, and how these policies are evaluated. We conclude with a discussion of how to approach policy co-production in ways that further self-determination and partnership at all stages of the policy-making process.

RESEARCH SITES

Four communities were chosen for our analysis of urban Aboriginal policy: the cities of Winnipeg, Thompson, and Brandon, and the Town of Swan River. They were chosen because they varied in size, location, and Treaty areas; they were generally felt to represent much of the range of likely urban Aboriginal policy production issues in the province. Winnipeg is the provincial capital, is located within the Treaty One area, and is the historic centre of the Métis Nation's territory. Brandon is located in the Treaty Two area and lies near the border with Treaty One territory. Swan River is in Treaty Four and Thompson in Treaty Five territory. All four communities have Métis communities represented by local councils. The Métis Nation played a central role in negotiating the *Manitoba Act* of 1870 and bringing the new Province of Manitoba into confederation.

According to the 2006 census, 15 per cent of Canada's Aboriginal identity population (175,395 people) resides in Manitoba. First Nations comprise 100,645 of that population, Métis 71,805, and 250 self-identify as Inuit (Statistics Canada 2008). Winnipeg has Canada's largest urban Aboriginal community with a combined population of 68,380 (roughly 10% of the city's total population). Aboriginal peoples make up 36% of Thompson's population (4,930 individuals). Close to 4,000 self-identifying Aboriginal people (10% of the city's population) live in Brandon.

This numerical snapshot masks the true diversity of Aboriginal communities in Manitoba. For example, there are approximately sixty-four First Nations located across the province (Assembly of Manitoba Chiefs 2008); seven Aboriginal languages are being spoken in Manitoba: Ojibway, Cree, Dene, Michif, Dakota, Oji-Cree, and Inuktitut (Aboriginal Languages of Manitoba Inc. 2008). This diversity is also reflected in Manitoba's urban areas where, in addition to the provincial diversity, there is a cosmopolitan diversity that includes many Aboriginal peoples from other traditional territories across Canada and around the world.

All four study communities have Aboriginal political and service organizations, including at the least a Métis local, a Friendship Centre, and an Aboriginal housing organization. In Winnipeg, there are many more such organizations; they range in programs and services from Aboriginal culture and spirituality to economic development, education to employment services and youth, elder, and family services. Evelyn Peters (2005) provides a historical contextualization of the evolution of Aboriginal community-based organizations in Winnipeg and the impact this evolution has had on the development of Aboriginal communities in this city. In addition to these organizations, Winnipeg provides a rare example – beyond the frequent presence of Friendship Centres in communities across Canada – of a city that has seen the development of a political organization with elected officials that specifically advocates for the interests of Aboriginal peoples (that is, First Nations, Métis, and Inuit). This political organization is called the Aboriginal Council of Winnipeg and was formed in 1990.

1 Aboriginal Justice – Winnipeg

Onashowewin Inc. is an alternative measures program serving Aboriginal peoples in Winnipeg that was started by Manitoba Justice, sponsored by the Aboriginal Council of Winnipeg and Southern Chiefs Organization, and governed by an Aboriginal board of directors.[3] Onashowewin seeks to apply principles of restorative justice to its alternative measures programs, namely, values of responsibility, inclusiveness, openness, trust, hope, and healing (Cormier 2002). Offenders are referred from the Crown Attorney's office to Onashowewin after being charged, but the individual must choose to participate. Offenders must take responsibility for their crime and work, through any of a number of programs (for example, Healthy Decision Program, Theft Under $5,000 Program, Auto Theft Program), at making positive changes in their lives and repairing some of the harm done to others.

The programs and staff at Onashowewin are funded through two separate annual contribution agreements, one with Manitoba Justice (Community Restorative Justice Program) and one with Justice Canada (Aboriginal Justice Directorate). Programs have been designed by Onashowewin staff in consultation with Aboriginal community members and Manitoba Justice. The objectives addressed by the programs have been largely prescribed by Manitoba Justice. Some program ideas that the staff felt would be particularly relevant to Aboriginal community restorative justice have not been among the programs endorsed by funders and are therefore not delivered. One example given by a participant was an idea for a program designed to help parents develop their roles in preventing crime among youth. It was this attempt by the board and staff to develop future programming outside the prescribed alternative measures objectives of Manitoba Justice that (at least in some part) prompted Manitoba Justice to take over governance of the organization directly.

In late 2007, the board resigned and Manitoba Justice assumed governance. As one participant put it, Onashowewin had been acting as an arm of the Prosecutions Service Division at Manitoba Justice to implement alternative measures to the traditional court system for Aboriginal offenders. The Aboriginal board of directors appears to have been seen not as an autonomous governance mechanism that set direction for the organization but as a means used by Manitoba Justice to situate the alternative measures program outside its offices and within the community.

One of the services that Onashowewin had hoped to take on was based on Section 718.2(e) of the Criminal Code as considered in the case of *R v. Gladue* (1999) where the Supreme Court noted that the incarceration rate of adult offenders in Canada was higher than in most western nations and this was particularly true for Aboriginal peoples. The Court emphasized that the purpose of 718.2(e) was to reduce this rate of imprisonment and spoke of the need to use restorative justice approaches in sentencing (not only Aboriginal sentencing but especially with respect to this group), even with respect to some violent offenses. Another case in 2000, *R v. Wells*, further encouraged the application of this section of the Criminal Code to restorative justice. In Manitoba, a "Gladue-Wells report" is prepared by order of a presiding judge. The report considers alternatives to incarceration given an offender's particular individual and community circumstances. Consideration of a Gladue-Wells report by the Court is a right, but the offender has to request it. At the moment Probation Services produces the report in conjunction with a pre-sentence report. Producing these reports, a central part of Aboriginal community objectives for strengthening restorative justice, was rejected by Manitoba Justice as a role for Onashowewin.

The Aboriginal Council of Winnipeg maintains a Justice and Human Rights portfolio and, in that capacity, hosted a Winnipeg urban Aboriginal community justice forum in 2006. The two-day community workshop was "an opportunity for members of the legal profession, Aboriginal political leaders, Elders, youth and citizens to dialogue on the important questions of how the Aboriginal community in Winnipeg can work within the justice system and courts in Manitoba to identify holistic ways to deal with urban Aboriginal crime in accordance with the values and beliefs of the urban Aboriginal community" (Aboriginal Council of Winnipeg 2007a).

The 2007–08 Work Plan of the Aboriginal Council of Winnipeg includes developing a proposal for creating justice initiatives that build on the 2006 forum, including an Aboriginal offender court report-writing service and an Aboriginal offender sentencing manual for use in trial courts (Aboriginal Council of Winnipeg 2007b). The court report-writing service would take the production of Gladue-Wells reports, for example, out of the Probation Services department. Under the stewardship of an Aboriginal Justice Committee, the Aboriginal Council of Winnipeg seeks to facilitate the creation of a sentencing manual that can assist trial judges in sentencing Aboriginal offenders in a manner that is based on traditional values and common threads within Aboriginal cultures in Manitoba in general and Winnipeg.

It appears that Manitoba Justice set the agenda for Onashowewin. There was co-production with Onashowewin staff of program alternatives, but decisions about which ones were to be implemented resided with Manitoba Justice, with Onashowewin responsible for actual implementation. Aboriginal social and political forces – organized through the Aboriginal Council of Winnipeg as part of its continued advocacy work – have articulated the need to expand the role for a community-based Aboriginal justice organization in the policy process. Upon examination, Onashowewin has not gone far enough – or been permitted to go far enough – to co-produce programs that would further community self-determination in the justice sector. On this basis, any benefits that may emanate from Onashowewin programs might be considered sub-optimal given the will and capacity in the Aboriginal community to work with Manitoba Justice at all levels of the policy process, not simply to implement Manitoba Justice policy under the pretence of community self-determination by an Aboriginal board and staff. It will be interesting to follow the progress of justice initiatives emanating from the Aboriginal Council of Winnipeg, which seems to be focusing on areas of justice most important to Aboriginal community members under the Criminal Code. Will Manitoba Justice support the priorities coming from the Aboriginal community and engage in policy co-production?

2 Municipal Aboriginal Policy – Winnipeg, Brandon, and Thompson

In 2003, the City of Winnipeg launched what was at the time the most ambitious Canadian municipal policy aimed at strengthening the working relationship between City Hall and Aboriginal urban communities. It was led by Councillors Dan Vandal (Métis) and Jenny Gerbasi and former mayor Glenn Murray. Murray was known for being an activist mayor; for example, during his term in office he had proceeded with an ambitious municipal housing policy and program and led the development of First Steps: Municipal Aboriginal Pathways (MAP). MAP "defines a policy framework – based on a number of key principles – to open the door to a new era of co-operation between the City and Winnipeg's Aboriginal community" (City of Winnipeg 2003, 1). The city's principal long-range policy and decision-making document, Plan Winnipeg 2020 Vision, included a policy statement to "promote self-reliant Aboriginal communities." MAP was launched as a secondary plan to guide Council activities in achieving the objective articulated in Plan Winnipeg 2020 Vision. There were five policy platforms or "Pathways" within MAP: 1) Employment, 2) Economic Development, 3) Safety, 4) Quality of Life, and 5) Outreach and Education. Each pathway had three "strategic initiatives" aligned with it and specific action plans were supposed to be developed by responsible departments shortly after the release of MAP. Action planning would also have involved developing implementation mechanisms, resourcing strategies, and timelines to targets.

Glenn Murray resigned as mayor in 2004 in order to run as a Liberal candidate in the federal election, not long after Council had unanimously adopted MAP in 2003. Councillor Vandal also resigned in order to run for mayor. Neither of these men, who had been popular in their previous positions, was successful in winning their bid to move up the political ladder. (Vandal was re-elected as a councillor, however, in 2006). This change in leadership halted progress on implementing MAP. The new mayor, Sam Katz, has not advanced the MAP project and has treated it as "the former mayor's baby," not one to which he wished to attend. In short, MAP became moribund shortly after it was born. However, it is still instructive to examine the ways in which the policy document was formulated and the lessons it offers for creating municipal policy to improve working relations with Aboriginal communities.

When Council instructed staff to begin work on MAP, an early issue for municipal officials was the extent to which consultation with Aboriginal communities should occur and at what time in the policy production process. One scenario considered was consultation with Aboriginal stakeholders in order to learn what their priorities were. It was determined, however, that this procedure could lead to a number of requests for intervention with which the municipal government would be ill-equipped to deal (that is, those involving policy sectors that are firmly within provincial and federal spheres of responsibility). Instead, the five pathways and the strategic initiatives were drafted in-house and taken to the Aboriginal community for feedback. Mayor Murray and Councillors Gerbasi and Vandal met with roughly 350 Aboriginal and non-Aboriginal community members at an inner city high school to present the draft and receive input. Reviews were mixed. While the concept of creating a working partnership between City Council and the Aboriginal communities was well received, the pathways and strategic initiatives outlined fell short of community expectations. To this criticism, the two councillors and the mayor replied that their work represented the first steps to a longer-term constructive partnership. Implementing MAP would involve using municipal programming and resources to address some areas, but would rely on partnerships with other levels of government to realize others. That partnership with other governments would come in the form of the Winnipeg Partnership Agreement (to be discussed later), which was brought into effect shortly after MAP was released.

One of the effects of MAP was raised expectations of what was possible in municipal-Aboriginal policy. The greatest regret of one of the key architects of MAP was that city administrators opted to produce the policy first and then pursue the funding from Council as a second step toward implementation. With the change in leadership, that crucial second step was never taken. Municipal investment in Aboriginal policy in Winnipeg has been deferred every year since

2004 and was deferred again in 2007 for consideration in the 2008 budget process.

Given that one of the lasting effects of MAP has been symbolic in the sense that it signals what kind of policy orientation is possible with Aboriginal communities, it is unfortunate that the process of formulating MAP was not more carefully contrived. The logic of deciding in-house what strategic initiatives would be possible and then taking those out to the community was a major flaw, and even less justifiable given that no funding was ultimately attached for implementation. Given the lack of resources to implement MAP, the project could still have made a valuable contribution if there had been an exemplary process of relationship building for long-term collaborative partnership between City Hall and the Aboriginal communities. One participant noted that the main political organizations in Winnipeg – including the Aboriginal Council of Winnipeg, Manitoba Métis Federation, and Assembly of Manitoba Chiefs – were indeed parties to a meeting with the mayor and councillors early in the MAP process, but inter-group conflict precluded the building of significant working relationships.

A positive appraisal of MAP came from an Aboriginal community expert working in the sport and recreation field. He argued that the existence of MAP gave his organization "a place to stand" when approaching City Council for assistance with sporting venues and other in-kind support. While this is a positive outcome, it could just as well be achieved by using the policy statement in Plan Winnipeg 2020 Vision to "promote self-reliant Aboriginal communities." The creation of a full secondary plan with specific principles and implementation objectives cannot be a legitimate basis for "opening the door to a new era of co-operation between the City and Winnipeg's Aboriginal community" if the Aboriginal community is not a full co-producer.

In the consultations carried out during this research, many Aboriginal leaders either did not remember MAP or noted that it sounded familiar but could not remember any specific information about it. In their minds, perhaps, MAP is vaguely recalled as a public meeting at a high school that did not translate into much on the ground. Had the MAP process instead focused first on creating a strong collaborative partnership with Aboriginal leaders based on mutual respect and driven by a desire to articulate shared objectives, it might have had a lasting impact. The approach taken by the city was a well-intentioned attempt to achieve a set of its goals through buy-in and participation by the Aboriginal communities. But, as one academic commentator (Belanger 2005) noted, although the consultation at the high school included about 350 people, it was not a deliberate effort to engage the Aboriginal community leadership as collaborative partners. It was a town hall meeting much like any other. It is easy now to look back on the process and criticize it, but it remains an initiative that was cutting edge at that time for municipal government and owed a lot to an activist mayor and two councillors who were eager to try new ways of working constructively with Aboriginal communities.

Quite different in its approach from Winnipeg, the City of Brandon's Community Strategic Plan (CSP) (City of Brandon 2006) does not refer to its relationship with Aboriginal communities or refer to Aboriginal peoples in its action planning. Brandon's CSP is described as the local community's "vision for the future of the city." This vision appears to neglect entirely, however, a significant portion of the local population, namely, the Aboriginal peoples. Indeed, the absence of the words "First Nation," "Métis," and "Aboriginal" from the document is striking, particularly given that specific ethnic groups and holidays are mentioned in the Cultural Diversity section. The City of Brandon, in its CSP, appears to make no differentiation between its Aboriginal citizens and any other new immigrants to the city. Such a position fundamentally denies the unique history of Aboriginal peoples in the settlement and contemporary life of Brandon. In this sense, by ignoring Aboriginal policy entirely, the City of Brandon makes a strong policy statement, one that places Aboriginal peoples as a nondescript minority group. Even this status is not articulated, however, in the CSP. For several interview participants, the reason for the policy inaction in the City of Brandon is an underlying racism that is perceived to be a significant barrier to bringing together Aboriginal and urban affairs. Certainly, the absence of Aboriginal-specific policy, especially in a major policy document such as the CSP, is a troubling statement about the city's relationship with urban Aboriginal peoples.

The City of Thompson appears to place greater emphasis than Brandon on its relationship with its Aboriginal residents. The past two mayors of Thompson have made significant efforts to build a strong relationship with local Aboriginal communities and surrounding First Nations. This is also reflected in the priority that the former mayor placed on including Aboriginal representatives on municipal policy committees. Still, according to interview participants, the burden seems to be on Aboriginal organizations to seek accommodation and involvement in existing policy arrangements, rather than participating as co-producers in the creation of new policy arrangements. Policy co-production with Aboriginal social and political forces did not occur in Winnipeg with MAP, and it appears not to have occurred to any great extent in Thompson, given the nature of its policy interface with Aboriginal urban communities.

3 Winnipeg Partnership Agreement – Component I, Aboriginal Participation

Winnipeg has a long history of tripartite agreements to combat economic decline in its inner city. In the 1980s and early 1990s there were two tripartite Winnipeg Core Area Initiatives. From the mid-1990s to the new millennium, the Winnipeg Development Agreement continued in similar style to bring resources and leadership from all levels of government to bear on inner city economic and social development in a relatively seamless intergovernmental fashion. Leo (2006) uses some of these initiatives as examples of what he terms "deep federalism" and "unbundling sovereignty." In 2004, the governments of Canada, Manitoba, and Winnipeg entered into another tripartite agreement, the Winnipeg Partnership Agreement (WPA), to continue this tradition until 2009. While all past inner city development agreements interacted in some way with the Aboriginal communities, the WPA is the most ambitious in its Aboriginal advisory mechanism and its focus on Aboriginal programming as one of four components of the agreement. The components of the WPA are 1) Aboriginal Participation, 2) Building Sustainable Neighbourhoods, 3) Downtown Renewal, and 4) Supporting Technology and Innovation. The overall goal of this combination of initiatives and coordinated government investment is to improve economic prosperity and quality of life in Winnipeg. Each government has committed funding up to $25 million over the five-year duration of WPA. Much of the money promised by different governments is not "new money," however, but is a redirection of existing funding envelopes for Aboriginal programs (Leo et al. 2007).

The first component – Aboriginal Participation – was launched in 2003 at the same time the Urban Aboriginal Strategy (UAS) pilot

program (discussed later) was beginning in Winnipeg. In effect, the
UAS pilot program served as the federal contribution to the Aboriginal Participation component of WPA. A motion approved by City
Council in 2004 to include $1.4 million in the 2005 budget process
by the City of Winnipeg for Component 1 has yet to be approved
by the mayor and Executive Policy Council. From year to year it has
been deferred to subsequent budget years. The Province of Manitoba has, however, invested in the Aboriginal Participation component and is largely responsible for the presence of this component in
the WPA.

The genesis of the WPA is linked to a combination of factors,
including the lineage of past tripartite programs, their success in
unbundling sovereignty, and the achievement of results in a shared
political space. There is a shared appreciation among governments
that downtown Winnipeg is an area that requires sustained public
investment in economic and community development. Senior staff in
all governments have experience working together in Winnipeg with
tripartite models and, as the prior Winnipeg Development Agreement wound down in 2001, there was considerable pressure from
community groups to continue investing in the city core. For our
purposes, the genesis of the Aboriginal Participation component is
of the greatest interest.

The (Manitoba) minister for Aboriginal and northern affairs, Eric
Robinson, was lobbied to support an urban Aboriginal strategy for
Winnipeg. According to a senior government official involved in the
process, Robinson was supportive but interactions between Aboriginal political organizations in Winnipeg were divisive and he felt
that he could not work with them together constructively. At the
same time, negotiations were underway between governments to
create the WPA. This was seen by Aboriginal and Northern Affairs as
an opportunity to include an Aboriginal component in the WPA, and,
fortuitously, the federal government was beginning to pilot its Urban
Aboriginal Strategy in Winnipeg at that time.

Robinson opted to work with his senior officials instead of with
the leadership of Aboriginal political organizations – the Manitoba
Métis Federation, the Assembly of Manitoba Chiefs, the Aboriginal
Council of Winnipeg, and the Mother of Red Nations Women's
Council of Manitoba – to create the Aboriginal Participation com-
ponent of WPA. It was not co-produced with Aboriginal leaders.
Today, however, an Aboriginal Partnership Committee – composed

of representatives from the Assembly of Manitoba Chiefs, Manitoba Métis Federation, Aboriginal Council of Winnipeg, Mother of Red Nations, five Aboriginal community members at large (mostly from Aboriginal community-based organizations), two Aboriginal youth, two representatives from the Aboriginal business community, representatives from the three governments, the United Way, the Winnipeg Foundation, and Aboriginal Elders (non-voting) – does make recommendations on implementing the policy/program. Decisions under the Aboriginal Participation component of the WPA start with the Aboriginal Partnership Committee (APC), which advises the WPA Management Committee (made up of senior government officials), which in turn takes direction from the Policy Committee (made up of politicians from all three governments). Proposals for program and project funding under the Aboriginal Participation component are reviewed by the APC, and the committee's recommendations are taken under advisement by the Management Committee.

At the outset, Aboriginal political organizations were opposed to the APC model because they felt that they should be able to administer a portion of the Aboriginal Participation component resources on behalf of their peoples. Further, the APC includes community members at large (often from community-based Aboriginal service organizations), government officials, and representatives from philanthropic organizations alongside Aboriginal political leaders. Once it was determined that the APC would be the mechanism for Aboriginal input into decision making, the APC felt it should have authority to make binding recommendations on funding decisions to the Management Committee. The APC is a compromise that responds to both the desire to initiate concerted activity in urban Aboriginal affairs and the need to create a governance mechanism that is perceived by decision makers as able to circumvent what was previously taken as prohibitive conflict between Aboriginal political organizations.

The Aboriginal Participation component of the WPA represents concepts of deep federalism. However, it does not have the tools to engage Aboriginal communities in a process of policy co-production that unbundles sovereignty among governments and incorporates communities according to the way they understand themselves and not according to preconceived notions of how governance should look (Leo 2006). The process for administering the Aboriginal Participation component was created by the provincial and federal governments without the involvement of Aboriginal communities.

The designated places on the Aboriginal Partnership Committee for political organizations, community members, and other business and non-Aboriginal philanthropic organizations do not emanate from consultation with the Aboriginal community. If consultation had occurred beyond initial discussions with Aboriginal political organizations, the decision-making/advisory mechanism would have perhaps been different: the presence of Aboriginal political organizations might have been reduced and the presence of policy and program experts from among the many Aboriginal community-based organizations in Winnipeg might have been increased. On the other hand, perhaps the committee composition would have been the same. In the following discussion of the Urban Multipurpose Aboriginal Youth Centre program, the concept of community nomination is discussed as a promising method for composing policy committees.

4 Urban Aboriginal Strategy – Winnipeg and Thompson

The Urban Aboriginal Strategy (UAS) was started in 1998 when pressure was placed upon government by senior (western) federal ministers concerned with the widening disparity in socio-economic circumstances between Aboriginal and non-Aboriginal urban residents. This urban "problem" was seen as a significant challenge to social cohesion in urban centres like Winnipeg, Regina, and especially Saskatoon. The federal view was that the problem should be addressed by coordinating its program investment in urban Aboriginal affairs with willing provinces and municipalities in order to maximize impact and to articulate that it "could and should not take full responsibility for issues facing urban Aboriginal people" (Privy Council Office 2002, 11, as cited in Walker 2005).

An earlier study (Walker 2005) examined the rationale for the UAS and its function of addressing homelessness in Winnipeg. Internal documents and interviews with UAS staff and community stakeholders pointed out that the implementation of UAS did not engage with Aboriginal urban rights to self-determination or self-government and did not further the realization of those goals. The UAS is a program driven by the goals of improving social cohesion and closing socio-economic gaps. Neither of these goals is incompatible with self-determination. Indeed, Aboriginal communities and organizations in urban areas may feel that the UAS facilitates new programming responsive to self-directed community goals.

However, facilitating mechanisms of Aboriginal self-determination is not an articulated goal of UAS. Consider this excerpt from an internal document:

> Policy differentiation on the basis of Aboriginality should be positioned not as the granting of extra rights and entitlements, but more the allocation of additional resources to certain groups of disadvantaged people on the basis of socio-economic and spatial criteria to assure equal access to basic opportunities and services enjoyed by all. This leads to a much more philosophical question in terms of the future treatment of Canada's urban Aboriginal population when the socio-economic chasm between Aboriginal and non-Aboriginal people has disappeared, that is, will it be necessary or preferable to continue policy differentiation on the basis of one's Aboriginality? (Privy Council Office 2002, 11, as cited in Walker 2005)

The federal budget in 2003 allocated funding for the UAS pilot project in eight urban centres, mostly in western Canada. Pilots ran from 2004/05 until the end of March 2007. As noted earlier, the Urban Aboriginal Strategy pilot project in Winnipeg was the first and most substantial component of the federal government's investment in the Aboriginal Participation component of the WPA. The Aboriginal Partnership Committee, started under the WPA as an advisory body, doubled as the *decision-making* body for UAS in Winnipeg, with some subtle differences. During the pilot project, the APC would make recommendations to the WPA Management Committee. Post-March 2007, with the pilot phase for UAS complete, the APC has become the decision-making body that adjudicates which proposals under the UAS in Winnipeg receive funding. Due diligence is conducted by federal government officials on project proposals to determine financial feasibility and compliance with national priorities, and a report accompanies the application to the APC, which then makes its decision.

The Winnipeg UAS has funded over sixty projects since 2004/05, including an urban Aboriginal housing planning process, support for school children and families, and programs addressing abuse against women. Under the pilot phase, the APC had little guidance about federal priorities and could recommend funding for a wide variety of project proposals. In the new phase, the federal government has articulated a set of national priorities focused on improving life skills, employment skills, entrepreneurship, and the situation of Aboriginal women, children, and families. As officials in Winnipeg noted, however, the national priorities are sufficiently broad that the Winnipeg community can still fit most project proposals within them. Project applications, however, outstrip available funds. For example, in 2005/06 it was estimated that there were almost three times more project proposals than the funding pool could accommodate.

Our examination of the UAS administration and implementation processes in Thompson showed that a mix of Aboriginal political and service organizations and representatives from all three levels of government have been appointed to the UAS local committee. The process of determining which groups were represented on or excluded from the local committee was described by interview participants as politically charged. Questions remain about how an organization is determined to be a legitimate voice for the urban Aboriginal population. The groups involved in the UAS local committee decide what issues are addressed through the program allocations. With the federal and provincial governments being the primary funders for urban Aboriginal policy and programs, and given that they hold seats on the UAS local committee, interview participants suggested that the federal and provincial funders were able to exert indirect control by their presence at the meetings where decisions were being made on how funding would be used at the local level.

The UAS is not structured on the principle of self-determination, yet perhaps it works to this end, given that federal parameters seem to be broad enough that communities can follow their own objectives in the use of funding. It is unclear to us to what extent Aboriginal organizations were originally involved in setting an agenda in urban affairs that government ministers then helped advance, ending with the creation of UAS. It appears, though, that within the UAS, Aboriginal selection committees do make near-binding decisions (the minister can always refuse a proposal) and in a sense are co-producing priorities at the local level within broad federal parameters (a characteristic of deep federalism), deciding on alternatives, and contributing to policy implementation. Aboriginal political and social organizations are certainly involved. A question returned to in the conclusion of this chapter is: what constitutes an appropriate technique for selecting the Aboriginal decision-making body?

5 Winnipeg Housing and Homelessness Initiative

The federal government's Urban Aboriginal Homelessness (UAH) component of the National Homelessness Initiative, implemented alongside the mainstream Supporting Communities Partnerships Initiative (SCPI) in Winnipeg, has been discussed in detail elsewhere (Walker 2005). It is worth discussing three results from this earlier study. The first is a criticism of the community planning process: it did not originally involve Aboriginal leaders in Winnipeg and this exclusion was met with concerted criticism from the Aboriginal community. As a corrective measure, a new supplement to the SCPI community plan was derived with the guidance of the Aboriginal Reference Group on Homelessness and Housing, a group created for this particular planning purpose. The review process for proposals under the UAH involved adjudication by the same non-Aboriginal committee (although there were some Aboriginal members) that dealt with proposals under SCPI. There was no restriction in the guidelines for administering the UAH against non-Aboriginal organizations drawing on the funds for projects that targeted Aboriginal people. With two main program criteria being a demonstration of project "sustainability" and "partnerships," organizations such as faith-based housing groups and the Salvation Army were able to meet criteria for funding most easily. Aboriginal organizations succeeded in getting proposals funded as well, but were never particularly comfortable with the fact that the UAH was not exclusively for Aboriginal organizations. Further, the large Aboriginal political organizations (for example, Assembly of Manitoba Chiefs, Manitoba Métis Federation) were disappointed early on that the UAH funding for Winnipeg was not divided up among their organizations to be administered through their own proposal selection committees.

The most recent recalibrations of the federal government's National Homelessness Initiative and SCPI-type programming are the Homelessness Partnering Strategy (HPS) and Homelessness Partnership Initiative (HPI). Under the HPI there is a designated Aboriginal component, which is similar in intent to the former UAH. (The Conservative government has diminished funding overall for homelessness programming, so there is little to discuss about the HPS).

In urban centres, one of two models for administering HPI funding is chosen to reflect what seems most effective given the local context. One model engages a "community entity" for delivering the HPI and the second model uses a "shared delivery" approach, where government and community stakeholders carry out the delivery together. In Vancouver, for example, Lu'ma Native Housing Society acts as a community entity. The community entity model applies in Edmonton as well. In Winnipeg, "the diversity of leadership" in the urban Aboriginal community is the rationale provided by Human Resources and Skills Development Canada (HRSDC) for employing the shared delivery model rather than appointing an Aboriginal organization or coalition of organizations to act as the community entity.

A Community Advisory Board makes recommendations on the selection of project proposals. Aboriginal stakeholders comprise roughly fifty per cent of the board's membership. The board advises on all project proposals, Aboriginal and non-Aboriginal. Thirty-five per cent of members are appointed (for example, municipal and provincial officials) and sixty-five per cent are elected by a Selection Committee chosen by HRSDC, following an open call to community members to invite applicants to express their interest and present their qualifications. This election process is based on the perceived success by government officials of the model used by the UAS/Winnipeg Partnership Agreement's Aboriginal Partnership Committee. HRSDC anticipates that the single community homelessness plan and advisory board will be sufficient to administer both the mainstream and Aboriginal portions of NHI funding. As under the UAH previously, non-Aboriginal organizations can apply for resources under the Aboriginal-specific funding envelope provided that the project targets that clientele. Process, according to an interview participant from government, is seen as paramount. In other words, if the community planning process is sound and the Community Advisory Board members are selected with diligence by the HRSDC-appointed Selection Committee, then the projects selected for funding will comply with (Aboriginal and non-Aboriginal) community needs and aspirations.

An official commented that it was intriguing that the HRSDC's Aboriginal Human Resources Development Agreement contracts were administered by the Assembly of Manitoba Chiefs, Manitoba Métis Federation, and the Centre for Aboriginal Human Resource Development, even though that model of self-management was not being used for the Aboriginal Communities portion of the HPI. It is still early to comment on how well the planning and advisory model for HPI will work.

Manitoba Family Services and Housing administers the housing portfolio developed under the discontinued federal Urban Native Housing Program and the Off-Reserve Aboriginal Housing Trust (AHT) money provided by the federal government. It is also responsible for Aboriginal housing policy development for urban, rural, and northern Aboriginal peoples in the province. It has an advisory committee to help administer the AHT funds, which is composed of a variety of political and service stakeholders and includes the Manitoba Urban Native Housing Association (MUNHA), an organization representing urban native housing organizations from across the province. The provincial government develops and implements policy with guidance from an advisory board made up of political and service organizations. Many of MUNHA's recommendations on program parameters under which the AHT resources are administered were adopted by the Province and discussed at a consultation with the AHT advisory committee. There appears to be a strong connection between recommendations from a housing planning exercise conducted by MUNHA last year and the program parameters selected by the province for allocation of the AHT funds.

The City of Winnipeg's Aboriginal Housing Program was officially launched in 2006 and explicitly pointed to the Municipal Aboriginal Pathways policy as its basis. On the Quality of Life Pathway, Aboriginal housing is noted as a specific strategic initiative. As mentioned earlier, MAP was never really implemented and the Aboriginal Housing Program is held up as one exception. In addition to the $160,000 that goes to each of the five designated Housing Improvement Zone neighbourhoods per year – which are administered on advice from neighbourhood associations and give effect to the Winnipeg Housing Policy and Implementation Framework – $200,000 is also designated to Aboriginal housing and administered on advice from MUNHA. The Aboriginal allocation can be used in any part of the city and is not confined to specific neighbourhoods. Although it draws on a small funding pool, the Aboriginal Housing Program is the most flexible of any of the government housing programs and is popular among Aboriginal housing organizations for doing things such as repairing existing units whose subsidy agreements with the federal government have elapsed or constructing landscaping and fencing for children's play areas.

The lineage of the Aboriginal Housing Program dates to 2004, when money from the municipal budget was left over and allocated to Aboriginal housing. In 2005, money was allocated in the budget for Aboriginal housing, although without a program framework. In 2006, a municipal housing official designed the program framework and submitted it to municipal colleagues and MUNHA for comment before having it ratified by Council. Officially, MAP is used as the policy basis for engaging in a specific Aboriginal Housing Program, something that could otherwise seem out of place for a municipal program.

At the provincial and municipal levels, Aboriginal housing organizations have had a comparatively direct role in the housing policy-making process, from agenda setting through to implementation. Co-production of policy seems most fruitful in sector-specific areas like housing if it involves Aboriginal community experts. It is in some ways remarkable that the city applied this approach to its Aboriginal housing program and consulted with Aboriginal housing organizations (through MUNHA) on the framework and implementation, but did not engage Aboriginal communities to the same extent in its production of MAP.

6 Urban Multipurpose Aboriginal Youth Centre Initiative – Winnipeg, Thompson, and Brandon

Aboriginal affairs programming at Canadian Heritage seeks to strengthen Aboriginal cultural identities as an important part of Canadian diversity. The Urban Multipurpose Aboriginal Youth Centre (UMAYC) program is directed at supporting the development of cultural strength and leadership among the growing population of Aboriginal urban youth. It is administered differently across Canada because it is often delivered through a third-party agreement with the National Association of Friendship Centres. However, in the largest urban centres across Manitoba, Saskatchewan, and Alberta, including Winnipeg, it is administered directly by Canadian Heritage. This direct funding of UMAYC is the result of a political decision attributed to Ralph Goodale, former Liberal cabinet minister in the Prairie regions. He determined that Friendship Centres were not an appropriate representative body within Aboriginal urban communities in large Prairie cities where First Nations, Métis, and urban Aboriginal political and service constituencies were more varied. Whether delivered by Friendship Centres or Canadian Heritage, decision making on program priorities and project proposals is done with an Aboriginal Youth Advisory Committee (AYAC).

There are ten members on the AYAC in Winnipeg, each of whom sits for a two-year term. Membership includes two Canadian Heritage program officers. The other eight members are selected by a general call for nominations through Aboriginal organizations, schools, and universities. In selecting the committee members from the nominees, Canadian Heritage tries to strike a balance by gender and by Aboriginal identity (that is, Métis and First Nations peoples). AYAC members represent Aboriginal youth while they sit on the AYAC, not Aboriginal political organizations. Participants described one of the major differences between the AYAC and the Aboriginal Partnership Committee (advisory for WPA; decision-making for UAS) as being that the AYAC works well as a group of informed Aboriginal youth, while the latter is still weighted more heavily towards Aboriginal political organization representation than perhaps it otherwise would be, had community nominations been used to select committee members.

Canadian Heritage officers defer to the AYAC for appraisal of community-relevance and the ranking of project proposals, but will not accept recommendations for projects where the financial risk or budget seem problematic. There are more project applications in a year than can be funded, but the number of applicants has gone down over time as the application process has become more rigorous and difficult for community organizations to complete. Most funded projects in a given year are repeats from previous funding cycles (roughly 95 per cent). In other words, it becomes easier to maintain funding once a track record is established and the program shows some success. Sustainability through funding partnerships is not a criterion of UMAYC, and funded programs can thrive or fold from year to year based on funding from Canadian Heritage. While organizations applying to UMAYC may also apply elsewhere in government for additional resources, UMAYC does not cost-share its project funding with other levels of government or other federal departments.

Three examples of programs perceived to be successful that have received a significant proportion of their funding from UMAYC are 1) Winnipeg Aboriginal Sport Achievement Centre run by the Winnipeg Aboriginal Sport and Recreation Association, 2) Big HART

(Heritage, Arts, and Recording Technology) program run by the Winnipeg Métis Association (service delivery arm of the Manitoba Métis Federation Winnipeg local), and 3) Growing Together – Youth Helping Youth Mentorship program run by Ma Mawi Wi Chi Itata Centre (an organization that provides culturally relevant supportive programs and services to Aboriginal families).

In Thompson and Brandon, the UMAYC is administered through the Ma-Mow-We-Tak and Brandon Friendship Centres respectively. The AYAC that reviews proposals for communities outside Winnipeg is composed of Aboriginal youth selected from communities across Manitoba, who gather periodically to adjudicate proposals from across the province as "blindly" as possible. While UMAYC funding is from the federal government, it is controlled by the Friendship Centres. Funding for projects is dispersed according to a detailed proposal evaluation process. From the point of receipt of the proposals, the process seems to be controlled by the Friendship Centres. This control has provided a reliable and familiar environment in which local Friendship Centres feel comfortable operating. In this case, the primary policy relationship is between the Manitoba Association of Friendship Centres, local Friendship Centres, and youth on the AYAC.

Research participants in Thompson compared the UAS and UMAYC programs. As discussed earlier in the chapter, the federal and provincial governments are the primary funders of the UAS, and government delegates on the UAS local committee were perceived by some Aboriginal stakeholders to be indirectly controlling how funding is distributed at the local level just by being present at "the table" where decisions are being made. This was contrasted with the UMAYC model in Thompson, where the Friendship Centre and AYAC make the decisions (although one must recall that this would be different in Winnipeg, where Canadian Heritage administers the program and has two program officers sitting on the AYAC with Aboriginal youth). It is unclear who originally set the agenda for the UMAYC initiative nationally, and whether it involved Aboriginal leaders in Ottawa or in communities across the country. We cannot say, therefore, whether policy co-production first occurred during issue identification and goal setting for UMAYC nationally. As with the UAS, however, communities may find project selection and implementation permissive enough in the context of local priorities that the principle of self-determination and some measure of co-production are approximated.

The UMAYC outcomes have been perceived as positive by all parties we met with, although, as with other programs, it was felt that funding was scarce compared with needs and aspirations, and that accountability measures for funding recipients were intensive, even at the application stage. A perceived strength of UMAYC is that Aboriginal political organizations have not been involved in adjudicating proposals and that the process relies on youth in the community who are nominated by their peers for their skills and leadership abilities. This perception was confirmed by program officials as well. Perhaps working with people selected from the community for their leadership or policy/program expertise is a promising practice for deep federalism in urban Aboriginal policy – quite different from defaulting to representatives of political organizations.

7 Urban Reserves – Thompson and Swan River

The designation of reserve status for urban lands acquired by First Nations through land claim settlements or purchase for economic, social, cultural, or political goals is becoming common in Manitoba. Recently, a prominent new urban reserve of the Long Plain First Nation was announced near downtown Winnipeg, which will house, among other things, a place of assembly for the province's First Nations. The federal government's *Additions to Reserves Policy* and the Manitoba government's *Treaty Land Entitlement Framework Agreement*, enacted within the past fifteen to twenty years, set out provisions and processes for the creation of urban reserves.

The City of Thompson and the Town of Swan River are both communities where urban reserves are in the process of being designated. Band councils have passed resolutions and forwarded them to Indian and Northern Affairs in order to transfer lands to reserve status. The province and respective municipal governments have been notified of the intent to designate the lands as reserves and asked to remove them from the local property tax base and domain of zoning, land use, and other municipal bylaws. In order to ensure compatibility between the development of the urban reserve property and surrounding municipal lands and infrastructure, the process of developing a Municipal Development and Services Agreement

(MDSA) between Band and City/Town councils is of central importance. The MDSA ensures compatibility of land uses, service agreements, and compensation for taxes lost in transition to reserve
status, and the adherence to standards and codes such as those that
concern fire, building, and infrastructure.

In Thompson and Swan River, the process of creating an MDSA
is underway. While the most formalized relationship for converting
land in an urban area to reserve status is between the Band and
the federal government, the most involved and strategically important relationship is between the Band and the town/city, yet very
little exists in the way of a formal process and the MDSA tends to
be negotiated differently each time. As one participant noted, it is
an important but uncertain and costly process for a small town to
undertake. Legal fees, to ensure that the MDSA is solid and can stand
for years to come, can strain the legal services budget for a small
town administration.

Although First Nations can use the services of the Treaty Land
Entitlement Committee of Manitoba Inc. in negotiating good
MDSAs, there is no entity to assist municipalities. It was surprising to
learn that the Association of Manitoba Municipalities provided no
services or advice to municipalities dealing with urban reserve negotiations. One participant noted, however, that he relied heavily on
his colleagues in other municipalities who had negotiated successful
agreements and compared notes with them; however, this was an
informal process based on personal relationships he had developed
over past years with other municipal officials across the province.

While the negotiation of urban reserves and their associated MDSAs
could be seen as an exercise in multilevel governance that included
federal, provincial, First Nation, and municipal governments, the
municipal government has little say about the nature of the resulting
policy or the timing of its implementation. The municipal government is only responsible for negotiating an MDSA with the Band
council and is "informed" of its obligation to do so. Municipal
governments are coming to terms with this process and beginning
to regularize it in their operations. However, understandably, it
is a process that was foisted upon them and to which they must
respond rather than with which they pro-actively engage. This situation may begin to change as both municipalities and First Nations
see the benefits of First Nation investment in urban lands, where
MDSAs provide good compatibility with municipal objectives and a

sufficient fee for municipal services that, over time, equals lost property taxes. Municipalities may begin to seek out First Nations with outstanding treaty land entitlements and encourage them to invest in urban holdings (Sully et al. 2008; Walker 2008b). This optimism must be situated against the more sullen backdrop of recent plebiscites in Thompson and Brandon, where citizens expressed their opposition to the introduction of local urban reserves.

CONCLUSION

In the seven policy fields reviewed in this chapter, there is no single model of engagement that can be pointed to as being overwhelmingly effective. Some of them, however, hold promise. Overall, policy in urban Aboriginal affairs is being *produced* by governments and implemented with Aboriginal communities. In some cases, there is involvement of Aboriginal communities earlier on in the policy process, but it is varied and it is hard to find consistency in practice. For example, the Province of Manitoba engaged with appropriate Aboriginal housing experts through the Manitoba Urban Native Housing Association to co-produce an implementation framework for the Off-Reserve Aboriginal Housing Trust policy. The same provincial government also decided it was too difficult to work with Aboriginal political organizations to co-produce the Aboriginal Participation component of the Winnipeg Partnership Agreement and worked through senior government officials instead. As a third variant to provincial policy development and implementation, the Onashowewin case shows how Aboriginal community-based organizations can be mechanisms for implementing provincial policy under the appearance of community-based policy and program self-determination but with little Aboriginal control at any stage of the policy process.

The City of Winnipeg was a national leader in its deliberate attempt to create a new relationship with Aboriginal communities in the city, yet it devoted virtually no time to building a relationship with Aboriginal community leaders prior to creating in-house a set of specific policy areas and action plans to pursue. Our view is that the policy never could have succeeded with a start like that. The advances made in the Aboriginal policy field by the City of Winnipeg, although imperfect, provide a stark contrast with the situation in the City of Brandon. The absence of a policy framework for relating to Aboriginal peoples or even a mention of this significant part of the community in the Community Strategic Plan seems surprising and can only harm attempts at inter-governmental work on the Aboriginal policy field. Without a policy that articulates a "place to stand" on the city's Aboriginal affairs, any resource contributions from the City of Brandon to Aboriginal programs will lack justification and direction.

At the federal level, the HRSDC's Homelessness Partnership Initiative, Aboriginal component, is administered in partnership with a community advisory board that is perhaps 50 per cent Aboriginal. The advisory board contains about half non-Aboriginal members. There is no restriction against non-Aboriginal organizations applying for funding earmarked for Aboriginal homelessness programming. Self-determination in the homelessness policy field is not occurring. Yet the same department, HRSDC, has Aboriginal Human Resource Development Agreements that are administered by Aboriginal organizations, which furthers the general implementation of self-government. Why the inconsistency in appreciation for self-determining autonomy, even within one government department in one province?

The assessment of urban Aboriginal policy in Manitoba shows that there are plenty of "voices" but not enough responsible policy co-production (Brudney and England 1982; Casey and Dalton 2006; Nyland 1995) with appropriate Aboriginal leaders and policy field experts. Instead, there is a confounding number of "stakeholders," from agenda setting to problem definition, generating alternatives, and policy implementation. Both the provincial and federal governments have been taking approaches to including the Aboriginal communities in policy processes that equate community leadership with heads of political organizations and policy expertise with political representation, and fail to take into account a variety of other elements of diversity. A more discerning and principled approach to policy co-production is needed.

In a policy process like the City of Winnipeg's Municipal Aboriginal Pathways, the city needed to examine its goal – which was to create a new relationship with its Aboriginal communities – and decide which Aboriginal community leaders or experts to co-produce the policy with. For a principles-based first steps document, community leadership might have been the best choice as key partners. For the subsequent development of specific policy fields and action plans, Aboriginal policy experts from among the well-developed set of community-based organizations might have been engaged. As Evelyn Peters (2005) has shown, Winnipeg has a very well-developed set of Aboriginal institutions, about a third of which have over twenty years of operation in a range of policy and program fields.

As mentioned, Winnipeg tried early on to include the leaders of the major Aboriginal political organizations, but the different organizations would not work constructively together. Perhaps the city should have engaged community leaders in the process instead of beginning and ending their efforts with political organizations. Many of the most well-recognized community leaders are not in elected political positions, yet they have tremendous legitimacy in their communities and years of experience with urban Aboriginal policy issues. The failure to involve Aboriginal leadership of any kind raises the question of whether the city should have tried to advance the policy field at all. The City of Winnipeg already had a policy statement in Plan Winnipeg 2020 Vision to promote self-reliant Aboriginal communities. The decision to take it further to create a full secondary plan with defined program and funding aspirations should not have been done by the city in isolation.

All levels of government noted problems with working with the large Aboriginal political organizations due to their unwillingness to work together constructively. This situation may be unique to Winnipeg or more generally to Manitoba and may not be the case in other provinces – we do not know. However, conflicts between Aboriginal political organizations should not be used as a justification for bypassing meaningful policy co-production and involving a varied group of stakeholders only late in the implementation process. Instead of proceeding "in-house" through government officials and bypassing policy co-production with Aboriginal communities, governments would do well to go straight to Aboriginal community leaders and community-based organizations. It is appropriate to include Aboriginal political organizations as well but they are not the beginning and end of the line for Aboriginal collaboration on policy production. A good balance of community leadership and community-based policy and program expertise, along with representatives of the main political organizations, would allow governments and Aboriginal urban communities to work together to co-produce policy and programs, from principles to action plans and implementation, whether through deep federalism, provincial, or municipal processes.

The principle of self-determination provides the central basis for policy co-production with Aboriginal communities, from agenda setting to implementation. The "nation-to-nation" principle in relations between Aboriginal and settler peoples resonates strongly with most Aboriginal participants we spoke with in this study and in previous work. Practical approaches to implementing self-determination in urban areas require that governments embarking on new policy make a conscientious and principled appraisal of what combination of community leaders and/or policy experts are appropriate as policy collaborators. The community nomination process used for the UMAYC advisory committee is a popular model and appears to work well.

We return now to the point made by Abele and Prince (2006) that "government-to-government" seemed to persist among staff at the Royal Commission on Aboriginal Peoples (1996) as a practical way to implement the "nation-to-nation" principle. In Manitoba, federal, provincial, and municipal governments dealing with urban policy development frequently try to involve Aboriginal political organizations, two of which (the Assembly of Manitoba Chiefs and Manitoba Métis Federation) are umbrella organizations for Aboriginal local governments in Manitoba (Band councils and Métis locals). This approach seems to have developed in response to the value seen in "government-to-government" approaches. We believe that this approach is problematic. Most of the Aboriginal governments represented by the provincial political organizations are not urban-based, and their attention and limited resources are focused mostly on rural and reserve community issues. This problem may be less acute where federal, provincial, or municipal governments work with Métis locals and tribal governments based, specifically in the area and where the urban First Nation population is reasonably homogeneous in tribal affiliation (for example, the Dakota-Ojibway Tribal Council in Brandon).

The attempt to apply the idea of urban-delimited Aboriginal *government* structures has mostly failed where it has been tried across Canada. Having said this, the Aboriginal Council of Winnipeg is still active, but its legitimacy as a *representative* body of urban government is frequently challenged, despite its accomplishments as an advocacy organization. Yet with all this, governments still try to impose a "government-to-government" framework when they seek to involve Aboriginal communities in urban policy processes. The principle of "nation-to-nation" is widely accepted by Aboriginal peoples in urban areas but "government-to-government" is not. The most knowledgeable and democratic representation on policy issues for Aboriginal peoples in urban areas may well be found among community leaders and staff at community-based organizations operating in specific policy fields rather than in Aboriginal government structures. Aboriginal political organizations have an important role to play, however, in issue identification, advocacy, and support to improve the quality of life of urban Aboriginal people; they also have a role to play in the creation of forums for public engagement. Including representatives of Aboriginal political organizations may be important in policy production processes, but no more so than including community leaders and community-based policy experts, especially when it comes to program design and implementation.

At the present time, with a few exceptions, governments are getting the policy collaborators wrong. They are drawing on political organizations when policy experts and community leaders are needed, or combining the two on committees and not giving any specific weight to the value of policy expertise over political organization imperatives. They are also undermining the principle of self-determining autonomy by having representation from a variety of non-Aboriginal organizations on decision-making bodies for Aboriginal policy fields. Finally, and most commonly, governments are not really co-producing policy with Aboriginal communities at all: they are simply striking broad-based advisory "tables," with lots of "voices," to assist with implementation of government policy that has been derived from agenda-setting onwards (until the implementation stage) without input from Aboriginal communities. This process may be a strategic way to placate the many "voices" in the Aboriginal communities, but it does not go far towards really co-producing urban affairs policy with those communities.

Aboriginal political organizations are well equipped to argue, as the Aboriginal Council of Winnipeg did in the Misquadis case, for self-determining autonomy in urban affairs and the importance of improving quality of life on Aboriginal peoples' own terms (Salée, Newhouse, and Lévesque 2006). But this argument must be distinguished from the process of policy co-production with

Aboriginal communities – based on the principle of advancing self-determination – where the appropriate collaborators will be experts in policy design and delivery from Aboriginal community service organizations with political organizations playing a supporting role. In summary, the point made by Calvin Hanselmann (2002) seems appropriate: all levels of government need to take responsibility for working with the service delivery experts on policy and program production and with political organizations on understanding issues and policy priorities emanating from the communities. It was explained to us by people at political organizations that they were "chasing" program and service delivery funding to make ends meet and they themselves noted that they ought to instead be devoting attention to issue identification and advocacy.

Leo's (2006) "deep federalism as process," where national policy is implemented with other state and community actors and creates new political space that unbundles sovereignty at the local level, is an appropriate model for federal Aboriginal policy. Federal parameters must be flexible enough to be tailored to local articulations of needs and aspirations. Leo points out how the National Homelessness Initiative failed on that front because it required that parameters suited to conditions in Toronto be applied in Winnipeg, where inexpensive housing stock was abundant. Walker (2005) shows how parameters from the SCPI program introduced into the Urban Aboriginal Homelessness program also disadvantaged local implementation by Aboriginal communities. Deep federalism is already present, with imperfections, in some urban Aboriginal affairs policy, such as the Urban Aboriginal Strategy and Urban Multi-Purpose Aboriginal Youth Centres initiative. Research participants generally preferred the UMAYC advisory and decision-making mechanism over that of the UAS in both Thompson and Winnipeg for two main reasons. First, the UMAYC relies on non-partisan youth for their expertise in decision making, whereas the UAS relies more heavily on political organizations. Second, the UAS has government officials sitting on the main advisory bodies, which is seen by some Aboriginal participants as perhaps unduly influencing the decision-making process. The UMAYC – at least in Thompson and Brandon – seems to place a more comfortable distance between the government officials as funders and Aboriginal community members as decision makers.

In pursuing deep federalism, it is crucial to get the mechanism for local Aboriginal governance correctly established in order to tailor broad national policy to local circumstances. Is the principle of self-determination being advanced through co-production? On the UAS committee in Winnipeg, for example, there are non-Aboriginal philanthropic organizations and government officials present. Is this the best way to advance self-determining autonomy? And are service-delivery experts and community leaders being used to tailor the policy to the local experience in what might be called localized co-production? Moving beyond "voices at the table" is crucial. Getting the right voices is essential because it is these participants who then bear shared responsibility for co-production, even if only a localized type of co-production designed to fit a broad national policy to a specific urban context.

Finally, our analysis of urban Aboriginal policy in this chapter has deliberately omitted an overarching concern in urban policy circles that was articulated in detail by Walker (2008c): how is policy in general being derived and administered by governments? The answer to that question is that it is being done for the short-term – even shorter under the present Conservative government – insecurely, and competitively. It is not entitlement-based but rather could be seen as a meta-governance technique that keeps many voluntary sector organizations busy with proposal writing to find enough program funding to keep their human resources budgets and some programming going from year to year, with little fat in the system to provide security for either jobs or programs. Aboriginal community leaders with a long history of activism and policy innovation have noted in interviews for this research and in past work that it is difficult to foresee significant protest for dramatic policy changes coming from the grassroots as it did in the 1960s and 1970s, partly because many of the people who would lead that activism have jobs in Aboriginal community organizations and are busy trying to secure short-term contract funding in order to maintain operating and program budgets. The urban Aboriginal policy field – like many other urban policy fields – is fostering a "winners" and "losers" approach to government spending on public policy and citizenship. For the purposes of this research, that concern with the general state of urban policy was bracketed, and we asked instead: how are Aboriginal affairs policies being created and implemented? On this front, we hope to have made a well-reasoned contribution to the debate on urban Aboriginal policy.

NOTES

1 The friendly exchange of ideas and data sources with Christopher Leo made our work easier and more enjoyable, and we thank him for his assistance. We thank Alfred Gay, Evelyn Peters, and Robert Young for their comments on earlier drafts. The research was funded by the Major Collaborative Research Initiative program of the Social Sciences and Humanities Research Council of Canada under the Multilevel Governance and Public Policy in Municipalities project directed by Robert Young from the University of Western Ontario.

2 See Andersen and Strachan (Chapter 4 of this volume) for another discussion of the concept of a "jurisdictional maze" as it pertains to urban Aboriginal policy.

3 We note that the federal government has authority for criminal law and procedure, ensuring some consistency in treatment across the country. The provinces have jurisdiction over the administration of justice in their respective territories. The Criminal Code of Canada, section 718.2(e) states that "all available sanctions other than imprisonment that are reasonable in the circumstances should be considered for all offenders, with particular attention to the circumstances of aboriginal offenders." Alternative measures to the court system and principles of restorative justice are also set out in the Criminal Code.

INTERVIEWS

Interview 1 – town official, Swan River, 17 July 2007
Interview 2 – Aboriginal service organization official, Winnipeg, 19 July 2007
Interview 3 – federal official, Winnipeg, 19 July 2007
Interview 4 – federal official, Winnipeg, 19 July 2007
Interview 5 – Aboriginal political organization elected official, Winnipeg, 19 July 2007
Interview 6 – municipal official, Winnipeg, 20 July 2007
Interview 7 – Aboriginal service organization official, Winnipeg, 20 July 2007
Interview 8 – Aboriginal community leader, Winnipeg, 20 July 2007
Interview 9 – provincial official, Winnipeg, 23 July 2007
Interview 10 – Aboriginal community leader, 23 July 2007
Interview 11 – Aboriginal political organization official, Winnipeg, 23 July 2007

Interview 12 – federal official, Winnipeg, 24 July 2007

Interview 13 – Aboriginal service organization official, Winnipeg, 24 July 2007

Interview 14 – two Aboriginal service organization officials, one Aboriginal community leader, Winnipeg, 24 July 2007

Interview 15 – provincial official, Winnipeg, 25 July 2007

Interview 16 – Aboriginal service organization official, Winnipeg, 25 July 2007

Interview 17 – Aboriginal service organization official, Winnipeg, 25 July 2007

Interview 18 – Aboriginal business organization official, Winnipeg, 26 July 2007

Interview 19 – two Aboriginal service organization officials, Swan River, 26 July 2007

Interview 20 – municipal official, RM of Swan River, 26 July 2007

Interview 21 – municipal official, Winnipeg, 21 September 2007

Interview 22 – Aboriginal political organization elected official, Winnipeg, 21 September 2007

Interview 23 – federal official, Winnipeg, 24 September 2007

Interview 24 – two Aboriginal service organization officials, Winnipeg, 24 September 2007

Interview 25 – federal official, Winnipeg, 12 October 2007

Interview 26 – municipal official, Brandon, 16 October 2007

Interview 27 – Aboriginal political organization official, Brandon, 16 October 2007

Interview 28 – municipal elected official, Brandon, 16 October 2007

Interview 29 – non-Aboriginal housing provider, Brandon, 16 October 2007

Interview 30 – non-Aboriginal service organization official, Brandon, 17 October 2007

Interview 31 – Aboriginal housing provider, Brandon, 17 October 2007

Interview 32 – Aboriginal political organization official, Thompson, 22 October 2007

Interview 33 – Aboriginal housing provider, Thompson, 23 October 2007

Interview 34 – Aboriginal service organization official, Thompson, 24 October 2007

Interview 35 – provincial official, Thompson, 25 October 2007

Interview 36 – municipal official, Thompson, 25 October 2007

Interview 37 – non-Aboriginal service organization official, Thompson, 25 October 2007

Interview 38 – Aboriginal service organization official, Winnipeg, 14
        November 2007
Interview 39 – Aboriginal service organization official, Brandon, 19
        November 2007

REFERENCES

Abele, Frances and Michael Prince. 2006. "Four Pathways to Aboriginal
    Self-Government in Canada." *The American Review of Canadian Stud-
    ies* 36 (4): 568–95.
Aboriginal Council of Winnipeg. 2007a. *Winnipeg Urban Aboriginal
    Community Justice Forum.* Winnipeg: Aboriginal Council of Winnipeg.
– 2007b. *Guiding Principle: Individual and Community Have Access to a
    Full Continuum of Justice Services to Ensure Fair and Equal Treatment.*
    Winnipeg: Aboriginal Council of Winnipeg.
Aboriginal Languages of Manitoba Inc. 2008. *About Aboriginal Lan-
    guages in Manitoba.* Available: www.ablang.com/about.html. Accessed
    3 February 2008.
Andersen, Chris and Claude Denis. 2003. "Urban Natives and the Nation:
    Before and After the Royal Commission on Aboriginal Peoples." *The
    Canadian Review of Sociology and Anthropology* 40 (4): 373–90.
Assembly of Manitoba Chiefs. 2008. *Manitoba First Nation Communities.*
    Available: www.manitobachiefs.com/amc/communities.htm. Accessed 3
    February 2008.
Barcham, Manuhuia. 2000. "(De)Constructing the Politics of Indigeneity."
    In *Political Theory and the Rights of Indigenous Peoples*, eds. D. Ivison,
    P. Patton, and W. Sanders, 137–51. Toronto: Cambridge University
    Press.
Belanger, Yale. 2005. "The Politics of Accommodation: Working Toward
    a Policy of Aboriginal Inclusion." Paper presented at *First Nations, First
    Thoughts* Conference at the Centre of Canadian Studies, 6 May, at the
    University of Edinburgh.
Bradford, Neil. 2004. "Place Matters and Multilevel Governance: Perspec-
    tives on a New Urban Policy Paradigm." *Policy Options*, February:
    39–44.
Brudney, Jeffrey and Robert England. 1982. "Urban Policy Making and
    Subjective Service Evaluations: Are They Compatible?" *Public Adminis-
    tration Review* 42 (2): 127–35.
Casey, John and Bronwen Dalton. 2006. "The Best of Times, the Worst of
    Times: Community-Sector Advocacy in the Age of 'Compacts'." *Austral-
    ian Journal of Political Science* 41 (1): 23–38.

City of Brandon. 2006. *Shaping Tomorrow Together: Brandon's Community Strategic Plan*. Brandon: City of Brandon.

City of Winnipeg. 2003. *First Steps: Municipal Aboriginal Pathways*. Winnipeg: City of Winnipeg.

Cormier, Robert. 2002. *Restorative Justice: Directions and Principles – Developments in Canada*. Ottawa: Department of the Solicitor General Canada.

Durie, Mason. 2003. *Ngā Kāhui Pou Launching Māori Futures*. Wellington: Huia Publishers.

Graham, Katherine A.H. and Evelyn J. Peters. 2002. *Aboriginal Communities and Urban Sustainability*. Ottawa: Canadian Policy Research Networks.

Green, Joyce. 2005. "Self-Determination, Citizenship, and Federalism as Palimpsest." In *Reconfiguring Aboriginal-State Relations. Canada: The State of the Federation, 2003*, ed. M. Murphy, 329–54. Montreal-Kingston: McGill-Queen's University Press.

Hanselmann, Calvin. 2001. *Urban Aboriginal People in Western Canada: Realities and Policies*. Calgary: Canada West Foundation.

– 2002. *Uncommon Sense: Promising Practices in Urban Aboriginal Policy Making and Programming*. Calgary: Canada West Foundation.

Hanselmann, Calvin and Roger Gibbins. 2005. "Another Voice is Needed: Intergovernmentalism in the Urban Aboriginal Context." In *Reconfiguring Aboriginal-State Relations. Canada. The State of the Federation, 2003*, ed. M. Murphy, 77–92. Montreal-Kingston: McGill-Queen's University Press.

Hunter, Anna. 2006. "The Politics of Aboriginal Self-Government." In *Canadian Politics: Democracy and Dissent*, eds. J. Grace and B. Sheldrick. Toronto: Prentice Hall.

LaGrand, James. 2002. *Indian Metropolis: Native Americans in Chicago, 1945–75*. Chicago: University of Illinois Press.

Leo, Christopher. 2006. "Deep Federalism: Respecting Community Difference in National Policy." *Canadian Journal of Political Science* 39 (3): 481–506.

Leo, Christopher, Martine Auguste, Mike Pyl, and Maria Bromilow. 2007. "Multilevel Governance without Municipal Government." Paper presented at the annual conference of the Canadian Political Science Association, 30 May – 1 June, at the University of Saskatchewan.

Maaka, Roger. 1994. "The New Tribe: Conflicts and Continuities in the Social Organization of Urban Māori." *The Contemporary Pacific* 6 (2): 311–36.

Maaka, Roger and Augie Fleras. 2005. *The Politics of Indigeneity: Challenging the State in Canada and Aotearoa, New Zealand*. Dunedin: University of Otago Press.

Magnusson, Warren. 1996. *The Search for Political Space: Globalisation, Social Movements, and the Urban Experience*. Toronto: University of Toronto Press.

Mercer, David. 2003. "'Citizen Minus'?: Indigenous Australians and the Citizenship Question." *Citizenship Studies* 7 (4): 421–45.

Minore, B. and M. Katt. 2007. *Aboriginal Health Care in Northern Ontario: Impacts of Self-Determination and Culture*. Montreal: Institute for Research on Public Policy.

Morgan, George. 2006. *Unsettled Places: Aboriginal People and Urbanisation in New South Wales*. Kent Town: Wakefield Press.

Nyland, Julie. 1995. "Issue Networks and Non-Profit Organizations." *Policy Studies Review* 14 (1–2): 195–204.

Peters, Evelyn J. 2007. "First Nations and Métis People and Diversity in Canadian Cities." In *The Arts of the State III: Belonging? Diversity, Recognition and Shared Citizenship in Canada*, eds. K. Banting, T. Courchene, and L. Seidle, 207–46. Montreal: Institute for Research on Public Policy.

– 2005. "Indigeneity and Marginalisation: Planning for and with Urban Aboriginal Communities in Canada." *Progress in Planning* 63 (4): 327–404.

Royal Commission on Aboriginal Peoples. 1996. *Report of the Royal Commission on Aboriginal Peoples*. Ottawa: Minister of Supply and Services.

Salée, Daniel, David Newhouse, and Carole Lévesque. 2006. *Quality of Life of Aboriginal People in Canada: An Analysis of Current Research*. Montreal: Institute for Research on Public Policy.

Sancton, Andrew. 2007. "Will the Toronto City-Region Ever be Self-Governing?" *Plan Canada* 47 (3): 25–27.

Statistics Canada. 2008. *Aboriginal Peoples in Canada in 2006: Inuit, Métis, and First Nations, 2006 Census*. Ottawa: Statistics Canada.

Sully, Lorne, Livia Kellett, Joseph Garcea, and Ryan Walker. 2008. "First Nations Urban Reserves in Saskatoon: Partnerships for Positive Development." *Plan Canada* 48 (2): 39–42.

Walker, Ryan. 2008a. "Social Housing and the Role of Aboriginal Organizations in Canadian Cities." *IRPP Choices* 14 (4): 1–18.

– 2008b. "Improving the Interface Between Urban Municipalities and Aboriginal Communities." *Canadian Journal of Urban Research* 17 (1) (Supplement): 20–36.
– 2008c. "Aboriginal Self-determination and Social Housing in Urban Canada: A Story of Convergence and Divergence." *Urban Studies* 45 (1): 185–205.
– 2006. "Searching for Aboriginal/Indigenous Self-Determination: Urban Citizenship in the Winnipeg Low-Cost Housing Sector, Canada." *Environment and Planning A* 38 (12): 2345–63.
– 2005. "Social Cohesion? A Critical Review of the Urban Aboriginal Strategy and its Application to Address Homelessness in Winnipeg." *The Canadian Journal of Native Studies* 25 (2): 395–416.

7

Conclusion

ROBERT YOUNG

The Aboriginal people living in Canada were central to this country's past, will be important in the future, and have opportunities and problems that are the focus of much current policy. They are only a small percentage of the total population, but their practical and symbolic significance is much greater. The relations between the majority society and Indians, Inuit, and Métis have been marked by deep paternalism for much of our history. They have also been marked by the deeply dishonourable behaviour of Canadian governments, which have, most notably, stolen land, refused to extend citizenship rights, and confiscated children. But there have also been episodes of co-operation that reach back to colonial wars and are now seen in constitutional recognition, court decisions, and widespread negotiations.

One front of co-operation is emerging in urban areas, and this is the focus of the works collected here. Most Aboriginal people do not live on reserves: they have increasingly come to live in municipalities and especially – like other Canadians – in larger cities. More and more public policies affect them and many are targeted towards them. The objectives of the research project that produced the chapters gathered here were, first, to document these policies, second, to analyze how they were formed, with particular reference to the structure of intergovernmental relations involved in creating them and also to the pattern of involvement of "social forces" (organized interests of all kinds and especially Aboriginal people themselves) in creating the policies, and, finally, to evaluate the quality of policy and make suggestions for improvement.

The coverage here is thorough. The New Brunswick study focuses historically on settler-Aboriginal relations in that province, particularly in the southern part of the province. In Alberta, Ontario, and Manitoba, each team of researchers studied policy in at least four municipalities of various sizes. This approach was taken in order to ensure representativeness. There is coverage of small and mid-sized towns, remote communities, and large metropolises. Documentary research has been thoroughly done, and the authors conducted 121 interviews with over 130 people. While the particularities of urban Aboriginal policy and the processes of its formation might be somewhat different in British Columbia or Saskatchewan or Newfoundland and Labrador, the coverage here is excellent and the results, we believe, are both reliable and representative.

In the Introduction, Evelyn Peters has provided an excellent overview of the terrain. The conditions of life are grim for many Aboriginal people in Canada's urban areas, but their capacity and agency persists, as does their culture. At the same time, she shows how the indigenous social melange is terribly complex, especially in the larger cities. Peters insists on two central points. First is the issue of jurisdiction, a fundamental problem underlying all policy in this field. The federal government has never explicitly acknowledged any responsibility for off-reserve Aboriginal people. While avoiding formal responsibility, however, Ottawa's engagement has been increasing, first with the funding of Friendship Centres, then through some exceptional programs, and now often through joint initiatives with provincial and municipal governments. Second, there is the issue of the right of self-government. Such a right does exist, but the problem in urban areas is to define the "self." A plethora of organizations can claim to speak for all Aboriginal people or for some of them. They range from the national political organizations to individual First Nations to relatively small and specialized service providers. Evelyn Peters argues that in practice, however, Aboriginal people find that "[t]heir main channel for exerting some control over aspects of their lives in cities is a variety of urban Aboriginal services organizations that have emerged in the last half century." That service-providing organizations manifest self-government is contested by other, competing organizations, particularly representative political organizations, but the issue of self-government is central to debates about urban Aboriginal policies.

The authors of the overview chapter about the federal stance towards urban Aboriginal people, Frances Abele and Katherine Graham, traced the "dynamics of policy engagement" between the government and Aboriginals. They identify four historical periods. In the current period, a new funding model is evolving in which federal officials are dealing not with the national Aboriginal organizations, which were at the fore in the period of high constitutional politics, but with smaller Aboriginal service organizations in urban areas. They note that the number of such Aboriginal NGOs tripled over the 1993–2000 period, testimony to the rapid change in the field. This new federal model was institutionalized through the Urban Aboriginal Strategy (UAS) that was created in 1998 and renewed in 2003 and 2007. Many observers take a rather rosy view of the UAS and paint it as an innovative horizontal initiative involving several federal departments. Others hesitate to criticize it for fear of helping to provide an excuse to terminate the funding it provides. It remains true in any case that the expenditures involved are small, and the funding is carved up finely, sliced and diced into a great many relatively small projects. The UAS helps matters, but it is hardly comprehensive.

We expect that the New Brunswick experience fairly represents that of the rest of Atlantic Canada (except for Labrador). There are relatively few Aboriginal people, and there are only low concentrations in urban areas. The UAS is not present in the province because no city meets the threshold of five per cent Aboriginal population. For New Brunswick, Karen Murray has provided a sensitive and nuanced historical account. She clearly shows how Aboriginal people have been regarded as the subjects of policy, even while the direction of policy shifted from on-reserve agriculture to segregation and then to (partial) integration. At the same time, indigenous people in the province consistently exercised their capacity in pursuit of their own objectives – resisting relocation, engaging with the market economy on their own terms, and slowly creating a set of representative institutions, including the New Brunswick Aboriginal Peoples Council, even as individual First Nations, such as St Mary's, became more assertive. Progress has been slow because of an extreme minority status, but the determination of the Aboriginal people has been bolstered by a series of important court decisions, and relationships with the provincial and municipal governments are being re-equilibrated.

The Ontario paper by Francis Abele, Russell LaPointe, David Leech, and Michael McCrossan makes an important and systematic contribution to the field of urban Aboriginal policy. While the stance of the provincial government towards Aboriginal people has oscillated widely as a function of the political party in power, municipal governments have been consistent in having very little policy explicitly about Aboriginal people. The situation in Kingston, where the indigenous population is small, rather resembles what was found in New Brunswick. In Thunder Bay, the municipal authorities are primarily oriented towards the local First Nation. There is much more activity in Ottawa, and one suspects this fact may be due to the large and well-educated Aboriginal population in the national capital. The Ottawa Aboriginal Coalition was able to generate a significant amount of research, and more research is being produced through the Urban Aboriginal Task Force. In Toronto, there is a long tradition of abjuring policy specifically targeted towards the problems of particular minority groups. This stance has informed policy about urban Aboriginal people (as it also does in the field of immigrant settlement). But there is change in policy taking place, as the UAS results in committees being established and funding being disbursed. Even earlier, there was targeting in housing and children's aid. Organization by indigenous people caused this. As the authors observe astutely:

> Cities and municipalities do not govern with practices that recognize special attributes of citizens in a way that the federal or even the provincial governments have come to do. Cities deal with residents and with neighbourhoods. Aboriginal rights and entitlements, whatever their legal bearing in cities, do not form part of the taken-for-granted governance framework of municipal governments. In this regard, we may learn from our case studies something about the importance of community organization to create local visibility. City governments respond to community organizations, and when Aboriginal service providers come together, they make it easier for cities to "see" needs and respond to them.

Rights discourse may yet become more prevalent in Ontario's municipalities; in the meantime, this is wise advice.

The research done by Chris Andersen and Jenna Strachan provides a fascinating vision of urban Aboriginal programming in Alberta. Here the province has taken the lead as the principal policy maker and service provider, with evident goodwill and a keen appreciation of the issues. But there is a vast array of actors and inadequate coordination in the sector, while programming tends to be short-term and project-based. There is a clear conflict between rights-based claims and needs-based policy. The provincial government is oriented towards needs, but Andersen and Strachan distinguish between general programs, those directed towards Aboriginal people, and those directed specifically towards urban Aboriginal people; they argue that the third category accounts for only a small proportion of all the services consumed by urban Aboriginals. The chapter is persuasive in depicting the complexity of this policy field, where three levels of government are involved with a great diversity of actors, many of which compete among themselves. Sometimes the conflict between groups is serious. The authors describe policy and the policy process in Cold Lake, Wood Buffalo, Edmonton, and Calgary and emphasize the dense organizational and programming systems in the big cities. In Edmonton, they found services related to arts and crafts, business and economic development, communications, education, employment, housing, health, women's issues, justice, sports and recreation, and youth and senior citizens. Despite this great complexity, the UAS is emerging as central because it has stimulated the formation of broad stakeholder committees in Calgary and Edmonton, along with greater municipal attention to Aboriginal issues.

For their study of Manitoba, Ryan Walker, James Moore, and Maeengan Linklater devised an innovative research design, which focuses on seven issues and policies and highlights how these policies played out in four municipalities. Manitoba is a significant province in the area of urban Aboriginal policy because of its high proportion of indigenous people and because it is often regarded as the source of many of the best practices in the field. This chapter raises important problems. First, the authors adopt a firm normative position in favour of the co-production of policy, that is, "a type of policy generation and implementation process where non-state actors are involved in the creation of policy, instead of only its implementation." We will return to this central theme later in the Conclusion. Second, they show that, in some urban areas, there is a distinct lack of municipal engagement. The Municipal Aboriginal Pathways initiative in Winnipeg was largely abandoned and in Brandon it seems that the authorities have been blind to urban Aboriginal issues. Third, the authors trace a consistent schism between Aboriginal political organizations and the service delivery agencies, one that was especially acute in the Homelessness Partnership Initiative and the Urban Multipurpose Youth Centre Initiative. The authors argue that there needs to be some division of labour. Governments should choose appropriate co-production partners and engage with political organizations to set the general agenda and with social service organizations to devise concrete policy and to implement it. This solution raises thorny issues. But the authors also insist on the deep capacity for policy making that exists in the Aboriginal communities of Manitoba: policy co-production certainly is possible.

COMPARATIVE CONSIDERATIONS

The studies gathered here are collectively broad in scope. They span four provinces and a large number of individual municipalities, and cover a lot of policy territory. So what general patterns are discernible? What conclusions about urban Aboriginal policy can be reached on the basis of this thorough research? Here we consider primarily the activism of provincial and municipal governments. Then we turn to more general questions.

When Calvin Hanselmann did his groundbreaking research for the Canada West Foundation, the federal presence was constant throughout the country: programs found in one municipality and province were also found in others (Hanselmann 2001, Figure 12). This remains the case, except that the UAS is differentiated by city. In cities where Aboriginals make up less than five per cent of the total population, UAS programming does not apply. Where there is a UAS in place, there is considerable variation across municipalities in what the funds are used for. There is also some variation within other federal programs. Homelessness initiatives, for instance, are delivered through a special entity or through shared delivery. Youth centres can be funded directly or indirectly. Generally, though, federal policy forms a uniform backdrop. And the same is true with the framework of Aboriginal rights, which were established ultimately by the Supreme Court of Canada and applied throughout the country. The New Brunswick study shows how court decisions such as *Corbiere* (1999) have been important in establishing the framework within which specific policies are generated and implemented.

Provincial governments vary widely in their engagement with urban Aboriginal issues. This is primarily a function of the demographic weight and distribution of indigenous people. There is relatively little concern in New Brunswick and the other Maritime provinces, while the government of Ontario is primarily concerned with conflicts over resource issues and some land claims, and urban Aboriginal issues are relatively less important. It is in the western provinces that there are large demographic pressures and opportunities. A typical view was expressed by David Hawkes (2005, 128): "Over the next ten years, Saskatchewan will experience a severe labour shortage unless one of two situations develop: either there is a massive immigration of workers or First Nations begin to attain the education and skills needed in the modern workforce. Given the historical difficulty in attracting skilled workers to Saskatchewan and given the youthful population of First Nations, the latter situation seems to be the wiser course." Economic considerations are not the only motive for engagement, of course, for there are real concerns about social cohesion and poverty and there are also straightforward political pressures from Aboriginal people themselves, but they are substantial ones. Moreover, where provinces are active in the field, they tend to play a dominant role because of their responsibilities for delivering a wide range of important social programs.

For their part, municipal governments have been largely inactive in the field until quite recently. Often, the stance was that urban Aboriginal policy simply does not fall within the jurisdiction or mandate of local governments. Alternatively, the field was treated as part of more comprehensive policies about non-discrimination and multiculturalism. Now, in many places, action is unavoidable because of demography and the UAS – where it is applicable. The degree of activism clearly varies as a function of the overall provincial policy framework, the amount of programming available, and how the provincial government prefers to have policy delivered. It also depends on political factors – the commitment of municipal political leaders, the strength and unity of purpose of local Aboriginal organizations, and, less obviously, the resistance to redistributive expenditures on the part of non-Aboriginal electorates.

The comparative work shows that perhaps the most distinctive feature of the urban Aboriginal policy field is the diversity and complexity of the social forces involved. These are not really "social forces" in the sense in which the term is normally used – organized interests of all kinds, which are part of civil society. Instead, these are organizations representing and providing services to people who have a constitutional right to self-government. This is a feature unique to this policy field, the implications of which will be discussed later.

GENERAL CONSIDERATIONS

As was mentioned in the Preface, these studies of urban Aboriginal policy constitute part of a much larger project about multilevel governance and public policy in Canadian municipalities.[1] While standing alone as a self-contained collection of research that is focused on a particular set of important issues in one policy field, this work can also help us address broader questions of concern to scholars, policy makers, and citizens. In turn, these questions can illuminate and situate the field of urban Aboriginal policy in Canada.

Some general questions concern intergovernmental relations (IGR), and how these help determine policy outputs. First is the issue of municipal-federal relations, which is an area of IGR that is receiving considerable attention after having been neglected for a long time. This neglect was perhaps understandable, given the longstanding constraints imposed on municipal governments by provincial legislation and the lack of federal interest in the municipalities. However, both of these conditions have changed. Local governments, especially big-city governments, have more latitude for initiative than in the past and Ottawa's longstanding interests in urban *issues* are now more likely to involve relationships with urban *governments*.

In urban Aboriginal policy, however, the municipal-federal link is not generally a close one. As the New Brunswick chapter shows, there are relations between the two levels of government when issues arise from reserves that are close to municipalities. Urban reserve creation also requires close coordination (Dust 1997). But the main mechanisms for joint or coordinated action are intergovernmental committees associated with federal horizontal initiatives, that is, policies that cross the boundaries of normal departmental responsibilities and that normally have localized implementation. These policies have included the Aboriginal Justice Strategy, the Urban Aboriginal Employment Initiative, the Aboriginal Human Resources and Development Agreements, and some housing agreements, along with the UAS itself. As Evelyn Peters notes in the Introduction, such multi-governmental and multi-departmental committees mean that the normal "silos" of departmental administration are transcended;

further "no government is seen as establishing a precedent in assuming responsibility."

Our studies show that the Urban Aboriginal Strategy has been a major stimulus to municipal involvement in this policy area and to engagement with federal officials. It is important that the UAS has a lot of scope for local initiative. While the rhetorical objectives of the program may change with the views of different federal governments, the actual delivery of programs and projects on the ground can meet locally expressed needs. The UAS now seems firmly entrenched in the federal policy suite, so municipal government activity will continue. Significantly, where there is no UAS in place – as in Kingston, Cold Lake, and throughout New Brunswick – there is much less municipal involvement with federal officials.

Municipal-federal relations are mediated and ultimately dominated by provincial governments. As Andersen and Strachan found, "the gulf between municipal and federal actors remains wide and though it does not seem to be widening, the provincial government remains the monitor, advocate, broker, and major partner in the design, implementation, and evaluation of urban Aboriginal programming." Provincial officials sit on joint committees with representatives of other governments, but it is they who are mainly responsible for the policies that must dovetail with federal and municipal initiatives. They have considerable discretion, as shown for instance by Ontario government support for Friendship Centres and by Alberta's Aboriginal Policy Framework. Ultimately, of course, provincial governments control municipal governments and they can exercise their jurisdiction in major policy areas, as was shown by Manitoba Justice taking over the restorative justice program.

If we turn to the resources brought to the intergovernmental arena, the picture is similar. Most of the money spent on urban Aboriginal people is provincial (though it may not be explicitly targeted to them). Some federal initiatives have been substantial. Among municipalities, the tendency is to resist spending in the urban Aboriginal field. Local governments generally do not perceive that they have jurisdiction or responsibility in this area, their role in social policy is minimal in most provinces, and they are acutely sensitive to being dependent on the property tax. On the other hand, the potential for autonomous action does exist, as was shown in Winnipeg during Glen Murray's tenure as mayor. Another important resource is expertise and information. Here again, provincial governments dominate, given their presence in education, health, social services, housing, and labour market training. However, municipalities have important assets too, given the knowledge of local officials about recreation, public health, libraries, and policing. In most cases, however, this municipal expertise is not focused on urban Aboriginal people in a coherent manner.

Another general question about policy is the role of politicians as opposed to officials in its creation. In the urban Aboriginal policy field, it seems that politicians have made a difference. Of course, most program and policy management becomes a matter of bureaucratic routine, and day-to-day decisions are taken by public servants – often by consensus in various intergovernmental committees. Yet it is clear that the vision and ideologies of politicians also shape policy. This fact is most obvious at the municipal level in Winnipeg, in the bold initiatives envisioned by Mayor Murray and then abruptly halted under his successor. Similarly in Thompson, mayors have worked hard to initiate relations with the Aboriginal community. At the provincial level, one is struck by the oscillations of policy in Ontario during governments led by Bob Rae (highly sympathetic to Aboriginal people), Mike Harris (uninterested at best), and Dalton McGuinty (sensitive and largely progressive). At the federal level, in the transition from the Martin government to the one led by Stephen Harper, enough flexibility existed in UAS parameters that programming on the ground was subject to no great change, but the overall direction and rationale of the program shifted substantially from social and cultural issues to matters of economic development. So, at all levels of government, politicians have been influential in shaping urban Aboriginal policy.

A final issue concerning IGR and the administration of policies and programs is whether they have been influenced by New Public Management (NPM) practices and, if so, to what effect. NPM consists of a variety of techniques that arise from a general orientation that governments should do less directly in the way of implementing policy but be more conscious and clear about establishing the direction of policy: government should "steer" rather than "row" (Osborne and Gaebler 1993). NPM techniques include using other actors to deliver services by contracting out, establishing competition between service providers to obtain efficiencies, implementing clear frameworks of accountability, and, on the "steering" side, breaking down traditional administrative silos and adopting a holistic approach to problems. In many respects, the delivery of much urban Aboriginal policy conforms to the precepts of NPM: non-governmental organizations have long been contracted to deliver services – and this trend is growing – there is competition in contracting, and accountability mechanisms are tight; further, the multi-departmental or supra-departmental structure of the UAS conforms to the model, and this conformity is mirrored in some provinces.

However, the studies gathered here reveal some problems with this mode of administration. The accountability framework is onerous. Smaller organizations in particular find it extremely time-consuming to provide the information that is required about the services delivered to clients. Reporting requirements are strict. Further, it is clear that at times many organizations bend program guidelines in order to meet pressing needs: either people are not technically eligible or clients need services not expressly mandated. In such instances, accountability chafes even more.

Competition is more problematic. In the urban Aboriginal field, it occurs at two levels. First, there is competition among organizations to be involved in setting program parameters or at least to sit on committees to provide advice about priorities and choose projects for funding. In this respect there are differences in approaches and interests between the major political organizations, and especially between Status Indians and groups representing Non-Status and Métis people. So, for example, the Métis representatives were absent from the core committee in Edmonton. At this level as well there is competition between service providers and political organizations. The latter tend to take an approach based on rights, which normally implies relations with federal authorities, while the former focus on needs, which implies relations with any governments that have resources to tap. We will return to this matter later. From the NPM perspective, the second form of competition – between service providers – is more central. To secure funding, Aboriginal organizations must apply for grants to provide services. They must compete against each other in many cases and also against large service providers that have many different clienteles. The supposed positive effects are efficiency and appropriate delivery of the services that are contracted for. But the studies here find many negative consequences. Preparing grant applications consumes a very large amount of time that could be spent on clients. Smaller organizations are disadvantaged in this process because they lack specialized expertise in law, budgeting, and accounting, though they may be much closer to potential clienteles. The treadmill of short-term project grantsmanship leads to staff burnout and high rates of turnover. And agencies must struggle to shift their goals and orientations as program parameters change. As Peters notes in the Introduction, "staff are trained, collaborative relationships are established, clients become aware of the program, and then the end of the project means either that staff are let go or organizations scramble to reconfigure programs to meet new granting criteria in order to retain staff and support clients. A large amount of time that should be directed towards service delivery is diverted to applying for funding and writing reports." In short, the competitive contracting-out model is often dysfunctional.

Breaking down silos and adopting a holistic approach can also have disadvantages. The UAS itself is highly decentralized and seems to operate flexibly and reasonably well. The Alberta case, however, seems mixed. There, responsibility for the Aboriginal Policy Initiative was conferred upon an interdepartmental committee of senior officials while programs were implemented by individual departments and interdepartmental partnerships. The result has been considerable overlap and duplication of programs – a "maze" of programs, according to Andersen and Strachan. It can be difficult and frustrating for potential clients to identify and access services.[2] On the other hand, there can be some benefits from overlap and duplication, one of which is that there are alternative sources of services for clients. There are also alternative sources of funding for agencies (and so some Aboriginal organizations do not register as such in order to maximize funding opportunities).

If the record of NPM is mixed in this policy field, the problems may not endure. There is real potential here for a softening of the model, as shown best by the UAS. At the local level, this program provides a forum for dialogue about shared and conflicting values and objectives. There is room for responsiveness to citizens, who are real actors as opposed to the "consumers" found in the NPM framework. Collaborative structures are emerging, with the prospect of defining needs and delivering services through broad coalitions of public servants from all levels of government as well as Aboriginal and non-Aboriginal organizations. In short, there are some signs of an emerging model rather like that laid out by Denhardt and Denhardt (2000), who described "the New Public Service" as part of their critique of NPM. This model involves an orientation towards service,

the creation of shared interests, deep collaboration, an appreciation of clients as citizens, and long-run collaborative relationships.
Where these structures and orientations are developing – mainly in
the major urban centres – one can be relatively optimistic about the
shape and administration of urban Aboriginal policy.

The second set of general issues that can be considered in light
of this policy field concern social forces, the organized interests of
all kinds that are involved (or not) in the policy process. The initial
question is which social forces take part in policy making. Participation provides scope for influencing the character of policy. Involvement even at the level of implementation enables social forces to
help determine the policy that is actually delivered on the ground
through the micro-level decisions made within the policy parameters.

Urban Aboriginal policy is noteworthy for the huge range of organizations involved or seeking to be involved in its formation. These
vary greatly in the amount of resources they command in terms of
expertise and money, in the size of their constituencies, and in the
bases of their legitimacy. First, there are the big national organizations, the Assembly of First Nations (AFN) and the Métis National
Council. In the period of "high politics" identified by Graham and
Abele, these organizations led the struggle for broad causes and
basic collective rights, including the right to self-government. With
wide constituencies and deep-seated legitimacy, they tend to insist
on a nation-to-nation relationship with governments. The AFN is
constitutionally rooted in individual First Nations that have a land
base on reserves and so has no direct urban constituency. Another
organization, the Congress of Aboriginal Peoples, purports to represent off-reserve and Non-Status Indians (and some Métis) as a coalition of other associations, but it has suffered from instability and
is very weak in the western provinces. The other national organizations have provincial wings, and there are also Métis "locals" in
most large municipalities in the west. Then there are individual First
Nations that have a land base and self-government arrangements.
Sometimes these First Nations are close to municipalities and aim
to exert influence there and provide services to off-reserve members.
Some First Nations have offices in nearby urban areas. Others, in
the west, have established urban reserves within cities.

In some municipalities, there are comprehensive umbrella organizations. The Aboriginal Council of Winnipeg is a rare example of an
association that includes all major elements of the urban Aboriginal

communities. The Ottawa Aboriginal Coalition provides another example. In most urban areas, the representational structure is far more fragmented. There are major multi-service providers, some Aboriginal and some not. There are the Friendship Centres, which have multiple and varied functions. Many have spun off other service providers, while in smaller municipalities the Friendship Centre is the only substantial organization in town. These Centres, unlike other service providers, have a pan-Canadian organization, the National Association of Friendship Centres, which provides advocacy at the federal level. Then there are specialized service providers, the numbers of which have dramatically increased in recent years.[3] In large cities, they are active in almost every conceivable area.

No other urban policy field has such a varied and complex set of stakeholders. But, of course, not all organizations merely speak for normal "stakeholders," because some formally embody the national status of their members and others are the main instruments of the right of self-determination in that they provide some control over aspects of Aboriginal people's lives in urban centres. The mix of groups varies in every locale and produces distinctive patterns of demands and pressures. This means that government officials often face a challenging task in locating interlocutors to participate in the policy process, a problem discussed by Hanselmann and Gibbins (2005) and stressed here by Walker, Moore, and Linklater in their study of Manitoba. The big split here is between political organizations and Aboriginal service delivery agencies. The authors of the Manitoba paper argue that if governments cannot work with political organizations, or if those organizations are in conflict to the point of deadlock, then governments should work with local community leaders, even if they are not elected, and with community-based organizations. More ideally, their view is that governments should deal with political organizations for agenda setting, advocacy, and public engagement while consulting community-based agencies about policy design and implementation.

This may be a satisfactory solution in theory, but there are some obvious problems. It is true that the political organizations tend to be anchored in the on-reserve constituency, but the counterpart to this is that the service providers are weakly organized at the provincial and federal levels of government. There is no effective umbrella organization in Ottawa, with the exception of the National Association of Friendship Centres. Collective organization is weak at the provincial level as well, and this weakness is crucial because most policy affecting urban Aboriginal people is generated there. Even municipally, it is rare to find stable and comprehensive coalitions of service providers. Second, many service organizations and much of the thrust towards targeted Aboriginal programming in urban Canada stand on one of two pillars. Either Aboriginal people have a right to self-government or, alternatively, have special rights – they are "citizens plus" – as a consequence of their Aboriginality (Cairns 2000) or urban Aboriginal people are instead a special needs group with particular problems that require policies to address them. There is no doubt that many initiatives in health, education, and housing available to Aboriginal people reflect concern about special need, but they gain legitimacy because of the special rights of Aboriginal people. The political organizations have fought effectively and for a long time for recognition of these rights. It is ironic to contemplate having them excluded from consultations about the exercise of these rights. Finally, if Aboriginal people have the right to self-government, then what justification is there for governments to choose the "appropriate" organizations to consult? Surely in this field, the choice of an interlocutor depends on the will of the community being consulted.

In this context, it is worth remembering that this whole policy area is new and evolving fast. It was only in 1995 that the principle of self-government off the land base was recognized by the federal government, most provincial governments only became engaged in Aboriginal issues at around the same time, and the universe of urban Aboriginal organizations is young and expanding. The UAS has drawn in new actors, including municipal officials. It is not surprising to see tensions and conflicts among those organizations that seek to influence policy making – between Métis and Status Indians and Non-Status Indians, and between political organizations and service providers. They compete for funding and they compete for influence; it will take time for mutual adaptation to occur within the system and for community legitimacy to flow towards the organizations perceived as effective and appropriate. In the meantime, and perhaps for the long run, it is worth noting that the studies gathered here also show that co-operation is not impossible and that strong representational coalitions can be formed to work with officials in shaping policy.

Leaving aside the involvement of Aboriginal organizations, we turn to another issue about social forces. It is always important to ask about interests that are *not* represented in policy making. In the urban Aboriginal field, the absence of business interests is remarkable. Many studies of municipal policy making focus on the role of business, and the general view is that this particular interest is able to achieve its objectives most of the time: it is preponderant (Tindal and Tindal 2009, 361–92). Either municipalities are constrained to meet business's needs by inter-municipal competition or their political leaders can enter stable coalitions (or "regimes") by allying themselves with business interests. It is true that most urban Aboriginal policy does not originate with municipal governments themselves; instead it occurs *within* municipalities, mainly at the behest of senior governments. Still, one would expect to find business engagement in any significant area of local public policy. This is not the case. In the studies collected here, there was some business interest in Aboriginal labour (and hence training) for the construction industry in Saint John, New Brunswick; a representative of the Calgary Chamber of Commerce participated in the Urban Aboriginal Initiative; and in Winnipeg, two representatives of the Aboriginal business community sat on the Aboriginal Partnership Committee under the Winnipeg Partnership Agreement. These are the only mentions of business involvement. Now business could have a negative influence, perhaps by supporting city governments that are not willing to engage in redistributive spending – as in Winnipeg under Mayor Katz – or by quietly acquiescing when local governments simply ignore Aboriginal issues. However, the lack of positive engagement is puzzling. The Canada West Foundation, which receives significant support from business, did much work to document the emerging problems and opportunities posed by growing populations of urban Aboriginal people and pointed out that a large proportion of the future labour force would consist of Aboriginal people (Hanselmann 2001). Further, the neglect by business of this policy area stands in striking contrast to its efforts in the field of immigrant settlement. In Ontario, for example, most major cities have seen the formation of large, multi-stakeholder coalitions led by business, which aim to speed the integration of recent immigrants into the labour force. Business organizations take an active role in monitoring and implementing immigrant settlement policy

(Stasiulis, Hughes, and Amery, forthcoming). A similar engagement in urban Aboriginal policy would certainly raise its profile and, in conjunction with other social forces, could produce more effective policy in municipalities.

The final general issue about social forces concerns *when* they participate in the policy process. This is an important matter, which is raised throughout the volume and particularly in the Manitoba study. It is important because it directly affects the degree of influence that organizations can have in shaping policy. Policy analysts generally distinguish several phases of policy making: agenda setting, problem definition, deriving policy alternatives, decision making, and implementation (Pal 2006, 97–236). Early involvement is advantageous. Organizations can have considerable influence at the implementation stage, for example, but only within the general parameters established by earlier policy choices, which rest in turn on how the problems and opportunities are defined, which in turn would not happen at all were the issue not to make it onto the policy agenda. Earlier involvement normally leads to greater influence.

Generally, Aboriginal organizations are involved at the implementation stage of the process: they deliver services and are consulted on the modalities of doing so. In Winnipeg, for instance, the Municipal Aboriginal Pathways, however welcome as a municipal initiative, were laid out before there was any consultation with Aboriginal groups. Similarly, most service providers apply for grants or contracts to deliver services that are defined as necessary by other actors. There is always some room for discretion in implementation, but this is a matter of embroidery on patterns determined elsewhere. In most programming examined here, Aboriginal organizations are policy takers.

There are some significant exceptions, however. Under the National Homelessness Initiative, there are funds segmented for Aboriginal projects, and Aboriginal organizations are engaged in adjudication. In New Brunswick, Aboriginal organizations helped to develop the Aboriginal Head Start program: they had a role in laying out alternative policies for decision. In the UAS, there has been an evolution from having Aboriginal representatives act in an advisory capacity (which occurs in other programs too) to having them make decisions about funding and project selection. As the Manitoba chapter discusses, Aboriginal organizations have had "a comparatively direct role in the housing policy-making process from agenda setting through to implementation." Aboriginal organizations have also occasionally engaged in research. This is extremely important because research questions and results lead to agenda setting and problem definition. In Ontario, the Urban Aboriginal Task Force commissioned research in five sites, and the very act of research stimulated organization on the ground and raised the profile of Aboriginal issues on the urban agenda. Research documents problems and helps define possible policy responses.

One final aspect of social forces' participation deserves mention. It is clear that urban Aboriginal people, through their representative organizations and service providers, have the capacity for effective involvement in policy making. This may not be so evident in the smaller communities. Andersen and Strachan note some sense of marginalization and impotence in the smaller places in Alberta, and in cities like Kingston there simply are not the numbers and capacity to do much more than provide advice and help make decisions. However, in the larger cities, all authors are in accord that the capacity exists within the Aboriginal community not only to consult, advise, and implement policy but also to assess needs, contemplate alternative solutions, and make decisions. From the perspective of self-government, this is a most significant finding.

ASSESSING THE POLICIES

A final area of analysis concerns the quality of the policies that prevail in the urban Aboriginal field. How good are they? How might they be made better? These are difficult questions to answer because we do not possess full information about the multitude of programs in existence, especially in the western provinces, where there is a plethora of programming that often involves many small projects. As well, as noted earlier, the field is in rapid evolution. But in any case, we need to clarify the criteria used for assessing the quality of policy, not least because our authors differ substantially in focus and attitude about evaluation. Abele and Graham, for example, mention effectiveness, efficiency, equitability, and optimality. For Walker, Moore, and Linklater, good policies are adapted to local circumstances, reflect "deep federalism," and are made through co-production with Aboriginal organizations. This last criterion is shared by Murray, who decries colonialist tendencies in policy making and by the authors of the Ontario chapter, who associate good

policy with the "self-organization of urban Aboriginal people."
Andersen and Strachan think that policy should be more coherent,
but they also insist that it can only become more practical, functional, legitimate, and innovative when Aboriginal social forces play
a stronger role at all stages of policy making. So the attempt here is
to discuss all these and other criteria of "good" public policy. In the
end, I will focus on the involvement of Aboriginal people in policy
making, rather than on the character of policy outputs or outcomes.

One common criterion is the speed with which policy is formulated. Does it lag behind the emergence of widely recognized
problems and opportunities? The urban Aboriginal field seems satisfactory in this regard now after a very slow start. The scope of policy
– the areas covered by programs – has expanded relatively quickly.
Indeed, change may currently be rapid enough that it is destabilizing,
especially in the view of service providers who deliver specialized
programs and who must struggle to adapt to new priorities. Apart
from this, policy gaps have been filled rather well (see Hanselmann
with Nyhof and McGuire 2002, Figure 6).

Other criteria are the scale and coherence of policy. Scale is always
an issue. One can always imagine further policy initiatives to solve
problems or to help realize opportunities. In the urban Aboriginal
policy field, it seems that scale is inadequate in smaller communities,
especially where Aboriginal populations form minor percentages of
the population. They may have distinct needs, but targeted programming is not available; indeed, this may be a cause of people's onward
migration to larger centres. In those cities, the overall scale of policy
is adequate, though there are shortfalls everywhere in functional
areas like housing. Policy coherence, however, is clearly a problem
– the Alberta chapter highlights this. Despite the goodwill of policy
makers – or perhaps in part because of their enthusiasm – there is
little integration of the many programs on offer. The lack of coherence and coordination results in overlap and duplication, which, in
Andersen and Strachan's analysis, poses major difficulties for clients
and service providers. The UAS was designed to allow for integrated
programming to meet the distinctive needs of urban Aboriginal
people in various places. There is flexibility enough for adaptation
to local conditions and also enough latitude that programs can target pressing needs. But the UAS has not evolved to the point that it
provides a coherent policy framework. In a narrower focus, housing and health policy each seem relatively well integrated, but the

overall suite of programs does not seem to be coherently and systematically fashioned, a situation that is perhaps inevitable given the jurisdictional uncertainties and avoidances that dominate the field. As Graham and Abele note: "[t]here has never been a comprehensive urban Aboriginal policy in Canada." At the level of individual municipalities, progress has been made. Mayor Murray's Municipal Aboriginal Pathways in Winnipeg were logically fashioned, and the Urban Aboriginal Initiatives in Edmonton and Calgary are promising. Municipal governments, however, have neither the power nor the resources to design comprehensive policy. The federal government avoids dealing with this problem, and provincial governments have created a patchwork of policies designed by individual departments and units.

Two further criteria often used to judge policy are effectiveness and efficiency. First, do the programs achieve their objectives, more or less? Second, do they achieve their objectives at a reasonable cost? We simply do not know the answers to these questions. There are too many programs, and they are too fragmented to assess effectiveness. In this light, the researchers whose work is collected here have been more inclined to focus on the process of policy making. So there is still no systematic examination of effectiveness, and Hanselmann's (2002, 12) conclusion is still true: "actors involved in urban Aboriginal policy-making and programming need to build the quantitative data that will allow for evaluations of policies and programming to assess what is working and what is not." This, however, may not be the immediate priority, as there are other considerations about what makes good policy and these may predominate.

If effectiveness cannot be evaluated, then it is impossible to measure efficiency. Efficiency concerns the cost of achieving some policy outcome. It cannot be measured in this field because, even though we can know the costs associated with a policy or program, we do not know what impact was achieved for the resources expended. Clearly, though, there is some inefficiency arising from how policy making is done in the urban Aboriginal field. The dominant policy paradigm in this field is to extend – usually on a contract basis – relatively short term, project-based funding. This funding mechanism produces instability that is costly, as the authors of the Alberta chapter stress. Less visibly, shifting program opportunities distort organizations as they strain to take on different functions and projects. Accountability mechanisms are also sources of inefficiency.

There is a trade-off between efficiency and accountability: the time and resources spent reporting are time and resources that are not being devoted to serving clients or to planning or managing better. The need for more flexibility in reporting procedures has been noted before (Hanselmann 2002, 12), but the situation has not improved and has probably worsened because of the federal government's *Accountability Act*.

There is a final criterion of good policy that is uniquely central to the field of urban Aboriginal policy. This is the extent to which Aboriginal people themselves shape the relevant policies. This consideration is not quite an issue of equity (another common criterion of evaluation) because equity normally refers to the distribution of policy outputs and outcomes rather than the roles played in generating policy. But Aboriginal involvement is a theme that runs through all of the chapters collected here. It is most explicit in the Manitoba chapter, where the authors insist on the need for "co-production" in policy making: they argue that Aboriginal representatives should be involved at all stages of the policy-making process. This involvement includes the definition not only of problems but also of the whole shape of the policy terrain (Pal 2006, 97–236). Fundamentally, the issue is how much Aboriginal people control the formation of the policies that affect them.

Using control over policy as a criterion of the "goodness" of policy goes beyond the usual arguments about participation and involvement. Often, it is held that policy is better if the subjects of the policy have a role in shaping it. This is sometime normatively charged, but it need not be. For instance, the effectiveness of policy can be improved through participation because those responsible for the policy receive better information from the public or interested groups than they would otherwise have. So participation improves policy makers' understanding of the system in which governments plan to intervene, and the resulting policy works better than it otherwise would have. Participation can also facilitate implementation. Resistance to new initiatives can be lessened when people have been consulted and have an understanding of the policy. The sense of meaningful participation helps promote consent in a manner like the traditional linkage between obligation and consent: one is only obliged to follow the laws of a regime if one has consented to its establishment. Further, participation in policy making may induce beneficial change among the participants. Here it is useful to distinguish "instrumental" from "developmental" participation (Pateman 1970). People participate instrumentally to achieve their desired objectives, but participation can have developmental consequences, as engagement in a process of ordered deliberation helps people to become better citizens. They are not simply becoming more informed, they are also learning tolerance, compromise, and the art of making mutually satisfactory arrangements through engagement in a process of collective deliberation. In sum, participation in policy making can be encouraged so as to generate better policy, ease implementation, and educate – broadly speaking – the participants. Policy planning very often involves a participatory component precisely in order to achieve these effects.

However, this sort of participation is limited. It does not reach the level of policy co-production. Once again, we can distinguish two broad meanings of participation. The first is participation *in* a process. People take part in order to realize their instrumental goals – their policy objectives. The structure of action (the process) is predetermined. The objective is to take part in a process to refine a policy rather than to determine collective goals. Participation may be stimulated by the people who control the process, for the reasons discussed above. All participants aim to have a "voice," that is, to play a part in decision making, but their influence may be unequal even over the long term since outcomes are dictated not by common interest but by negotiating power that is based on the resources brought into the policy-making arena. In contrast to this view is participation *with* others. This concept implies sodality, that is, an association of mutual aid or action. Fellowship is the primary characteristic, and action would not occur without the participants. People do not join an already structured process but join together towards some common end or join to decide on goals. Within the group, members are fundamentally equal, as is their influence on decision making over the long term. This situation produces a commitment to collective projects because the absence of a structured hierarchy removes resentment of decisions seen as imposed. It also produces the developmental effects of participation, as noted earlier.

This categorization is simple – a pair of ideal types. Nevertheless, it serves to distinguish involvement (or partial participation) in an established process from full participation, where actors come together to determine collective goals and a wide range of issues is open for decision. The latter is the sort of participation that would characterize the co-production of policies in the urban Aboriginal field. Full participation is an ideal that is sought by many, but it is elusive. First, it is impractical on a mass level: it is available only to relatively small groups of individuals or to representatives in decision-making bodies. More broadly, modern states are simply not direct democracies. In our system, elected representatives ultimately exercise sovereign power; they control government and its processes. Finally, governments, subject to democratic control, establish the framework of governance within which social forces and other actors participate. Final decision-making authority rests with governments, and they are accountable to electorates. This is the essence of representative democracy. Policy co-production involving Aboriginal people, or, more extremely, the delegation of decision-making power to Aboriginal people themselves would be a substantial departure from this model. Is it appropriate to deviate from these basic principles in the case of Aboriginal people? If so, why?

One simple reason for such a departure is that Aboriginal people are different from the majority society. They have different histories, different cultures, and different political traditions; most important, they have different rights. These are not only the extra rights that might adhere to Aboriginal people as "citizens plus," but also a right to self-government. This extends now with practical certainty only to First Nations occupying a land base, but there is also such a right for urban Aboriginals, though the modalities of its exercise are not clear. How policies affecting urban Aboriginal people are made is very important because this involves self-government.

Another reason for allocating decision-making power to Aboriginal people is that Canadian state structures and policies have treated them dishonourably in the past – including the recent past. This odious treatment should have some bearing on the majority society's willingness to accord, now, an equal role (co-production) or even a predominant role in making policy about urban Aboriginal people.

In an influential work, Alan Cairns (2000) presented a very sharp analysis of the *Report* of the Royal Commission on Aboriginal Peoples and of its emphasis on separateness and nation-to-nation relationships. He pointed out that the Commission badly neglected urban Aboriginal people and off-reserve Indians in general. He argued more broadly that the Commission's analysis neglected the political dynamics of the majority society and its interactions with

Aboriginal people, including their relations with the federal and provincial governments. In particular, the nation-to-nation approach diminishes and attenuates a sense of common citizenship and weakens the fellow-feeling needed to sustain political support for flows of resources to Aboriginal people. This may well be true. But the view, which doubtless is shared in less sophisticated terms by many in the majority society, neglects too much the burden of the past. The fact is that many of the problems that are meant to be addressed by flows of resources to reserves and to services for urban Aboriginal people are themselves the legacy of past dishonourable treatment by the majority society. That society often has taken – and sometimes still does take – a general attitude of colonialism and paternalism and it has implemented specific policies that have impoverished Aboriginal people and gravely eroded their cultures and self-respect. As a consequence, the majority must be prepared to countenance and support the maximum possible self-determination of Aboriginal people. In policy making, the guiding principle should be that Aboriginal autonomy and the right of self-government need to be put into effect. This principle should take priority over issues of efficiency and over the problem of what others might regard as poor decisions. Participation in policy making must go far beyond the level of involvement and the attempt to harness the developmental effects of participation to the ends of the majority society. Cairns (2000, 63) quotes a former minister of Northern Affairs and Natural Resources, whose position on the issue of participation in 1963 is a perfect example of the paternalism of the past that still endures in many quarters today: "[t]he prime condition in the progress of the Indian people must be the development by themselves of a desire for the goals which we think they should want."

The conclusion of this discussion of participation is that Aboriginal people have special rights to determine the policies that affect them, especially those that target them. They have a claim for resources to support these policies and programs, one that is based in part on the damaging and dishonourable treatment that has often been inflicted on them. In general, participation in policy making is not a criterion of a good policy: poor policies may have involved a lot of participation and at times citizen participation can make policies worse by any reasonable measure. However, policies about Aboriginal people are different. *By definition*, policies that do not rest on their full participation are sub-optimal. Against the measure of full autonomy, the co-production of policy is a minimal, barely satisfactory standard to determine whether a policy is a good one. By this criterion, many of the policies examined in the research presented here do not measure up.

CONCLUSION

The chapters in this book have provided a rich, detailed, and thought-provoking view of urban Aboriginal policy in Canada. This is a unique policy field because of the jurisdictional issues involved and the special rights of Aboriginal people. It is also a dynamic policy field. There has been a great deal of recent innovation, as both the policies being generated and the players taking part have evolved rapidly. There are many new Aboriginal organizations anxious to play a role in shaping and delivering policy, and there is increasing involvement by federal, provincial, and municipal governments. There are many uncertainties to be overcome in sorting out the responsibilities and relationships among these governments and in achieving stable coalitions among the organizations that compete to represent Aboriginal people and to deliver services to them.

This is a field with difficulties, yet there are grounds for optimism. In major cities, Aboriginal organizations and leaders have developed the capacity to define both problems and opportunities and to design and implement policy. Their chances to do so are increasing. We can expect that the occasionally destructive competition between them will diminish through mutual adjustment and the availability of more resources. These resources should flow because governments are clearly tending to increase the priority they place on issues involving urban Aboriginal people. One can hope that they are wise enough to extend as much autonomy as possible so that Aboriginal people themselves make decisions about priorities and solutions; that is, to design the policies that affect them. If so, policy will improve.

NOTES

1 For results from some other parts of the project, see Young and Leuprecht (2006), Lazar and Leuprecht (2007), Sancton and Young (2009), Carroll and Graham (2009), and Tolley and Young (forthcoming).

2 In this context, the listing of urban Aboriginal programs and organizations by the cities of Edmonton and Calgary is a laudable initiative.
3 For Edmonton, compare Hanselmann with Nyhof and McGuire (2002, Appendix 1, 18–19) with City of Edmonton (2008).

REFERENCES

Cairns, Alan C. 2000. *Citizens Plus: Aboriginal Peoples and the Canadian State*. Vancouver: UBC Press.

Carroll, Barbara Wake and Katherine A.H. Graham, eds. 2009. "Special Issue on Federalism, Public Policy, and Municipalities." *Canadian Public Administration* 52 (3).

City of Edmonton, Aboriginal Relations Office. 2008. *Guide to Aboriginal Edmonton*. 2008–2009 edition.

Denhardt, Robert B. and Janet Vinzant Denhardt. 2000. "The New Public Service: Serving Rather than Steering." *Public Administration Review* 60 (6): 549–59.

Dust, Theresa. 1997. "The Impact of Aboriginal Land Claims and Self-Governance on Canadian Municipalities." *Canadian Public Administration* 40 (3): 481–94.

Hanselmann, Calvin. 2002. *Uncommon Sense: Promising Practices in Urban Aboriginal Policy-Making and Programming*. Calgary: Canada West Foundation.

– 2001. *Urban Aboriginal People in Western Canada: Realities and Priorities*. Calgary: Canada West Foundation.

Hanselmann, Calvin, with Carolyn Nyhof and Julie McGuire. 2002. *Enhanced Urban Aboriginal Programming in Western Canada*. Calgary: Canada West Foundation.

Hanselmann, Calvin and Roger Gibbins. 2005. "Another Voice is Needed: Intergovernmentalism in the Urban Aboriginal Context." In *Canada: The State of the Federation 2003 – Reconfiguring Aboriginal-State Relations*, ed. Michael Murphy, 77–92. Montreal and Kingston: McGill-Queen's University Press for the Institute of Intergovernmental Relations, Queen's University.

Hawkes, David. 2005. "Rebuilding the Relationship: The 'Made in Saskatchewan' Approach to First Nations Governance." In *Canada: The State of the Federation 2003 – Reconfiguring Aboriginal-State Relations*, ed. Michael Murphy, 119–32. Montreal and Kingston: McGill-Queen's University Press for the Institute of Intergovernmental Relations, Queen's University.

Lazar, Harvey and Christian Leuprecht, eds. 2007. *Spheres of Governance: Comparative Studies of Cities in Multilevel Governance Systems*. Montreal and Kingston: McGill-Queen's University Press for the Institute of Intergovernmental Relations, Queen's University.

Osborne, David and Ted Gaebler. 1993. *Reinventing Government: How the Entrepreneurial Spirit is Transforming the Public Sector*. New York: Penguin.

Pal, Leslie. 2006. *Beyond Policy Analysis: Public Issue Management in Turbulent Times*. 3rd ed. Toronto: Thomson Nelson.

Pateman, Carole. 1970. *Participation and Democratic Theory*. London: Cambridge University Press.

Sancton, Andrew and Robert Young, eds. 2009. *Foundations of Governance: Municipal Government in Canada's Provinces*. Toronto: University of Toronto Press and The Institute of Public Administration of Canada.

Stasiulis, Daiva, Christine Hughes, and Zainab Amery. Forthcoming. "From Government to Multilevel Governance of Immigrant Settlement in Ontario's City-Regions." In *Fields of Governance 1: Immigrant Settlement Policy in Canadian Municipalities*, eds. Erin Tolley and Robert Young. Montreal and Kingston: McGill-Queen's University Press.

Tindal, C. Richard and Susan Nobes Tindal. 2009. *Local Government in Canada*, 7th ed. Toronto: Nelson Education.

Tolley, Erin and Robert Young, eds. Forthcoming. *Fields of Governance 1: Immigrant Settlement Policy in Canadian Municipalities*. Montreal and Kingston: McGill-Queen's University Press.

Young, Robert and Christian Leuprecht, eds. 2006. *Canada: The State of the Federation 2004 – Municipal-Federal-Provincial Relations in Canada*. Montreal and Kingston: McGill-Queen's University Press for the Institute of Intergovernmental Relations, Queen's University.

Contributors

FRANCES ABELE is a professor in the School of Public Policy and Administration at Carleton University and Academic Director of the Carleton Centre for Community Innovation.

CHRIS ANDERSEN, a Metis originally from Saskatchewan, is an associate professor in the Faculty of Native Studies at the University of Alberta and founding editor of *aboriginal policy studies*. His research interests include the dynamics of Aboriginal identity in law, the rise of "statistical literacy" in Aboriginal organizations, and the policy dynamics of urban Aboriginal issues.

KATHERINE GRAHAM is professor of public policy and administration and senior advisor to the provost at Carleton University. She has been undertaking research on urban and Aboriginal issues for over thirty years.

RUSSELL LAPOINTE is a doctoral student at Carleton University who also works for Indian and Northern Affairs in the Statistical Analysis Directorate. He is currently examining the social and economic conditions of urban Aboriginal populations.

DAVID J. LEECH holds a PhD in political science from the University of Ottawa. He is currently a senior advisor with the Department of Fisheries and Oceans in Ottawa.

MAEENGAN LINKLATER is operations manager for Mazinaate Inc., a native-run and operated publishing company located in Winnipeg, Manitoba. He is vice-chair of the West Broadway Development

Corporation, and a board member of the Aboriginal Council of Winnipeg, the Manitoba Writers' Guild, and the Aboriginal Writers' Collective of Manitoba.

MICHAEL MCCROSSAN is a PhD candidate in the Department of Political Science at Carleton University. His doctoral research focuses on the spatialization of legal knowledge and the constitutional rights of Indigenous peoples.

JAMES MOORE has a master of city planning degree from the University of Manitoba. He is currently a land use planner with the City of Kelowna and is a member of the Canadian Institute of Planners.

KAREN BRIDGET MURRAY is associate professor of Political Science at York University. Her research and teaching focuses on urban governance and poverty in Canada in comparative perspective.

EVELYN PETERS is a professor and Canada Research Chair in geography at the University of Winnipeg. Her research has emphasized working with a variety of urban Aboriginal and government organizations on issues facing First Nations and Metis people in cities.

JENNA STRACHAN is Metis, originally from northern Alberta. She received her BA Hons in Native Studies in 2008 from the Faculty of Native Studies, University of Alberta, and is currently employed by Westbank First Nation in BC in the Intergovernmental Affairs Department.

RYAN WALKER is an associate professor in the Department of Geography and Planning, University of Saskatchewan. He is past-chair of the university's Regional and Urban Planning Program and is a member of the Canadian Institute of Planners.

ROBERT YOUNG is professor of Political Science at the University of Western Ontario and Canada Research Chair in Multilevel Governance.

Index